First published as an EBook in the UK by Malcolm McEwan
in 2017
mmcewan@madasafish.com

I dedicate this book to my kids.

(In the hope that they might even read it)

A LITTLE PREAMBLE

I shouldn't be giving this one away because it is such a powerful technique - but nobody will read this, right?

If you ever get stopped while driving always tell the police officer, "I'm glad you stopped me because..."

That is a good start. It is non-confrontational. It will distract the officer from his original aim. Curious why you are glad he stopped you. That minor traffic offence you committed will go to the back of his mind.

The next part of the technique involves the 'why?'

Adapt the reason you give for being glad he stopped you to your situation. Your reason should fit in with what you are doing or where you are going. There should be no need to lie.

"I am looking for directions to..."
"Can you tell me where the nearest toilet/pharmacy/petrol station is?"
"I'm lost."
"I'm not feeling well."
"My car has been playing up."

Police officers join the job to help people. Redirecting their attention from issuing a minor ticket to helping a member of the public is something they would prefer to be doing. It makes them feel good to help others. It works at a base psychological level. Thus, if you get it right, they forget their reason for stopping you and assist you with your problem. As an afterthought, they might say something like; *'Oh, by the way, get your taillight fixed,'* or *'keep your speed down,'* or *'remember to use your indicator.'*

It is a win/win situation. The officer will feel good for helping you, and you get away with a quiet word in your ear. The method does not work if you fall out of your vehicle drunk or have committed a hit and run or other serious offence.

STOP PRESS:

This technique also does not work if, like me, you get stopped by a police officer who has read this book, therefore knows this modus operandi and doesn't believe you are bursting for the toilet (I wonder if I can sue for a new pair of trousers?).

So without further ado, here is my final effort in the trilogy of police memoirs documenting the amusing circumstances, crazy scrapes, nonsense and shenanigans that went on. There is no central plot to follow. You don't have to be a police officer to recognise the characters - they appear in every walk of life. You don't have to want to be an outstanding police officer either. I wrote this book to record the comical cases and hilarious situations I experienced during my thirty-year career in the police.

I changed the names to protect the guilty, embellished stories and took literary licence. Although, the most ludicrous stories are probably true.

THE MICHAEL PARKINSON TELEVISION INTERVIEW

British broadcaster Michael Parkinson (best known for his long-running talk show, *Parkinson*), said *'Muhammad Ali was the most extraordinary man I ever met'*. But who was the second?

The following happened when Michael Parkinson came out of retirement for one last chat show:-

Parky: I'd like to welcome to the studio tonight Malky McEwan, best-selling and award-winning author of *How to be the most outstanding cop in the world*.

APPLAUSE

Malky enters, embraces Parky and takes a seat.

Parky: Welcome, Malky. Can I call you Malky or should I call you Inspector McEwan?

Malky: Malky is fine. I'm no longer an inspector.

Parky: Now, Malky you have written *'How to be the most outstanding cop in the world'* do you think anyone can become an outstanding cop?

Malky: In a silly way, yes.

Parky: In a silly way?

Malky: Yes, in a silly way. That's the title of the book. *'How to be the most outstanding cop in the world - in a silly way!'*

Parky: I see. What I'm interested in sharing with the audience is your experience with the not so outstanding cops you came across in your career.

Malky: That's not fair. They were all outstanding… in their own way.

Parky: PC Penfold?

Malky: Er… um… Yes, PC Penfold, in his way was outstanding.

Parky: Not as a cop though.

Malky: Probably not.

Parky: In your previous books you have described cops who were a little inattentive. If there is a puddle on the road, they would step in it and get wet. There are others you described as unlucky; they see the puddle, sidestep to avoid it and still get soaked as a car drives through the puddle splashing them. You say PC Penfold was both inattentive and unlucky?

Malky: Yes. He would be the one that would jump the puddle to avoid getting wet, then land on a jobbie, slip and fall back into the puddle and then get splashed by the passing car.

Parky: Does he appear in this book?

Malky: He makes a brief appearance, yes. Like the time he they asked him to play in goal for the police football team.

Parky: What happened?

Malky: They were only ten minutes into the game and he had already let three goals passed him. He kicked the ball so far out of play it cleared the fence surrounding the ground. PC Penfold shouted, 'I'll get it,' chased after it, climbed the fence and didn't come back. Everyone thought he went to the pub. Nobody bothered because without him they only let in another two goals the whole game.

Parky: Oh that's funny?

Malky: That wasn't the funny part. The next week they were ten minutes into their next game when PC Penfold climbed back over the fence into the ground. He raised the ball above his head and shouted, 'Found it!'

Parky: So will the reader learn anything from him about being an outstanding cop?

Malky: Of course, learning from other people's mistakes is way better than learning from your own.

Parky: Is that how you learned to be an outstanding cop?

Malky: I don't profess to have been an outstanding cop. For me policing was like sex.

Parky: Like sex?

Malky: Yeah, I fumbled around for a bit, not really knowing what I was doing and I was never sure how long it would last - but, oh boy, it was fun!

Parky: Do you have any good advice for anyone who wants to join the police?

Malky: I think the main thing is to have good posture.

Parky: Good posture will make you a good police officer?

Malky: Pretty much, the two words that help there are 'nipples leading'.

Parky: Look the part, project a good image, I get the idea. So this book is all about the funny incidents that you came across?

Malky: The silly incidents, the crazy characters and the stupid things that happened, yes. I think reading about what happens in the police and thinking about how you will deal with those situations will prepare you for what you may encounter.

Parky: It pays to be prepared?

Malky: Yes, but if not at least you will get a laugh.

Parky: So Malky, what was it like when you first got promoted to Inspector?

Chapter 1

IT'S A MYSTERY

It was a mystery. How did that man with so much nonsense in his head get to be an inspector? He was still as immature as the day he joined, and that was over twenty years ago. He has the mentality of a sixteen-year-old. The mind of a teenager, more concerned with drinking beer and having shenanigans than being serious about 'keeping people safe' and all that senior officers stand for. But there he is, two pips on his shoulder, scrambled egg on his hat and a warrant card to prove it. It was quite worrying. How was he going to fool them all in this role? He had only just about managed it as a sergeant. Seven years left on the job before he would retire! Seven years as an inspector in charge of sergeants, cops and every serious incident that would come his way. How was he going to cope for that length of time?
  Better get on with it, I suppose!

I turned away from the mirror, stepped out of my new office and made my way into the briefing room. It was time to introduce myself to my new shift.
  Rows of cracked plastic chairs faced a desk and a computer in the briefing room. The walls bare except for peeling paint and one yellowed poster giving the fire safety regulations. Sergeant Dougie Dougieson sat at his computer and waved me to the seat next to him behind the desk.
  "Good morning everyone," I said nodding at my new troops.
  "Good morning inspector," they replied in unison.
  "Carry on sergeant," I nodded at Sergeant Dougie Dougieson to continue with his briefing.
  Sergeant Dougieson scrolled through crime returns, night logs, and various other briefing tools on his computer, reading out the pertinent bits to the cops In front of us. I switched off to what he was saying and looked at each of the officers on my new shift. I tried to remember their names and

what my predecessor (Inspector Charlie McNugget) had said about each of them. Getting a background on the staff was something that all supervisors did before taking over a new shift. We like to know who the workers are, who the shirkers are and who we had to watch like a hawk. The simplified version was - good guy, good guy... blank.

I had twelve cops on my shift (on paper at least). Seven of them were sitting in front of me. F division, a large, heavily populated and crime ridden area, needed more than twelve officers to police it properly. It was ridiculous to expect that we could do a good job with twelve, yet here we were making do with seven. I discussed it with Charlie McNugget, despite having a shift of twelve cops, in reality he never saw all on duty at the one time.

So where were they all?

One was pregnant. PC Stubbs declared herself 'up the spout' the week before I was due to start. A day later they moved her to the poisoned chalice that was the Resource Management Unit (RMU). Nobody liked the RMU. Don't get me wrong, the people were nice, they were just doing their job. It was just that their job involved shattering the dreams of the average cop, disappointing sergeants who wanted more staff and gazumping inspectors by getting chief inspectors to deny requests for overtime. Cops had to put all leave requests through the RMU, and they followed a formula; all requests denied if it meant the shift went below minimum staffing levels. Sergeants contacted the RMU to query why they were below minimum staffing levels; the RMU pestered chief inspectors to authorise overtime to cover but, as there was no money, the chief inspectors would tell them to pass on to inspectors that they should risk manage the shortfall.

'Risk manage', what a wonderful phrase. It meant taking responsibility for threats of damage, injury, liability and loss but don't pay overtime. So the boss set minimum staffing levels based on average demand not maximum need. When below minimum staffing levels (levels the bosses had set) they said 'risk manage it.' While inspectors, sergeants and cops risk managed the multitude of emergencies they dealt with you could bet your backside the boss who refused to pay for cover was tucked up in bed sleeping like a baby.

Yup, the RMU got it in the neck from everybody.

PC Stubbs would remain there until she had to leave to give birth after that she would be off for six months maternity leave. In the unlikely event she returned to my shift, we still wouldn't see her for at least a year. Despite that, she still counted as one of my twelve on the group strength.

One cop, PC Malingery, was on long-term sick leave. PC Malingery's doctor diagnosed him with 'nervous disability.' He'd only turned up for one day in the past eight months. I learned that his last appearance was the day before his sickness benefit ran out. A day later he'd be on half wages. Inspector McNugget sat him down for the prerequisite 'return to work' interview. PC Malingery complained of cold hands, shortness of breath, heart palpitations, dry mouth and feelings of panic, fear, and uneasiness. The next day he signed off sick again with anxiety disorder. Anxiety is a real thing. Cops can suffer from it like anyone else. However, I never met anyone who was so anxious they couldn't come in to reset their sick pay. With his sick pay reset at least he didn't have to worry about going to half pay for another six months. Despite that, he still counted as one of my twelve on the group.

They seconded two officers to a major enquiry. One was an ex-detective constable, and one was an aspiring detective constable. The ex-detective constable had put himself forward for the promotion process and didn't get it. Not enough street experience they had told him, he had been in a specialised role for too long. Addressing this, he asked for a transfer back to uniform to gain street experience. He had only been back in uniform for three days when a major enquiry kicked off, and they transferred him straight him back into the CID - they needed his specialised experience.

The wannabe detective constable was there to gain experience. I didn't expect to see either of them back in my group; the major enquiry looked as if it would go on for years. I was right, the ex-detective went on to get a temporary detective sergeant's rank and slotted right back in; the aspiring detective got made up from aide to a permanent position. Despite that, both still counted on the strength of my group.

The fifth missing cop was down in the cells. PC Millstone hadn't been locked up but probably should have been. The custody suite was considered a 'critical place of business' ever since a Fatal Accident Inquiry into the death of a prisoner two years before, (in another force) resulted in that force being heavily criticised for having too few staff on duty in their custody suite. Thus the instruction had come down from the top floor that an additional officer was to assist in our cells. Our senior officers wanted no similar criticism directed towards themselves. We had to provide the additional officer for custody from the front-line. No matter if there were no prisoners in custody, no matter how busy the streets were, no matter that another front-line officer was out there getting a kicking, we had to provide an officer to assist in the cells. Inspector McNugget made the shrewd decision to send PC Millstone.

PC Millstone was a liability. The type of cop you could scold for being argumentative, and he would reply, "No I'm not."

He spent more time and effort trying to get out of doing a job or trying to cut corners than it would take to do the job in the first place. Sergeants followed at the back of him sweeping up the mess he left. He took so much supervising that the custody suite was, in fact, welcome to him.

I once heard an inspector cajole him by saying, "C'mon PC Millstone, hurry up and get that done. You are getting lazy."

To which he replied, "Not me - I've always been lazy."

I first met PC Millstone when I was a sergeant. I had called into the custody suite to interview a prisoner, a job normally allocated to a cop. However, it was one of those nights when calls rained down like a thunder-plump and cops ran around in a frenzy trying to deal with them. I popped across to F Division custody to do it myself. Otherwise, it wouldn't get done, an opportunity missed.

"I need to interview Brian S. McNutt," I informed PC Millstone who was sitting at a table behind the charge bar reading a magazine. "Everyone is busy, so I have popped across to do it myself. It shouldn't take long, so I was wondering if you could corroborate me for five minutes?"

In Scots law, we required corroboration for everything. I couldn't interview on my own, so I needed someone to sit with me.

"I can't."

"You can't, why?"

"I have to be here to assist the custody sergeant."

"I know, but it will only take five minutes."

"Doesn't matter I need to be here, just in case."

"Just in case what?"

"Just in case a prisoner buzzes."

"I checked the computer before I came across, you only have one prisoner, and that prisoner is Brian S. McNutt - the guy I need to interview."

"But what if another prisoner comes in?"

"Well, the custody sergeant and the PCSO (Police Custody Support Officer) will be here to deal with them."

"But they might need me after that."

"We will be finished by then."

"But what if you aren't?"

"I will. I only have to charge Brian. It will take five minutes."

"What if it doesn't?"

Just at that, the custody sergeant returned to his office with his PCSO on tow. I would seek his help in getting PC Millstone off his backside. He surely wouldn't have an issue leaving himself and a PCSO to deal with anything that came in in the next five minutes.

"Hi Grant,"

Sergeant Grant McTrumpster acknowledged my greeting with a nod.

"Grant, I am looking to interview Brian S. McNutt, could I borrow PC Millstone to corroborate me, it should only take five minutes?"

"If he is not doing anything, that should be fine."

I looked at PC Millstone sitting at the table reading his magazine. I gave him a look and a nod that said 'come on then, let's go'.

PC Millstone pulled the cuff up from his left jumper and made a point of reading his watch.

"That's six o'clock Sarge, I'm now on my break," he said looking at Sergeant McTrumpster for his support.

I expected Sergeant McTrumpster to tell PC Millstone to get off his backside and go with me to corroborate my interview with Brian. But no. Sergeant McTrumpster turned towards me, put his hands on his hips and stood to face me, legs apart and said, "Oh well, maybe you could come back."

Inside I was boiling with anger. Aghast at the audacity of PC Millstone and irritated with Sergeant McTrumpster's lack of backbone. However, I can well keep my feelings to myself. I am a poker player in these situations. I knew if I said what I thought I would just antagonise them. I needed to use the art of persuasion. I'd read 'How to win friend's and influence people' and learned from it. So I weighed up my choices and pondered the best course of action.

Then I kicked Sergeant McTrumpster in the nuts, grabbed PC Millstones magazine, a copy of Good Housekeeping, rolled it up and stuffed it up his arse.

At least, that is how I like to remember what happened.

Every day PC Millstone came in, got changed into his uniform and went to assist in the cells. Despite that, he still counted on the strength of my group.

I looked at the remaining seven in front of me. Two cops were due to go on their annual leave at the end of the week; Sergeant Dougieson allocated them time to get their paperwork up-to-date before they went off on holiday.

Despite that, they still counted towards the strength of my group.

On paper, it looked like I had twelve cops to call upon to go to calls, deliver citations, follow-up enquiries, attend road accidents, deal with sudden deaths, and all the myriad of other things that cops do. The reality was that we were two calls away from having no-one left to deal with anything.

Another factor I had to consider was the individual abilities of each of the seven cops in front of me. I think this is one thing that senior officers are most apt to forget.

We can't all be as good as you Chief Inspector!

They forget that they were young once too. I had three cops at varying stages of their probation. PC Scott Bungle was just out the packet and still had some wrapping stuck to him - literally in his case, his shirt collar still had the card insert in it, and he kept fiddling with it as it was irritating his neck. Not one of his colleagues made any move to alert him to the fact that the card was still underneath his collar, preferring to grin at their coworkers and point out the probationer's plight with a sneaky nod of the head. It was difficult to assess how many months it would take for this fledgling to become a useful member of the police force - maybe it would take years.

The second youngest probationer, PC Dinah McBarrie was the polar opposite. With only three months service everyone who knew her expected that she would effortlessly work her way up the ranks. Over the next two years, I would come to appreciate her undoubted intelligence, her work ethic and her dedication to duty. There were only two things against her, two things she could do nothing about; her sex and her baby face. Sexism and always looking like she had just graduated from primary school, meant that she didn't shoot through the ranks as quickly as she deserved - although she did pretty good.

The third probationer was PC Fatty McWhirter. There was more fat on a chicken wishbone left out to dry on a windowsill than on Fatty McWhirter. Fatty wasn't his real name but everyone called him Fatty. A few weeks later I was wandering through the report room when the phone rang, I answered it, and a middle aged female voice said, "Is Fatty there?"

"I'm sorry he is out at the moment, can I take a message?"

"Aye, jist tell him his mother called."

It is part of the Scottish psyche to veer towards irony when applying nicknames. Thus 'Wee Wendy' will be six feet two and twenty stone, 'Big Barry' will be vertically challenged and 'Irish Tony' was actually born in Macclesfield.

Despite not having a lick of fat on his bones even Fatty's mother called him 'Fatty'. I'm not even sure of his real first name now. It might not surprise me to learn that he had been christened Fatty at birth.

Fatty was a likeable character, always cheery, always obliging but always worth the watching. On the one hand, Fatty would be first to volunteer for every call that came in, on the other, he often never got around to going to it. Not that he didn't intend to go. Fatty found himself tied up with something else and never got there. When he made it to a call, he had the opposite effect of King Midas (King Midas, is remembered in Greek mythology for his ability to turn everything he touched into gold). In Fatty McWhirter's case, everything he touched turned to shit. Simple enquiries would end up more complicated than the Enigma Machine. Every police station in the country has a Fatty McWhirter, someone renowned for their ability to turn an ordinary situation into a major incident. Most police officers reading this will be thinking of a particular person right now - their very own Fatty McWhirter. If you are a police officer and you are reading this, and you can't think of anyone at your station who fits this bill, then I'm sorry to tell you that **YOU** are your station's, Fatty McWhirter.

There are occasions when some Fatty McWhirter types slip through the net and end up getting themselves promoted. That is when all hell breaks loose. Sergeants have to oversee everything that the cops do on their shift.

Fatty McWhirter types who become sergeants always complicate everything. There has been many a time when cops have been dealing with an incident in a perfectly professional manner when their own 'Sergeant Fatty McWhirter' has intervened - mayhem results. To prevent mutiny, the bosses promote the Sergeant McWhirter types to inspector just to get them out of the road. It is a route to a promotion that can take a 'Fatty McWhirter' type all the way to Chief Constable. If you are a senior officer reading this, the next time you attend a high-level meeting look around the table, you will identify at least one 'Fatty McWhirter' type. If you can't, then I'm sorry to tell you that **YOU** are the Fatty McWhirter in the room.

So that was Fatty McWhirter. Unfortunately for him, he had one other slight issue. Fatty was obliging; he would get involved in anything and everything. I couldn't fault his enthusiasm. The issue was that he had a severe allergic reaction to doing paperwork. Seriously, he would deal with an assault, take a statement from the victim, take statements from the witnesses, get medical evidence, have the victim's injuries photographed, arrest the accused, charge the accused, fingerprint and photograph the accused then let him go. That was it. Nobody got to hear of it because Fatty didn't put a single piece of paperwork in about it. He knew he had to do it, he knew how important it was, yet he couldn't bring himself to do it. I have heard it said there are three things that will get you into bother as a police officer; procreation, productions and paperwork. With the first two you need to get caught - with paperwork it catches up with you every single time.

Fatty McWhirter got the bullet. I occasionally bump into him when I am out and about. Fatty is still cheery and always stops to speak and have a chat. A likeable character. He is always keen to tell me what job he is doing now. He was a car salesman, that didn't last - apparently, they have paperwork too. Then he tried working for the council as an administrator - he got sacked for failing to ensure matters were properly filed. He became a call centre operator - let go due to his inability to keep customer notes.

What Fatty needed was a job that didn't involve paperwork. The last time I met Fatty I was encouraged to hear he had found his ideal job. A job that saw more paperwork passing through his hands now than ever before, but he didn't get into bother for it. He is perfectly happy in his position as a bin man.

So that was the probationers. The remaining four in front of me were fully fledged cops with varying lengths of service.

The oldest at forty-two was PC Jim Park, ex-army, five years service and already disillusioned. He wasn't a bad worker; he was just fed up with all the red-tape that went with the job. In the army he shot people came back and slept like a tired dog. In the police, he went out arrested people then came back and had to put all the details on a computer, write a report, complete a vulnerable person report, fill in an arrest sheet, create an intelligence entry, update the call card, etc., etc. I think he was more disillusioned because he wasn't allowed to shoot people anymore, "I mean, we should be allowed just to shoot them, fur fecks sake!" he forever bemoaned.

The cop with the most service was PC Jane McSweggan, twelve years in the job. *Twelve years service! Where are all the cops with more service than that?*

It might come as a surprise to some politicians (who have increased the minimum length of service of a police officer from thirty years to forty years) that there is a shelf-life to being a front-line police officer. There is only so much trauma a person can deal with, only so much abuse (physical and verbal) that a person can take, and only so many new initiatives from senior officers that front-line officers can endure before it has a negative effect on their health. Cops get to the point where they think 'I've done my time' and look for cushier numbers, desk jobs, specialist units, or promotion. At least with a promotion they get paid a little more for being on the front-line.

PC Jane McSweggan was nearing the end of her tether. It wasn't hard to spot, she had that dead look in her eyes, everything she did was mechanical, there was no love for her job, and there hadn't been for several years. She was going through the motions. Turn up for work, do what you have to do and go home - often via the pub. She wasn't interested in promotion; didn't have the energy to sit the exams or jump through hoops. Still a useful member of the group, she knew how to do the job properly and could teach probationers that knowledge. However, the enthusiasm she once showed had long since been knocked out of her. She turned up at the same houses and dealt with the same people for the same things too many times.

"Your role is to build high-performance teams and motivate people to do their best work," the Chief Constable had told me on the day he had promoted me to the rank of inspector.

How do you motivate the likes of Jane McSweggan?

Her main priority was to get through the day without being spat on, sworn at or stabbed in the back. Dealing with the dregs of society drained her of all hope for humanity. When she returned to the office, the demands of bosses, Procurator Fiscals, Report Checkers, new initiatives, paperwork, Crime Recording Standards, and the Crime Management Unit drained her further.

What could I possibly say to her that would get her motivated again?

"I'd like to motivate you and turn you into an integral member of our high-performance team," I said.
           Jane hit me with a double positive, "Aye, right!"

PC Kenny McBride had four years service. He'd been to university got a degree in marine biology then spent the next five years working as a barman in London.
           "Why did you do marine biology?"
           "I like fish," he replied.
           "So why did you then spend five years working as a barman in London?"

"I like fish," he replied again, this time with a wink.

The appeal of life in London waned. Living in a cupboard that cost the same as a mansion in Scotland forced Kenny to do something new with his life; he moved back to his childhood home, joined the police and settled into his new lifestyle. With only four years service, he was already cynical. He was pessimistic about his promotion prospects. Mocking of senior officers, and their knee-jerk reactions to everything. Sceptical of any efforts to improve working practices. Sarcastic with his supervisors, contemptuous of other departments, in particular the Traffic Department (but then so was everyone else), and disparaging of the way cops from other groups dealt with things, leaving him to pick up the pieces. Yup, he was just like every other cop.

So how do you know who will be a good cop or not? How do you decide if they are a good guy? Here is a test for you. The last two on my shift had three years service, I'll describe them, and you decide which one would make the best cop.

PC Danny McCabe always wanted to be a policeman. He applied to join the police the moment he left school but was advised that he was too young and inexperienced. Still intent on joining he went to university and got a degree in criminology. On the day he received his BA he applied for the police again, and this time he got in. At police college, he won the academic prize. He cruised through his probation and was highly praised for his report writing. Despite having only three years service, he was trusted to take on a probationer of his own and teach him the job. He sat in the front row of the briefing, uniform pressed, boots polished, notebook at the ready.

PC Ally McArthur used to work at the zoo, fed up with monkeying around he applied for various jobs including the police. He scraped his way through police college with middle-of-the-road exam results, middle of the road fitness tests but managed to keep to the left side of the road on his driving test. He scraped through his probation and was now sitting up the back of the briefing room jacket unbuttoned, a cup of coffee in one hand and a piece of cake in the other. The crumbs dropped onto his black wicking shirt every time he took a bite. It wasn't clear if he was listening to the sergeant or not.

Obvious isn't it?

You would think you would be a fool to choose PC McArthur over PC McCabe. McCabe a motivated cop, keen and made an effort. McArthur had fallen into the job, the first one he got a reply from, there was no burning desire to be a policeman. He was slovenly, lazy and apathetic. So who would you choose?.

Well if you read the descriptions again, the clue is there; PC Ally McArthur was a keeper. (C'mon he used to work at the zoo).

Oh, suit yourself!

Sergeant Dougieson finished his briefing.

"Would you like to add anything inspector?"

I had given this some thought. I was now in a position of authority; In charge of this group and responsible for everything they did. I would be the most senior officer on duty when the bosses had all disappeared off home. Back shifts, night shifts, and weekends. The times when the most serious things happened. We rarely got rapes, murders, serious assaults, robberies and the like Monday to Friday 9 a.m. to 5 p.m. These things happened when people were drunk, late at night, and when we had the least amount of police officers on duty.

"Your role is to build high-performance teams and motivate people to do their best work," the Chief Constable had told me.

I had thought about that too.

I wanted to get off to a good footing. I worked on my management style as a sergeant and felt I had developed a good working relationship with my teams. I'd experienced bad management working practices in the past and learned from them. I didn't like being micro-managed, so I didn't micro-manage. I didn't like it when supervisors took credit for my work, so I always gave credit where credit was due. I praised good work in public and when things didn't go according to plan, I examined these things in private - always with the view they were learning experiences. I didn't like bullies, so I never bullied people. I didn't like it when supervisors were indifferent or apathetic, so I always took an interest and paid attention to what my staff said. I didn't like supervisors who thought they were better than everyone else so I listened to opinions and was willing to change my viewpoint or at least give people the chance to prove that they could do what they said they could. I was there to support and develop everyone on the group.

Conscious I'd never worked as an inspector in F division before, even although I was with the same force, there were things we did different from station to station. I vowed not to criticise any practices that were different. Nobody likes getting told they are doing it wrong or hear the words 'At my last station we did it this way'. That just annoys people.

In 2013, the police in Scotland merged the eight forces into just one, we all became members of Police Scotland. A lot of changes took place. A lot of our practices came under some criticism for being outdated and ineffective. Not long after we merged, I had to attend a training course regarding the way we dealt with domestic incidents. Domestic violence is unacceptable. It became a priority for the government, who made it a priority for the police. That wasn't a bad thing, a high proportion of murders are committed in the domestic setting. The thing was, I had to sit through a training course telling me this. A senior officer who had worked at another force before our merger into Police Scotland, explained the new procedures we were to adopt. He went on at great length about how important it was and how we needed to adhere to these new procedures. The new procedures turned out to be the very same procedures we had been using in our force for the past twelve years. The actual step diagram he showed us was the same one we had been using - identical in every way except the colour, instead of green it was now yellow. So I vowed not to be that man.

I planned to show my new team respect, pay attention to them, know their names and learn all about them. I planned to smile, value their work and develop their trust. I suspected that they would be just as anxious at having a new inspector. I had my introduction prepared. I wanted to put them at ease as quickly as possible. I didn't want to be the fearsome inspector I remembered from my time when I started. I wanted to be approachable; I wanted to be open-minded, and I wanted to earn their respect. Helping the group make a success of themselves would be the best way to build a good working environment. A good working environment built on mutual trust, honesty and decency is the best way to build high-performance teams. That is my opinion.

"Yes, I'd like to say a few words…"

The radio crackled into life, "That's a grade one call to the Sports Bar in the High Street, fight in progress, repeat fight in progress."

Sergeant Dougieson and the entire shift rose from their chairs as one. Three seconds later the room was empty.

So much for my motivational first speech. It was time to get my jacket.

THE MICHAEL PARKINSON TELEVISION INTERVIEW

Parky: You discuss senior officers a little more in your latest book, there are fewer stories about members of the public. Is that a conscious decision?

Malky: There are some hairy incidents with members of the public in this book too. It is just that I dealt more with senior officers as an inspector than I did as a cop or a sergeant. I wrote about what I experienced.

Parky: Do you think your stories put senior police officers in a bad light?

Malky: On the whole, I have to say our senior officers were good at their jobs. If compared to other industries you would probably say they were excellent. There were some shining examples of dedicated, courageous and expert leadership.

Parky: But not all of them?

Malky: All of them were excellent some of the time. Some were excellent all of the time, but all of them weren't excellent all of the time. That's where my stories come in.

Parky: That makes sense - I think. Is that why you wrote about Chief Inspector Chumley?

Malky: I didn't mind Chief Inspector Chumley. We had different ideas, and that made it frustrating for me, but I think I probably frustrated him as much he did me.

Parky: Were his meetings actually known as the 'Hindsight Meetings?'

Malky: They were the morning meetings that chief inspectors run in every police office, everywhere across the country. I would be surprised if there isn't a single cop anywhere that doesn't refer to them as the 'hindsight meetings'.

Parky: You mention the Dunning-Kruger effect, what is that exactly?

Malky: The Dunning-Kruger effect, is a recognised psychological effect. It is all to do with a cognitive bias where people have difficulty in recognising their own incompetence, and that leads to inflated self-assessments. Delusions of superiority if you like. I abbreviated it to 'Dunker'.

Parky: Dunker?

Malky: Yeah, **Dun**ning-**K**ruger - Dunker! It was my pet name for some people.

Parky: Did they know what it meant?

Malky: Of course not. That's the thing about the Dunning-Kruger effect, people who suffer from it don't realise they suffer from it. If you ask a 'Dunker' the difference between ignorance and apathy they will reply - 'I don't know and I don't care.'

Parky: Do you think that applied to Chief Inspector Chumley?

Malky: Well I used to call him 'Dunker' to his face, and he thought it was a term of endearment. He thought it was something to do with the way he always dipped his biscuits in his tea. Although, he wasn't a total Dunker. I believe there is a sliding scale. I don't think of those internal misperceptions as either on or off. People have a dimmer switch. It varies.

Parky: So on a scale of one to ten where would you put Chief Inspector Chumley?

Malky: Well if Donald Trump is a ten and Gandhi is a one then Chumley would be a seven or eight.

Parky: Where would you put yourself on that scale?

Malky: Is that a trick question?

Parky: I wondered if it was relevant?

Malky: Self-insight is tricky at the best of times. So is the question, do I recognise the extent of my inadequacy?

Parky: Do you?

Malky: Dunning and Kruger, the psychologists who discovered the effect, also found that people of high ability tend to underestimate their relative competence. I always worried that I was doing the right thing. I was always interested in other people's points of view. I tried to weigh up everything before acting.

Parky: So you didn't make mistakes?

Malky: I didn't say that. I just found it interesting to make observations about people when they did stupid things.

Parky: You have been frank and honest with this book, does it worry you it might offend someone?

Malky: I've no intention of offending anyone. That is why I changed the names.

Parky: But surely some of your colleagues will recognise the people you have written about?

Malky: Yes, well that certainly happened with my first two police books.

Parky: Does that worry you?

Malky: Yes, it worries me. I only ever wanted to tickle, inspire and make people think. I apologise to anyone who takes offence.

Parky: So would you consider removing any stories if someone asked?

Malky: I'd consider it. I have put my email address at the end of the book so people can get in touch.

Parky: You have an interesting perspective on being an inspector - can you tell us about that?

Chapter 2

THE THING ABOUT BEING AN INSPECTOR

The thing about being an inspector is that you don't get to have as much fun as you used to.

On the day they took my stripes away and presented me with two pips, they gave me a slip of paper to take across to Health & Wellbeing. There I had to hand the slip of paper to the receptionist, she nodded, grim-faced, and asked me to take a seat in the corridor on a cracked plastic chair. It was an uncomfortable chair, made all the worse because as I fidgeted to get more comfortable the skin of my buttocks got caught in the crack and sent me jumping into the air dragging the cracked plastic chair with me.

It was a long wait punctured only by the sad souls passing as they entered to get various ailments assessed and diagnosed so they could decide which department would take them while they were recovering. The ones that were not unwilling to catch my eye looked even more forlorn as they exited.

"Resource Management Unit?"

"Yup!"

After an interminably long time sitting with one bum cheek on the rim of the chair to avoid the crack, the receptionist popped her head around the door to get my attention, "You can go through now," she said.

All inspectors have to go through this procedure. It is a prerequisite you have to agree to before accepting the promotion.

The room was bare, except for a heavy wooden chair. Leather straps hung down from the arms and further straps dangled from the front two legs.

A man in a white coat with a white face eyed me up and down before bidding me to take a seat. Then he secured my arms and legs to the chair using the straps, pulling them tight, there was no escaping. A nurse entered the room. She had a clipboard in her hands and went through a list of preset questions; What medications you are on? How often do you have sex? Have you ever seen a monkey eat chocolate? Although, I don't profess to remember them word for word.

She took my temperature, then my blood pressure. She measured my pulse and noted all the details down on the form secured to the clipboard. Satisfied that all was in order the man in the white coat provided me with a strong local anaesthetic before carrying out the surgical removal of my sense of humour.

Honest that's what happened!

The process of getting to Chief Inspector is even more Draconian. With the addition of an extra pip, they have to go through the process again just to ensure that there are no tiny little growths of humour spreading their way back in. The sense of humour sac has to be well and truly scraped out and then flushed of all funniness. Once removed the surgeon implants an extra large sarcasm gland in the vacant space. The result is a zombie-like senior officer devoid of all sensitivity in his biting scorn and mockery. It is a huge price to pay for the equivalent of an extra *McFlurry* in the wage packet.

The higher the rank, the worse it gets. A newly promoted superintendent, on his way out the door, gets handed a letter in a sealed and official-looking brown envelope. He has to take the letter with him to the 'psychiatrist's office'.

The psychiatrist's office is situated in a back street identified only by a small plaque showing all patients should enter via the side door. There the superintendent meets the psychiatrist. It would be easy to mistake her for someone who had just spent the weekend at the first Glastonbury Festival in 1970. She ushers the superintendent to an upstairs room and guides him to sit on a stained couch of faded floral vintage upholstery. Then she starts a course of memory erasure.

Memory erasure is the selective artificial removal of memories from the mind. There are many patients who benefit from this process; sufferers of post-traumatic stress disorder, drug addicts, war veterans, victims of violent crime and those who voted for Donald Trump.

In the case of the superintendent, the process he or she undergoes is for the express purpose of erasing all recollections of cock-ups, boobs, blunders, gaffes and bungling incompetence exhibited in his or her career.

At least, that is what it seems like.

Chief Inspector MacSever was to be my boss at F Division, and he came with a public health warning. I don't mean he had a big red warning triangle stamped on his forehead or anything, but whenever anyone congratulated me on my promotion to inspector they would ask the question, "So where are you going?"

"F Division," I would reply innocently.

This reply would elicit a sharp intake of breath, the furrowing of the brow and the follow-up question, "Ooh, how do you get on with Chief Inspector MacSever?".

Chief Inspector MacSever was in charge at F Division and as you will guess, had a reputation. He was infinitely confident in his abilities and just as infinitely scornful of everyone else's. I sounded out another inspector who worked in F Division, "How do you like working with Chief Inspector MacSever?"

He drew his cheeks together, furrowed his brow and inhaled so deep a breath he could have sucked up a firkin of beer in the one go, "Have you never worked with him?"

"No. But I heard he was the type of cop that would charge his granny."

"He was the type of cop that would shove a copy of the Road Traffic Act up his grannie's arse if that would get him another rung up the ladder."

"It can't be easy working for him then?"

"It is terrifying. You can't please the man. I call him 'Aye but'"

"iButt?"

"Aye, 'aye but', you just can't please the man."

"How do you mean?"

"You'll find out."

Well, I did find out.

A couple of weeks later, Chief Inspector MacSever called me into his office for a chat. Despite being in my forties with twenty-three years police service under my belt, I felt like a schoolboy called to the headmaster's office for a telling off. I was strangely nervous. All the stories about the brutal MacSever had played on my mind. I was only just in the door, and I was wondering if I had done something wrong. Maybe it was something I hadn't done. I likened this to a virus; the fear spreading from the other inspectors. Not just them, all the sergeants and every single one of the cops seemed to panic as if in terror when they heard Chief Inspector MacSever's footsteps coming along the corridor. Jackets were buttoned up; hats thrown onto heads and quick exits made. Those who couldn't escape the office daren't look up. All eye contact avoided. They studiously typed on their computers or made notes in notebooks, anything to look busy and avoid his dreaded eye or the horror of him actually speaking to them.

It was with a little trepidation, then, when I stepped into his office and he ordered me to sit in the low seat in front of him. I slumped into the soft seat, knees level with my chest and looked up at him on his high swivel chair behind his desk.

"Inspector McEwan, how are you settling in?"

"Very well, thank you," I replied.

"How are you getting on with Sergeant Dougieson?"

Ah! A fishing expedition.

"Sergeant Dougieson seems like a good lad, from what I have seen so far he has a good handle on the shift, and they seem to be working for him."

"Aye, but…?" he posed this as a question.

"No buts."

Chief Inspector MacSever looked at me in the eye, then ever so slightly raised an eyebrow. He didn't say a word. It was the oldest trick in the book. That quizzical look, accompanied by the awkward silence is a technique I have used myself. It is a great way to coax someone to keep talking. It is the additional unplanned conversation that can trip someone up.

A fishing expedition.

Unfortunately, with all my trepidation and big guppy mouth, I took the bait.

"Well, no big buts anyway, er... um... when I say big buts I don't mean *big butts* if you know what I mean. There aren't even any small busts, I mean, er... um... not busts - buts, no tiny wee buts, er… um… you know not like tiny wee bums, oh buttocks. I mean there are no 'howevers, yets or stills'.

"No exceptions, you mean?"

"Yes, that's what I mean, no exceptions."

"Come now, Inspector McEwan, there are always exceptions to the rule," his eyebrow had come down from its elevated position.

"Well, so far sir, I haven't come across anything of any great concern."

"So you have minor concerns?"

"Eh… No, nothing like that."

"Aye, but…?"

"No buts," *here we go again,* "…I mean, no exceptions."

"Aye, but his time management isn't the best, is it?"

"Time management? I haven't had a problem with his time management. So far he is always last to leave the office."

"There you go," MacSever sat back in his chair and folded his arms, "time management."

"That's not what I meant. I meant that Sergeant Dougieson always makes sure the troops are back in and have their work up to date before he goes home."

"Aye, but…?" the slightly raised eyebrow was back.

I changed tack, "Well if that is what you think, sir, I'll keep my eye on it."

"Aye, but… he forgot to put a write off on the logs last night."

"Write off? What write off?"

"You mean you don't know? You're supposed to be in charge of the group, and that means taking responsibility for your sergeant."

"Yes sir, that is my fault, I accept full responsibility. I am liable on this occasion because I don't know about it. What exactly was the entry he forgot to put on?"

He ignored me.

I bet he made that up just to rattle me.

"I'm looking to get this station working like clockwork, Inspector McEwan, and that starts with you and your group. There are not enough drugs cases going through the uniforms. We can't just leave it all to the drugs squad; they have bigger fish to fry. The cops out there must come across drugs all the time, and I see nothing to suggest they are doing something about it. Do they wear blinkers out there?"

I presumed that was a rhetorical question and didn't answer.

"I could go out just now and score myself a bag of heroin in a jiffy."

Really! You know how to score a bag of heroin for yourself?

"Cops just don't seem interested anymore. In my day…"

Here we go.

"…it was just something we did as a matter of course. I was always looking for self-generated work."

Oh, yes, that was when you had twice the cops on the street and half the calls that they have now

"I want something done about it. I want every other Chief Inspector across the force to know that I have the best detection rate."

Now we've got to the bottom of it - it's all about you.

There was no point in arguing with him. He didn't want to know I only had seven of the twelve cops on my group strength on duty. He couldn't care that five of them seconded or off sick. His talk was his way of ticking the box in the leadership manual. He had had his chat with his new inspector, he set out my responsibilities, what he would hold me to account over and gave me a clear instruction that drugs were his priority. I left his office well and truly encouraged, enthused and motivated to be getting on with the job - like that time I had to wait a week to have a colonoscopy.

I relayed Chief Inspectors MacSever's priority to the shift at the next briefing.

"If we could put some effort into detecting a few drugs cases that might keep him off our backs."

Sergeant Dougieson nodded and then tasked the team with what they had to do. He allocated one crew a sudden death that would tie them up for most of the shift. He gave another crew door-to-door enquiries for a series of housebreakings that had occurred over the weekend. That would tie them up for most of the shift. The last remaining crew he tasked with attending the outstanding calls - we had thirty-two on the list, and that would only get reduced if no more calls came in. I wondered how we would ever get any additional self-generated drugs cases. It was always like this.

About a week later Sergeant Dougieson popped into my office.

"Just to let you know inspector, I've had the lads working on drugs."

"What drugs have they been on?"

"Not them. The drugs problem."

I perked up, "And?"

"Well, Jane McSweggan has come up with some information. The Quigley brothers are dealing cannabis."

"Where did she get this information from and is it corroborated?"

"It is anonymous, but we know that they have been charged for drug dealing in the past."

"Is there any recent intelligence?"

"Nothing new, no."

Sergeant Dougieson knew he needed reasonable grounds to get a search warrant.

"No judge will grant a warrant on one anonymous tip off, is he?"

"No a judge won't, but a justice of the peace might."

Justices of the peace or JPs come from all walks of life and do not need to have a legal qualification. They are volunteers, of proven good character, who sit in place of a judge in minor criminal cases in the district court. While they undergo some training, they get advice from a qualified clerk during court proceedings. They also have the authority to grant a search warrant, when a judge is not available out of court hours. They must be satisfied by information on oath that there are reasonable grounds for suspecting the specified matters. JPs are all of good character and value and respect the police. Thus when a police officer chaps their door at one o'clock in the morning looking for an urgent search warrant, they rub the sleep from their eyes and deem that it must be serious. They nod at whatever we tell them and sign on the dotted line.

I considered the information Sergeant Dougieson had presented, "Where do they stay?"

"They have a small cottage on the outskirts of town."

"Could we put a watch on it?"

"There isn't anyone available. The whole shift is tied up and have custody reports to do."

"Okay, get your civvy jacket, and I'll borrow an unmarked car from the CID."

It was a Saturday morning. I parked the unmarked CID motor across the river from the cottage. Far enough away so it wouldn't draw attention from the Quigley brothers but close enough to see if there were any comings or goings from their cottage. The morning turned into the afternoon. Nothing much was happening, but it was a pleasant day to be out of the office. There were no movements from the cottage. Two ducks on the river amused us as they dived under the water to forage. We picked one each and made it a competition to see who's duck stayed under the longest. We were both surprised when mine remained submerged for an impressive thirty-three seconds. Then they stopped and sat on the calm water preening themselves. We waited some more. Occasionally our attention was drawn to dog walkers who crossed the viaduct to our left and disappeared into the forest on the other side of the river. We were still there when they returned, dogs muddy and carrying sticks. Then our luck changed.

Two youths appeared from behind us, passed our car and walked to the viaduct. They didn't have a dog. That was interesting. Hooded youths tend not to go for a walk in the woods. They turned right once they had crossed the viaduct and headed towards the Quigley's cottage. Even more interesting. From our position we couldn't see the front door of the building, the two youths disappeared from view. A moment later one of the Quigley's exited the back door, he climbed a small metal fence and entered the cornfield at the rear of the cottage. Partially hidden we saw him traipse diagonally through the field and enter a metal shed right down by the river. No one would guess it belonged to them. In the meantime, the two youths came back into view at the front of the cottage. They aimlessly waited. The Quigley brother we had seen at the metal shed returned, and within a minute of entering the rear of his house, the two youths were walking back over the viaduct. Unfortunately for them, they would walk right past us.

I clicked open the bonnet catch, got out and fiddled with the engine. Sergeant Dougieson opened the boot and rummaged around. As the two youths walked by the unmarked CID car, they found themselves sandwiched between a smiling plain clothed sergeant and an equally pleased plain clothed inspector. It couldn't have worked out better. We searched them, found a bag of herbal on each of them and after checking out their details via the control room were delighted to find that both had arrest warrants in their names. A plan formulated in my head.

I didn't need to worry about our two youths warning the Quigleys; they would remain in custody to appear in court on the Monday for their warrants. They turned out to be quite obliging and provided full signed statements to the fact that they had got their drugs from the Quigleys. I sent two cops to obtain a search warrant from an obliging JP and for it to include the authority to search the metal shed. The next morning, instead of having a normal briefing, we would take the whole shift down to the Quigleys and execute it.

Sunday morning came, and the night shift inspector handed me the responsibility for two vulnerable missing person enquiries. I left the drugs raid in the hands of Sergeant Dougieson.

When I eventually got back to the office Sergeant Dougieson had a smile a mile wide. I had a smile wider than his when he told me that the Quigley brothers were in custody and let me in on what he had found. I couldn't wait to see Chief Inspector MacSever's face when he turned up for the morning meeting on Monday.

"What are you looking so smug about," were MacSever's first words as he entered the meeting room.

Monday morning meetings started at 8 a.m. These were fraught affairs when chief inspectors go over everything that happened over the last three days. MacSever was a particularly demanding chairman; he expected answers to everything.

"What happened at the road accident on Friday afternoon? What were the injuries? Has someone been in touch with the driver's parents? What size of engines did they have? What colour were the cars involved?"

I mean - REALLY! - What difference does that make to him? It reminded me of the Monty Python sketch where King Arthur and his knights come to the Bridge of Death, and the bridge keeper asks three questions, which they must answer truthfully before they can cross, the third question being 'What is your favourite colour?' Sir Galahad of Camelot replies 'Blue... er no it's actually...' and at that, he is tossed into the fiery pit.

I gathered my thoughts and rattled off an answer to Chief Inspector MacSever.

"The young driver was using his mobile phone and crossed into the opposite lane where he had a head on collision with an old couple coming the other way. All parties were taken to the hospital, but the young driver got released later on. I think his parents collected him. The elderly couple sustained whiplash injuries and remained in hospital overnight for observations, but they are out now. The Ford Focus ST used by the young driver has a two-litre engine and has about 252 brake horsepower, it does nought to sixty in about 6.2 seconds and has a top speed of 145 mph. The elderly couple drove a 1.1 litre Suzuki Alto; I'm not sure that a Suzuki Alto can reach 60 mph. The Ford was yellow, and the Suzuki was blue, er no it's actually..." I said and at that point expected to be tossed into the fiery pit.

"Aye, but," Chief Inspector MacSever interrupted, "was he speeding?"

"No. We have independent witnesses saying he was just pulling away from the traffic lights and the maximum both cars were doing was only about ten miles per hour, thankfully."

We went through three days of logs, crime returns, and other business like this. Finally, Chief Inspector MacSever came to his priorities.

"What are you doing about my priorities?" he looked directly at me.

"Well Chief Inspector, yesterday Sergeant Dougieson obtained a drugs search warrant and turned the Quigley's cottage down by the viaduct."

"Aye, but he didn't find anything in the house did he?" MacSever had obviously read the crime report but missed one significant part. I smiled at myself.   What a joy it is to sit in a morning meeting and get one up on Chief Inspector MacSever. He represented all the worst of the bullies in the job and all the back end of a sewage outlets I had come across in my life. Times like that you have to savour. The juiciness of knowing I would rub it right in made me almost drool.

"Well no sir, other than about three thousand pounds in cash…"

"Aye, but that doesn't prove a drugs case, does it?"

"No, not that in itself sir, but the cannabis factory they were operating at the bottom of the field behind their house kinda proves it. We have statements from witnesses speaking to them selling it, we have their fingerprints all over the shed they were growing the cannabis in, and we also have their full and frank admissions they owned the shed and started a cannabis factory in it. There were so many plants, and so much bagged cannabis we reckon the street value must be nigh on half a million pounds."

Stick that up yer pipe MacSever.

"Aye, but, his productions are always a mess aren't they?" He replied.

THE MICHAEL PARKINSON TELEVISION INTERVIEW

Parky: I'm interested in the way the police promotion system works.

Malky: Yes?

Parky: There seem to have been a few different systems used over the years.

Malky: Yes, if there was one constant it was 'change'.

Parky: Why have there been so many?

Malky: The old 'bun fight' needed revised, it was such an antiquated way to promote someone. The police needed something that was fair, and above board. Unfortunately every time they put a new system in place there was someone who disagreed with it.

Parky: You had a good idea for a new system?

Malky: Yes, I did some reading and research into it and 'The Sweetie Jar Principle' impressed me most. It brought the most competent leaders to the top. It was fairly simple and cheaper to implement than other systems and any organisation that used it seemed to thrive.

Parky: Did you suggest it to senior management?

Malky: I explained how it worked to two different Chief Constables.

Parky: So what happened?

Chapter 3

THE SWEETIE JAR PRINCIPLE

My promotion to inspector took place at a time when interest rates rose to 5.25%. Things seemed to be going downhill, and it wasn't long before the world experienced an almighty financial crash in the worst economic disaster since the Great Depression of 1929. House prices fell, yet mortgage costs spiralled. Many ordinary people lost lots of money and some ended up with no roof over their heads. All of this resulted from the subprime mortgage crisis that started in America and quickly spread its diseased tentacles across the globe. Several observant money-men saw it coming and scooped up billions of dollars into their coffers by betting against the accepted investing wisdom. Some banks struggled, and some failed spectacularly. The Dunning-Kruger effect was like a virus; it spread with epidemic proportions across the banking sector. The effect meant that bankers couldn't see it coming - blinded by their incompetence.

They needn't have worried. Politicians shored up the finances of all the banks, bailout packages amounting to trillions of dollars dished out to keep all the banking Dunkers in their high-paying jobs. They continued to receive bonuses that would support a small country. So, when a politician retires, resigns or gets voted out of public service and goes on to give a talk to a group of estate agents in New York about Brexit or something and gets paid twice his yearly salary for an hour or two, it makes me think; *'What the hell did they do to deserve that?'*

It was enough for me to raise an eyebrow at the politicians. Others raised a similarly suspicious eyebrow at the police promotion process.

You would think the performance review process would link to the promotion process. It didn't and never has. As far as I could see there was little connection between performance and promotion. There will be those that will tell you it is linked, that there is a procedure to make the two connect, but that is just naïve. I'll tell you why it is not.

There have been many promotion processes over the years, all variations on a theme. When I started out, long before I was even to consider going for promotion, they had 'The bun fight'. The bun fight was where senior police officers, heads of department, got together in a wee room and argued about who they should promote. There would be a ding dong argument and whoever shouted loudest for their favourite, would get him or her promoted. I'm not sure why they called it ' The bun fight', but I pictured several of our more intimidating senior officers throwing various choices of patisseries at each other. You might think it a fair method of promoting someone, particularly if you were a member of the police football team (a disproportionate number of which seemed to end up with scrambled egg on the skip of their hats). That might be a surprise to all conspiracy theorists who thought it was the Freemasons who ran the show. The police had, long ago, moved on from funny handshakes to kicking balls and showering together. (For all I know that's what the Freemasons did too, but I am only surmising).

As time moved on the feeling grew that promotion through favouritism was not a good way to run the police force. So they introduced another promotion process. The new process involved a complete revamp of the way we did things. The 'bun fight' was consigned to a metal storage container at the far reaches of the rear yard at headquarters where it remained under lock and key - and would only ever see the light of day if all common sense and rational thought were to vacate the premises.

The Human Resources Department (HRD), spent months researching the subject and came up with a new system. This new system was, of course, abandoned by the next Chief Constable, whose preference was for something he had more control over. That was something that happened with every new Chief Constable. As soon as the new incumbent took up the role, HRD would be tasked to come up with something new and supposedly better.

The new Chief Constable was of the opinion that every single senior officer below him had been promoted beyond their ability. As demonstrated by the 'Peter Principle'. The 'Peter Principle' is a management theory which states that employees stop getting promoted once they reach a rank in which they are incompetent. A multi-national company that finds itself saddled with an ineffective executive nudges the underachiever into a job which he can do no harm ('Stevie, we need you to sort out our branch office in Timbuktu') I know it happened in the police. Competent cops earned a promotion to sergeant; competent sergeants received deserved promotions to inspector and so on. However, they did not get promoted further if they are incompetent in their new role. That is the 'Peter Principle'. Once they no longer perform effectively, they stop being promoted, and thus managers rise to their level of incompetence. Unfortunately, it wasn't always that the police had a branch office in Timbuktu.

For those of you that disagree and consider that you did not or are not being promoted further because of some other reason - it's probably because your immediate boss is incompetent and **doesn't appreciate just how good you are**. See, the Peter Principle works!

The Human Resources Department was a wonderful development from the 'Personnel Department'. The name change was not mere cosmetics. The department encompassed all the best ideas concerning hiring, evaluating, training and compensating employees. HRD focussed on the people side of management. It introduced practices to deal effectively with the staff in the organisation. It was there to provide advice and identify proper processes in the way management dealt with all aspects of employee development. The police is undoubtedly a more professional organisation because of HRD. So here is my problem: why do they have to be so bloody irritating?

I bring this up because the new Chief Constable decided we needed a new appraisal process. He wanted to dispense with typed reports and introduce a computerised system. He discussed it with HRD and left them to get on with it. It wasn't a bad idea. The current process was open to human error. I say error, I mean incompetence and apathy. The guidelines were clear; once a year every single person in the organisation, cleaner, cop, chief inspector - you name them, is supposed to have an annual appraisal (performance review). The line manager should have a one-on-one chat and provide useful feedback about their job performance. Each appraisal should become a historical record and contribute to professional development.

Nope!

Few managers submitted appraisals in time, and often not at all. I recall going four whole years getting no feedback whatsoever. What was HRD doing?

It seemed simple. HRD sent out an appraisal form to the line manager, the line manager carried out the one-on-one chat, filled out the form and sent it back through the chain of command. If it didn't arrive back, HRD should contact the line manager and chase it up. If that didn't work, they should alert the line manager's boss. If that didn't work, it should be part of the feedback on the line manager's appraisal, simple.

Computerising the appraisal process didn't seem such a bad idea.

In due course, they developed the new system. Then HRD put it in place, with no form of training.

It was a different system from which we were used to. It used unique computer software. Due to there being no training and it not being intuitive we had issue after issue using it. HRD had spent a lot of time working on it, getting to know the ins and outs, ironing the out the faults, and adding in fixes until they figured that it was perfect. So perfect they could introduce the new software system to every police office and everyone would intuitively know how it worked and what we were meant to do.

I can pick up a smartphone swipe the screen open, click on any app and intuitively use it without having to read screeds and screeds of instructions. On my Dad's eighty-fifth birthday we presented him with an iPad. His first tablet and he clicked away immediately. Within minutes he was absorbed in a game of *'Solitaire',* and we got on with raiding his drinks cupboard and eating his cake.

Sorry to be the bearer of bad news but the new computerised appraisal system was an almighty load of bollocks - a head full of lice wouldn't leave you scratching your head as much.

It didn't quite roll out as smoothly as HRD thought it should. It spluttered, coughed and rolled along as if someone had left on the handbrake.

Our Chief Constable was a nice person who exuded intelligence and competence. He was a personable man who took an interest in what people thought. He was concerned about his staff and what they thought about the way the force ran. He wanted to know what he could improve. So, he visited every inspector in his Force. My turn came. He sat in my office, and we chatted about various matters. The subject of the new Appraisal System and promotion process came up. He had heard a few moans and groans about it and wondered what we could do to improve it. I voiced my concern we still hadn't got it right.

"Okay, so what would you do?"

"I think we should roll out training for the new appraisal system."

"You don't think it is simple enough?"

"No, I don't. We wouldn't be having all the problems we are having with it if it was simple and intuitive to use, but it isn't. At the moment we are like dogs sitting waiting for a treat, but we can't understand the instructions, so we sit, beg, give a paw and wag our tails in the hope that we hit on the right thing that HRD want us to do. It is an incompetent back end of a sewage outlet that thinks just because they understand something everyone else will too."

"You think HRD are incompetent arseholes?"

"You are maybe reading things into that that I didn't say."

"It would be time intensive to provide that training, and it is time we can little afford."

"It will be more expensive in the long run if we don't carry out training - even if HRD were to cascade the training, it would be more sensible than doing nothing. If there is no training in it, then almost everyone will take ages to learn the new system or scratch their heads forever more."

My nice Chief Constable contemplated what I had told him and nodded. He seemed to agree with me.

"What about our promotion process?"

It is normal for moaners, naysayers and the like to have no idea and say they don't know, quick to criticise, slow to come up with a better solution. In my case, I had given it some thought. I had researched the topic and concluded that the 'Sweetie Jar Principle' would be easy to adopt and implement. Convinced it would give the best results. It had proven to do just that elsewhere.

"What is the Sweetie Jar Principle?" he asked.

"Oh, you probably don't want me to waste your time telling you about that. I once discussed this with your predecessor, and he told me it was interesting but... 'that will not be happening' he said."

His predecessor, Chief Constable Handy McDandy, had been the guest of honour at a sporting event I was taking part in, I was chairman, and he sat at my table. After the dinner, speeches, and prize giving he loosened off his tie, and we got talking. I took the opportunity to tell him about the 'Sweetie Jar Principle'. After explaining all the ins and outs, he dismissed it out of hand. 'Interesting but that will not be happening!' he told me. So when my new Chief Constable asked about it I answered, "Do you really want me to tell you?"

"Yes, what is the sweetie jar principle?"

"You won't be interested, I haven't spent five years developing it. It is just something I know that some companies use."

"I am interested, tell me about it. That is why I am here. I want to know what people think, I like to hear good ideas and if they have merit, I am the type of person who will implement them," he encouraged me.

So I explained that the 'Sweetie Jar Principle' was a promotion process used by some successful companies in America and other parts of the world. The basis came from the theory that the more people involved in choosing who should be promoted, the more likely you would come up with the right person.

The theory originated from experiments where they compared results from one person guessing how many sweeties were in a jar to increasing numbers of people guessing and then taking the average. One person guessing could be right but in all likelihood would be wide of the mark. However, if you took ten people, and they all guessed, and you took their answers, added them up and divided by ten you would come up with a closer approximation, ending with a better guess than one person. If you took one hundred people and did the same, you would get an even more accurate answer. It is, in fact, a scientifically proven principle. The sum of all knowledge available will give a more reliable approximation than singular subjective speculation. The best way to know the correct number of sweeties in a jar is to count them out. If you can't do that, then the best is to ask as many people as you can to have a guess and then take the average.

Some companies took this principle and adapted it to their promotion process. One company had a simple way of doing it. If a position came up in their company, they advertised that post for suitably experienced interested parties. This part qualified the candidates in that it identified people interested in doing the job. Putting themselves forward showed ambition on their part.

The company then sent out a ballot to every employee, from CEO to cleaner. Everyone had a vote, and each vote counted the same.

Not everyone voted, not everyone voted for the same person, but at the end, the person who got the most votes got the job. What the company found was that people liked to vote for good communicators, hard workers, competent managers and inspirational leaders. Nobody wanted to be managed by an idiot or by some over ambitious paranoid schizophrenic lunatic.

Those that were ambitious realised that to get on in the company, they couldn't just suck up to their boss and hope for a bit of nepotism. The company found that, as a direct result of the process, people worked harder, worked together better, were more engaged and the best people rose to the top. It was a neat solution, fair, above board and it worked. The particular company I looked at took it one step further; the winning candidate was put on probation for one year. That meant that they could see if they were suited to the role. It also meant that they were counting the sweeties.

How do you tell how many sweeties are in a jar? Answer: count them. What if you can't count them? Answer: ask as many people as you can to have a guess.

You can't know how well someone will perform in a role until they do it so choosing wisely in the first place then assessing the performance was all part of their system. How did they assess the performance at the end of the year? They went back to everyone in the company and asked them to rate how the person had done. It is great for identifying if they'd squashed a round peg into a square hole. The 'Sweetie Jar Principle' was fair - it did away with nepotism, discrimination, and incomplete knowledge of a candidate. The 'Sweetie Jar Principle' was effective - it identified the best candidate. The 'Sweetie Jar Principle' helped businesses thrive - the hardest workers, the inspirational leaders, the innovative thinkers, the great communicators all rose to the top. The 'Sweetie Jar Principle' was economical - the process was simple and cheap to operate.

I explained all this to my new Chief Constable, and he listened with his hands entwined, chin resting on his two index fingers, nodding appropriately, considering everything I said.

"What do you think?" I asked him.

My new Chief Constable looked at me, seemed to deliberate over his answer, after a large pause his face creased into a great big cheesy grin, and he said, "Interesting… but that will not be happening!"

THE MICHAEL PARKINSON TELEVISION INTERVIEW

Parky: Why do you think they didn't take on 'The Sweetie Jar Principle?' I mean it sounds like a perfectly reasonable process, and it proved to work elsewhere.

Malky: I wasn't given a reason. I think it was probably too radical a step.

Parky: Or maybe they felt they should decide because that was what they were paid to do?

Malky: The Dunning-Kruger effect?

Parky: Yes, because they thought they knew best?

Malky: I remember when I was a kid, and I asked my Mum or Dad if I could do something, and before my request was out of my mouth, they would have said 'no' cuffed me on the head and sent me to bed. It felt like that.

Parky: Did you ask to go out to play in the park or something?

Malky: Yeah, something like that - but mostly it was for taking the petrol canister out the garage and asking for matches.

Parky: Can I take you back to the title of this book. It is quite a different title to your first two. I was expecting this title something like 'The really IDIOTIC thing about being an INSPECTOR?'

Malky: Yes, let me explain.

Chapter 4

HOW TO BE THE MOST OUTSTANDING COP IN THE WORLD (Not in a funny way)

It was late in December in a year when a lot happened. Sad things like earthquakes, riots, air crashes and popular beat combo band members died. Okay - that just about describes any year. Adele was riding high in the charts - still any year. *Wham* had just been on the radio singing *'Last Christmas'* and *'Fairytale of New York'* was now being belted out by *The Pogues* and *Kirsty MacColl* - doesn't help does it? Okay, I'll narrow it down, it was the year we had the heavy snow that covered all of Scotland. Things came to a standstill.

I'd woken at 6 a.m. to see my entire world carpeted in six inches of snow. I like the snow, it's nice. I like watching it fall, with anticipation of building a snowman later with the kids. This morning it was falling like millions of plump miniature pillows rushing to cover the ground and carpet it white. I smiled to myself. That was until I remembered that I was the duty inspector that morning. I grimaced.

The police are always in for a busy time when it snows. First, we have road accidents to contend with. Without fail idiots will look out their windows and think 'That's nice', jump into their car and expect to travel to their work at the same speed they always do. That's when accidents happen. We have to deal with the smashes and crashes, old people slipping and falling. All sorts of problems caused by the weather, the snow makes it difficult even to do normal police work.

I considered walking to work, but I knew the road gritter would have been along the main roads, so I left my house earlier than normal and nursed my car out the drive. My car cramped over the fresh fall until I hit the main arterial route where the gritter had spread its load. I navigated my way through the slush to the office.

My first job was to get the police yard cleared. The night shift had taken all the cars off the road because of the dangers of driving on slippery roads. That is fine at five o'clock in the morning when there are no calls to attend. Soon it would be rush hour, and a flurry of calls would descend on us like the snow had. They hadn't considered us and not only was the yard covered in six inches but so were the police vehicles. My entire shift, the sergeant and I pulled on wellies, grabbed shovels and made a start. I say my entire shift - one officer was missing, Constable Winston Thackerton Fenchurch Jones.

Constable WTF Jones had called the office and left a message for the sergeant explaining that his car was stuck. My sergeant and I assumed that Constable WTF Jones would now be late for work. Understandable given the continued fall of snow, which was getting heavier.

The calls came in. A trickle of minor calls became a flood, and then a deluge. The entire shift went their separate ways to deal with accidents and other urgent matters. The calls kept coming in. No sooner had we cleared one accident another one happened elsewhere. About two hours into the shift I radioed in to find out if Constable WTF Jones had made it into the office. No-one had seen him. I asked the controller to phone him for me and find out where he was and what was his estimated time of arrival. I got a message back to say there was no reply on his house phone or his mobile. I left instructions to keep trying.

The snow eased up. The calls eased too. The rush Hour passed, and the improving state of the roads, along with the lessening traffic helped give us a little breathing space. It was now 10 a.m. I headed back to the office and spoke to my office clerk.

"Have you seen Constable WTF Jones?"

"No, he hasn't arrived in yet."

"Has he been in touch to say when he will be here?"

"No, and he still hasn't answered his mobile or house phone."

This news concerned me. If a police officer cannot travel to his work because of the weather if possible, he or she must report to the nearest police office. Constable WTF Jones lived eight miles away, so I didn't expect him to walk to our office. His home, however, was only one mile away from Police Headquarters. So I expected that if he couldn't extricate his car from the snow, he would make his way into Police Headquarters on foot and we could arrange transport for him to our office from there. At least he would have access to a computer and could get on with his work. I checked with Headquarters and no-one there had set eyes on him. What if something had happened to Constable WTF Jones?

I dropped everything and drove to his house. I had my fingers crossed that nothing had happened to him. I'd wrapped myself up in the morning's events, and it was now three hours into our shift. There had been no further word from Constable WTF Jones. His car had got stuck in the snow, he had made us aware, but he had failed to answer his mobile or home phone since. I had left messages on both his home answering machine and his mobile answer phone, yet he hadn't been back in touch. He hadn't made it into Police Headquarters although he could have walked there in twenty or thirty minutes. I had the duty sergeant there check the canteen, the muster room and even the toilets. It was the sort of situation that makes your gut sink.

It took me twenty-five minutes to drive to Constable WTF Jones's house. Had it not been snowing I would have been there in fifteen. I turned into Constable WTF Jones's street and noted that it was on a hill. I stopped my car at the bottom. I didn't want to chance getting stuck as well, so I got out and made my way up on foot. Halfway up there were people dressed in anoraks and parkas and furry boots, with shovels clearing the snowfall from the roadway. A combined effort by the residents to have the first snow free road in the area. It wasn't until I reached them that one man, who was wearing a hooded anorak, looked up from his efforts and I saw that it was Constable WTF Jones. He looked surprised to see me.

"Hello Inspector, what brings you up here?" he said all innocent.

"You!" I said, hardly able to contain my anger.

"I was just helping my neighbours clear the street."

"You are supposed to be at your work. We have been phoning you every ten minutes for the past three hours. I have left messages on your mobile phone and your house phone asking you to contact me immediately."

"Oh, my mobile is charging in the house."

I gave him a withering look. I didn't want to explode in front of members of the public that would be unprofessional (I'm plenty unprofessional enough in private). I think the expression on my face said all I needed to say.

Okay, I promised you in the title information on how to be the most outstanding cop in the world. First, I need to tell you a story.

As a police officer, you have a responsibility. That responsibility is fundamental to the role. A constable of the law has a duty to guard, watch and patrol so as to protect life and property, preserve order and to prevent the commission of offences. A constable is given powers and privileges to carry out those duties. The execution of those duties is intrinsic in the way an officer of the law should conduct himself. Police officers are there to serve the public, deal with emergencies and keep people safe. All the powers conferred on a constable bestows a responsibility to do his or her duty. And you can't do your duty if you are shovelling snow outside your house. Constable WTF Jones's realisation of his situation spread over his face as it flushed red and carried on down to his brass neck.

"What do you want me to do, Inspector?"

"I want you to get in my car, and I'll take you to work."

"I need to get my stuff, Inspector, do you want to come in?"

"I'll wait in the car," I said and about turned and marched back down the hill. I was furious, fuming mad. Too resentful to wait where I could still see him. I needed to vent my annoyance. I'd kept a lid on it, but I have to admit I was struggling. Constable WTF Jones had seriously damaged my trust in him. He had not only breached his duty, but he had shown utter disrespect and contempt for his colleagues left to deal with every call that came in. He had taken his oath to serve the functions of a constable and obligations to the public and his colleagues and disregarded them to shovel snow with his neighbours. I try not to swear because repeated unnecessary profanity only diminishes the effectiveness. Thus when I do swear it has more effect, more meaning. People interpret it as more serious when a non-swearer swears. So I can tell you this, as I sat in my car waiting for Constable WTF Jones to gather his stuff and join me for the ride back to the police office, I was fucking angry, and I needed to calm the fuck down.

Constable WTF Jones opened the car door and climbed in. I drove off. He had taken ten minutes to gather his stuff and join me in the car. It was enough time for me to calm down from enraged to infuriated. Enough that I didn't launch into a thunderous outburst of scathing criticism and condemnation regarding his suitability to be a police officer. Instead, I held it in. I didn't say a word. I drove in angry silence.

Constable WTF Jones made the mistake of filling the void.

"I get the impression that you are a little peeved with me inspector?"

A little peeved! Seriously? 'A little peeved'.

I chose my next words with care.

"Son," - I couldn't bring myself to use his name or even call him 'constable' - "I am more than a little peeved, so if you know what's good for you just you sit there nice and quiet and I'll talk to you about it when I'm good and ready."

I still needed time to calm down before I felt I could speak to him - in a professional manner that is.

I drove on. The dipstick next to me couldn't keep up the silence and after just one minute decided that he had better apologise.

"I'm sorry, Inspector; it was just that when I got back to my flat, my car got stuck in the snow and I couldn't get it out. I thought it best to phone in and leave a message for the sergeant."

Wait a minute. When he got back to his flat?

"What do you mean, 'when you got back to your flat?'"
	"I was staying at my girlfriend's place, and I had to go back home to get my stuff before I came to work."
I looked him up and down; Constable WTF Jones was still dressed in his anorak, non-police trousers and a pair of wellington boots.
	"What stuff?"
	"Just my sandwiches and stuff."
	"Sandwiches and stuff?"
	"Yeah, my lunch."
	"Where is your uniform?"
	"In my locker at the office."
	"So what did you need to go back into your house just now?"
	"I needed to get my sandwiches."
	He wasn't making his situation any better.
	"How far away does your girlfriend stay?"
	"About fifteen miles away. But it took me a lot longer to get back in the snow."
	"You mean you managed to drive fifteen miles in the snow back to your house but couldn't get from there to your work?"
	"Well, I kinda got stuck."
	"You didn't think to park at the bottom of your street and walk up?"
	"No, I suppose I should have. I drove into my driveway so I could get turned, but I couldn't get the car back out."
	"Wait a minute. There was no car in your drive when I was up there."
	"Um, no, my neighbour helped me push it out."
	"So your car isn't stuck anymore?"

Constable WTF Jones might have been shovelling the snow when I saw him, but he was now shovelling an even bigger hole for himself.

"No. It's out."

"So why didn't you come to your work?"

"I thought I'd better help the rest of my neighbours get out of the street, so I got my shovel and started clearing the road for them."

He said this as if it made up for everything. As if it was the right thing to do. As if clearing snow was his career as if it were more important for him than coming into his work to do the job he was paid to do. As if it was more important than attending emergency calls and helping those in real need, more important than assisting his colleagues and not leaving them to do everything.

"Why didn't you tell me your car wasn't stuck anymore? You could have driven yourself to work!"

"I thought I better do as you told me."

It might surprise you to know I didn't stop the car, get out and go around to Constable WTF Jones' side, open his door and drag him out. I didn't then handcuff him to a lamppost, and I didn't then get back into the car and reverse over him. That's how much I have grown. That's how outstanding I am.

I carried on in silence, dumbstruck. At the office, I let the sergeant speak to Constable WTF Jones, telling him I would talk with him the following day. It would give him a chance to reflect on the day's events and give me a chance to compose myself. I wondered if it was a little cruel letting him worry about what I would say to him for a whole twenty-four hours, but I seriously doubted that Constable WTF Jones thought he had done anything wrong.

That night I lay in my bed and couldn't sleep. The Constable WTF Jones situation kept burrowing through my head and wouldn't go away. I was consumed with anger then irritation and then frustration. I was trying to decide on how best to deal with the situation and what I would say to him.

I have mentioned the Dunning-Kruger effect. It is possible that Constable WTF Jones is a 'Dunker'. I thought about it long and hard. Just maybe Constable WTF Jones wasn't a 'Dunker' maybe he was a normal person with normal thoughts and feelings. Maybe it was the police training at fault, or maybe his tutor cop or the company he kept or even my expectations.

I don't recall there being any training we got regarding our duty, our responsibility our need to be dependable when I was at police college. Sure we learned about the Police (Scotland) Act, and our primary duties to protect life and property, to preserve order, serve citations, etc. We were taught that in the same way we were taught the rudiments of theft, poaching and pissing in the street. Nobody sat us down and said, "Do you truly understand what it means to be an officer of the law?"

Maybe I should blame his tutor cop? Perhaps Constable WTF Jones's tutor had been a lazy, self-serving, useless, incompetent dunker. Constable WTF Jones could have learned from that and followed suit. I have heard it said 'you are the average of your five best friends'. My Mum and Dad certainly kept tabs on who my siblings and I hung around with, even in those days they knew it makes a difference who influences us. Let's face it - your friends are your friends because you are alike and you end up doing what each other does. If that is not the case, you are hanging around with the wrong people. As a police officer, you might have to make some hard decisions when it comes to friends. The thing is, if you don't make those hard decisions quick there will be a lot harder decisions to come.

Then there were my expectations. I was now an inspector. I had more than a quarter of a century to shape my beliefs and understanding of what it means to be a constable. I was a cocky little upstart when I joined, and I didn't know diddly squat. Why should I expect an officer like Constable WTF Jones to be any different? His priorities were different to mine. He didn't have a wife and a family to feed, I did. When I was his age, my priorities were probably along the same lines as his. Earn enough money so I could afford to buy beer for the Dutch courage to ask a girl out.

The day after Constable WTF Jones failed in his duty I called him into my office. I sat him down, and we had a chat. After our chat, I put it behind me, and I moved on. We all make mistakes, and Constable WTF Jones made a monumental mistake. As epic as it was, nobody got hurt, nobody suffered unduly, and nobody died.

The problem is, all of those things could have happened. So to prevent that happening again I spelt out to Constable WTF Jones where I felt there was a flaw in his thinking and why. I hoped that under the same circumstances he would not shovel snow - other than to create a path for himself so he could to get to his work. So the first step in being the most outstanding cop in the world (not in a silly way) is to not make the same colossal mistake as Constable WTF Jones.

THE MICHAEL PARKINSON TELEVISION INTERVIEW

Parky: Your story about Constable WTF Jones is not quite the same as your other stories in your books.

Malky: No, I suppose it has more of a serious tone to it.

Parky: I think there is a great message there, why did you feel the need to tell us about it?

Malky: I had a moment of sudden and great awareness. Here I was telling all the silly incidents, the crazy characters and the stupid situations I had encountered in my career, but there was more to them than just amusing anecdotes. These were tales I wish I had read about when I first started. I could have learned how not to be a police officer, what silly things I shouldn't do and I could have been a better cop from the outset. I wasn't going to include the Constable WTF Jones story at first. I had it in my head it wasn't funny enough. Then I thought, what if another Constable WTF Jones comes along and does the same thing?

Parky: Someone could get hurt, someone could suffer, and someone could die?

Malky: Exactly, perhaps the next Constable WTF Jones might read this and then in a similar situation he might take a more conscientious course of action.

Parky: You are trying to make police officers accountable for their actions?

Malky: Nah! I'm just trying to make them laugh. Who am I trying to kid?

Parky: Yes, but it also relays an important message?

Malky: Of course, I'm being stupid, dunkers, by their nature, won't be reading this. They already think they are outstanding.

Parky: That may well be true. Only good cops will read this book. However, you have another story about an officer that beggars belief. I believe he was even more frustrating to you than Constable WTF Jones. Can you tell us about Sergeant McBullyboy?

Malky: Maybe later. I'd rather tell you about some good cops.

Chapter 5

THE LEGENDARY TONY MALONEY

Had the 'Sweetie Jar Principle' been employed there is every likelihood that Tony Maloney would have found himself promoted a good few rungs further up the ladder.

Occasionally there are characters in the Police who are such a rich source of stories they become legends. Their escapades passed on between cops like folklore. Tony Maloney was just such a legend. Normal rules for Tony did not seem to apply. If I could have sourced all his colleagues over the years, I could probably have written a series of books about his exploits alone. His career took him from the beat to the CID where he remained for the rest of his service. He retired as a detective sergeant. Those that knew him will have no difficulty in identifying his anarchic sense of humour.

I first heard about Tony Maloney when I went to the CID. While he worked in a different station, our paths did cross. He was always smartly tailored and somewhat solemn looking. My first impression was that he was a studious individual. A man who took his job seriously and not one for nonsense or hilarity. He had an air about him born of inner confidence. There was never any doubting his capabilities, his colleagues and even his supervisors treated him with something akin to reverence. He was an interesting character, but I didn't know just how interesting until I heard of some of his exploits.

The indications were there in his early days; these were the days when prisoners could smoke and custody sergeants invariably smoked themselves. Sergeant Grouch asked Tony (a young probationer at the time) to go to the shop and buy a packet of Kenistas Club cigarettes for him.

"What if they don't have Kenistas Club?" young PC Tony Maloney asked.

"Just get me anything," Sergeant Grouch replied irritably.

About twenty minutes later Tony Maloney appeared back at the custody suite and placed a 2lb bag of tatties on the counter.

"What's that?" enquired Sergeant Grouch grumpily.

"They didn't have any Kenistas Club… and you said to get you anything."

There were, of course, many other stories about Tony Maloney and his antics. My favourites were always his successes in interviewing - although he applied some unconventional techniques. To explain:-

In olden times 'Violating Sepulchres' was a common crime. The crime involves the 'wicked and felonious' stealing of dead bodies. The Burke and Hares of long ago would plunder newly laid graves, steal any valuables buried with the deceased and sell the corpse to unscrupulous doctors. Those found guilty by the courts were banished for 'seven years beyond seas'.

We still regard Violation of Sepulchres as a heinous crime, albeit these days it is rare. Doctors no longer require illicitly obtained cadavers on which to practice their skills. Stealing dead bodies just doesn't happen that often. The buried stay buried. That was until two drunken lads, Scuzz and Guffy (two gentlemen of low moral standing), decided it was a good idea to dig up the grave of Mrs Higginbotham.

Mrs Higginbotham died in 1756 at the unripe age of thirty-two. She was interred at the town cemetery and given a grand looking commemorative headstone by her rich family. Scuzz and Guffy dug her up in the mistaken belief she might be worth a bob or two. Unfortunately for them, they were seen making their way back to their block of flats in the early hours of the morning carrying heavy bags and looking suspiciously grubby.

The violation of the grave was reported in the morning. There was nothing to tie Scuzz and Guffy to the crime, other than the reported sighting of them carrying something heavy. It was, however, the belief of those investigating that these two lads of low moral standing were stupid enough to have been responsible.

The initial investigation gathered no further direct evidence. The suspicion remained that Scuzz and Guffy were responsible. Their homes were searched but nothing was found, due to the lads having woken the next day and, realising that a bag of bones and a skull would be of no use to them whatsoever, they got rid of the evidence. They disposed of Mrs Higginbotham's remains in a nearby bin. The bin had collection happened before the police arrived to detain them. Mrs Higginbotham ended up getting re-interred at the local dump.

Scuzz and Guffy were detained and brought in for questioning. Scots law, at the time, allowed that suspects could be held for six hours while further enquiries were carried out. That gave the investigators time to interview them. Both had been capable, careless and culpable enough in their lives not to have gone without this ignominious experience before. The advice of their lawyers to 'say nothing' still rang in their ears. Scuzz and Guffy braved it out for the first few hours; they said nothing. The smirk on their faces told of their guilt, but that was insufficient to take to court. Without an admission they would remain free and clear - and they knew it. The officers knew they were guilty. Innocent people don't say 'no comment'. Innocent people are keen to deny it. People who are Innocent do everything to help the police understand why they didn't do it. In the eyes of the interviewing officers, their 'no comment' replies made them as culpable as would an admission of guilt - not in the eyes of a judge though.

The officers tried every standard interviewing technique. When that didn't work, they tried a few unorthodox ones too. It was to no avail. There was nothing else for it; it was time to call in the legendary Tony Maloney.

Tony attended at the custody suite and listened to the detaining officer's plight and nodded. He quickly understood their predicament. They had less than an hour of the detention time to go before they would have to release them without charge. They needed Scuzz and Guffy to admit to digging up Mrs Higginbotham. Tony mulled over the situation for a moment then said, "Get me my lab coat."

The next interview the lads received was from a serious looking man in a lab coat (Tony in disguise). He was wearing a white paper mask and was carrying an unusual looking device with a pointer which he described as his 'Geiger Counter'. Tony explained to them he was a government scientist. Following examination of the violated grave, they discovered evidence of contamination. He explained to them that anyone who had been in contact with the grave itself had been rushed to the Decontamination Unit in Dundee. Anyone who had touched the body needed to go there now or… The peril they were in remained unsaid.

Sweat formed on both Scuzz and Guffy's foreheads.

Tony, looked serious, his lab coat gave him an air of trustworthiness. He explained to them it was their decision. If they hadn't touched the body, they would be fine. If they had, then they needed to go to the Decontamination Unit, or they would have to suffer the consequences.

Tony produced his 'Geiger Counter' and informed them he needed to check them over. If the Geiger counter registered more than seven beeps, then they would have to remain in quarantine no matter what. That meant staying in custody. If they wanted medical help, they needed to attend the Decontamination Unit in Dundee. The two of them were not sure what to do. Until this troubling news, they thought they were free and clear.

Tony, in his official-looking lab coat, pointed his 'Geiger Counter' at Scuzz. The machine whined then went 'beep'. Tony put on a serious expression and counted 'one'. The machine beeped again, and he counted 'two'. On the seventh beep, Scuzz cracked and admitted the crime.

"Okay, okay, it was me, what the hell am I contaminated with?"

Guffy quickly followed suit when he went through the same process.

"All right, I admit it. We dumped the bones in the bin. What disease have I picked up?"

Tony, said nothing. He nodded to the two detectives investigating the case then left the room.

"Are you going to take us to the Decontamination Unit in Dundee now?" Scuzz and Guffy asked in unison.

"Naw," smiled the detective, "we will take you to the Decontamination Unit in HMP Barlinnie."

Tony Maloney contrived to make his police career an interesting and eventful one. His escapades were of much amusement to his colleagues, but that was not his primary concern. His primary concern was to do his job to the best of his ability and have enough nonsense in the process to keep himself amused. His exploits were a simple garnish that made his work even more palatable. He relished his job, but when the opportunity arose for him to spice it up and delight with some anarchic prank, he didn't hesitate. And there lay the problem.

For all his success, Tony Maloney worried senior management. The stories of his escapades filtered through and they discussed him in whispers on the carpeted offices of the top floor. Like the time Tony brought a prisoner back for an interview and found himself at the back of a lengthy queue in the custody suite. He informed the custody sergeant that he would be in the canteen with his prisoner, the PCSO went looking for him when it was his turn and found Tony and his prisoner happily playing a game of pool. On another occasion, one of his prisoners got caught re-entering the police office with a large bundle wrapped in old newspapers.

"Where have you been?"

"DC Maloney asked me if I was hungry and gave me ten pounds to get two fish suppers, one for him and one for me."

The senior officers were less inclined to think of his pranks as amusing high jinks. There was always the possibility that his mischief could come unstuck and thus he was a direct threat to the credibility of the organisation. Even more worrying for them - he might be a direct threat to their credibility and careers. The senior management deliberated in private over each incident involving Tony. They worried that he would go too far and get caught. The potential for embarrassment to themselves was ever present, a catastrophe in their eyes.

Not that they did anything. The Chief Constable and other senior officers weren't stupid. They couldn't come right out and admit that they knew what he was up to. There had to be some plausible deniability. Thus Tony's shenanigans went on unchecked. There were no calls for Tony to come in and be spoken to. Professional standards weren't asked to investigate. Either Tony was lucky, or he was clever. I plumped for the latter.

My thoughts re-affirmed when I found out what the senior officers knew. It is an incredible tale that just seems, even now, too absurd to be true. Had this been a story about anyone else I would have dismissed it as complete nonsensical fiction. It is inconceivable that an officer could have carried this off. However this wasn't just any officer, this was Tony Maloney. As implausible as the story may be, I have no doubts it happened as described.

Detective Sergeant Tony Maloney was a regular attendee at court where, as a witness, he presented evidence led by the Procurator Fiscal. He dealt with many cases and was a regular witness in court. Michael Savage, the defence lawyer in a forthcoming trial, where Tony was to be a witness, was a veteran of the court. While named as 'Michael' in the papers, court dockets, etc. his clientele all knew him as 'Mike'. Mike was an imposing figure. He stood 6' 6" in height and weighed in at a good 260 lbs. His voice boomed in court when he spoke, and there wasn't a Procurator Fiscal, a witness (whether a civilian or a serving officer) or judge who didn't find him intimidating. His leaning towards the bar as an occupation was not some unselfish belief in justice or his way of expressing his conviction for a more civilised world. Drawn to it because of his ability to exercise his imagination in the interpretation of the law. His reading of the truth was a singularly objective affair that objective being to win. His courtroom style was to browbeat the opposition into submission. Michael Savage had had many a run-in with Tony Maloney, yet not once had he got the better of him. He had simply been unable to intimidate Tony the way he intimidated others. Tony remained calm, unflustered and composed during cross-examination. Michael Savage always ended up the one to get frustrated when Tony Maloney was in the witness box.

When Mike's tactic of browbeating witnesses didn't work, he resorted to another technique. He would cease his bullying and apply his secondary strategy. His lesser approach involved becoming calm; he would lower his volume and adopt the façade of a friendly uncle. It was a simple technique. Michael Savage asked a question and once the witness answered he would cock his head to the side and wait. The pause and his cocked head indicating his expectation that there should be more to the answer than the witness gave. The witness, who was already uptight, would become even more anxious and spout forth all sorts of additional information. In their confusion, Mike would pick up on some small matter, and the witness would end up wobbling like jelly on a roller coaster.

Michael Savage tried this technique on Tony Maloney. Tony answered his question, resting his hands on the witness box. Mike cocked his head to the side and looked directly at him, not saying a word. Everyone in the court turned their heads back to Tony expecting some further explanation or embellishment. Tony remained silent. The judge, annoyed by the pause in proceedings, looked up and glowered at Michael Savage. Chastened by the glower, Michael Savage continued, "You said you found the property in the boot of my client's car?"

"Yes," replied Tony.

Mike paused, looked at Tony, cocked his head and waited. The whole gallery of the court also turned towards Tony, expectant of further explanation. Tony pulled his hand up towards his face, turned the back of his hand towards himself and inspected his nails. He had no intention, whatsoever, of providing any further explanation or statement.

Mike tried his technique again, only to get by an implacable one-word response. "Yes," or "No," was all Tony would say.

Mike's fury rose within him until he exploded.

"ARE YOU COMPLETELY INCAPABLE OF GIVING ME ANYTHING OTHER THAN A ONE-SYLLABLE ANSWER?"

Tony Maloney took his eyes off his nails and looked Michael Savage in the eye. This time he paused. He looked at the accused in the dock; he looked at the crowd in the gallery. Tony then turned his head to the judge and in reply to Michael Savage's outburst said, "No."

On another occasion Tony gave told the court he had called at a house and heard a disturbance inside.

"I heard the accused verbally abuse his wife and threaten to punch her."

"Objection, your honour," Mike stood to address the Sheriff, "Detective Sergeant Maloney can't possibly say it was my client who said that, not if he was on the other side of the door. I move that his evidence is stricken from the record as unsatisfactory."

As Mike waited on the Sheriff's judgement, Tony piped up, "Away and boil yer heed."

Mike turned towards Tony, furious. "What did you say?"

"How do you know it was me that said anything?"

"I heard you."

Tony turned towards the Sheriff, "How can Mr Savage say I said that, your honour? He had his back to me. I move that his evidence is unsatisfactory."

Tony Maloney rankled Mike, infuriated by the mere mention of his name. Inside he seethed and plotted the time when he could get his own back. He wanted to get Tony Maloney in the witness box and embarrass him the same way he had humiliated him. Michael Savage had lost his temper because of Tony Maloney. He had been unprofessional. He had gone astray, and this failing had been on show to everyone in the courtroom that day. Now he wanted the opportunity to get his revenge on Tony Maloney. He was confident he could control his temper, he was confident he was smart enough to show up any witnesses, including Tony Maloney. He wanted the chance to prove it.

Then his chance arrived.

Michael Savage almost whooped in joy. His opportunity to get back at Tony Maloney appeared in the form of one of his regular clients, a drug taking thief by the name of Benjamin Brown.

Ben Brown had grown up surrounded by a family of wasters. His father was an alcoholic and died young leaving his wife and family to support themselves, not that he did much supporting when he was alive. Ben's mother had also taken to the gin and was drinking herself into an early grave. Ben's brothers were a motley crew of thieves and vagabonds, role models that would help him in his thievery but abandon him to his fate at the slightest inkling of trouble. Thus Ben Brown ended up in jail as often as the local dry cleaning company who had the contract to clean the cell blankets. Ben Brown was thus on first name terms with his long-time lawyer 'Mike' Savage.

When Ben Brown first appeared in Michael Savage's office and told him his story, all Mike could think was 'I've got him, this time Tony Maloney has gone too far.'

Tony Maloney's reputation preceded him. He was undoubtedly a great investigator, known for his detective skills. He was an excellent interviewer, had a sound knowledge of investigatory procedures. He was also the most thorough of crime scene managers. Fortunately for Michael Savage and his intent on revenge, Tony also had a penchant for mischievousness.

For anyone else, this would be a career suicide. I used to think of us all as having an imaginary self-destruct button sitting on a desk. In quieter moments most people look at it and ponder what would happen if they pressed it. They give it a touch, just a caress, but not enough to activate it. Then they ignore it and get on with their work. Tony Maloney struggled to ignore his self-destruct button. It sat in front of him, goading him to press it. It was like blowing up a balloon. Some people blow it up, tie the end and then they have a balloon to play with, they can kick it around as much as they like. Tony just kept blowing that balloon, the pressure on the inside increasing until - BANG - it explodes in his face, he couldn't help himself. He liked to blow up lots of balloons and have fun kicking them about, but sometimes he blew them up too far.

On a whim, now and then Tony pressed his self-destruct button. It would go - BANG! Incredibly, like magic, after everything exploded, Tony left smiling at his naughtiness. But he always came out unharmed, not a scratch on him. He would simply go about his business, and people walked away scratching their heads wondering what had happened.

Word got out that Tony Maloney could be in trouble, he'd been cited as a witness in the case against Ben Brown. Ben's lawyer, Michael Savage, had made it known that this time Tony had gone too far. There were grumblings in senior management offices, people whispered behind his back, and there was a general feeling that this time there was no way out. The rumour circulated that Michael Savage would haul Tony over the coals. This time he had him. Benjamin Brown had given him the ammunition to bring him down. As soon as DC Tony Maloney presented his evidence for the Procurator Fiscal, Michael Savage would stand up and ask such probing questions as to his conduct, that the case would fold there and then. Mike's clients had related stories to him about Tony before, and until then, there was nothing he could do about it. This time it was different.

On the day of Ben Brown's trial, DC Tony Maloney was duly called into the witness box. Dressed in his dark three piece court suit, he looked like an expert and had a calm and competent demeanour. He presented his evidence, under guidance of the Procurator Fiscal. He came across well. The judge nodded through his evidence accepting all he said. There were no reservations.

Then Michael Savage stood up in his best pin-stripe suit, calm and professional. But there was more. Today he had a wry smile and would relish cross-examining DC Tony Maloney. Ben Brown had told him what had taken place during his interview under caution and it was so outrageous that Mike knew it to be the truth. That his client had admitted to the crime at the time was not his concern. His job is to throw doubt on the circumstances. After the cross-examination of Tony Maloney he knew there would be doubt, and he felt confident he could secure a 'not guilty' or at the least a 'not proven' verdict.

Ben was a regular rogue who had a string of theft convictions. He had been arrested for housebreaking (burglary). Seen near the scene of the crime at the material time, the evidence showed that he had later sold property stolen from the house. The rules of the court meant that Ben Brown's previous convictions could not be brought up during the trial. According to Ben he'd been detained and taken to the Police Station where two CID officers had interviewed him at length regarding the crime. He told Mike that he had remained uncooperative and made 'no comment' to all the questions. Nearing the end of the interview the door opened and a man wearing a fancy dress rabbit suit entered. The 'rabbit' hopped over to the table, sat down and interviewed him. Ben thought it all one big joke, and he had smiled and gone along with the nonsense and admitted to the crime but only as part of the ongoing repartee with a man in a rabbit suit. The rabbit took notes in a notebook.

The lawyer turned to Tony in the witness box and looked Tony in the eyes.

"DC Maloney, I have to put it to you that you entered the interview room wearing a fancy dress outfit?"

"A fancy dress outfit?"

"A rabbit suit!"

"A rabbit suit?"

"Yes. You entered the interview room wearing a rabbit suit, and in that suit, you farcically interviewed my client?"

The lawyer planned to catch Tony unawares. Everyone assumed his client would plead guilty and Tony wouldn't be required to give evidence. Now Tony was in the witness box he would present the court with the ridiculousness of wearing a fancy dress rabbit suit to interview a suspect.

Wide-eyed Tony Maloney looked at the lawyer; taking his time he looked at the judge then he looked around the packed courtroom. He took in everybody. His face cracked a smile, then it became a grin, and from there he couldn't help himself, he burst out laughing. There were only two people in the courtroom that didn't follow suit, Michael Savage and his client Benjamin Brown. Everyone else, including the judge, burst into raucous laughter. A rabbit suit, indeed!

Eventually, calm restored. Mike Savage's plan to embarrass Tony Maloney had backfired. He was now sporting another red neck, and his client sat in the dock looking confused.

Michael Savage waited until the last snigger died away. The judge put his serious face back on and motioned for him to continue. Mike turned to Tony Maloney and asked his final question. His plan was that this question would put Tony Maloney in his place. It would identify him as a maverick. Everyone would know the admission his client provided was a fabrication. He'd expose Tony Maloney as a liar, and his client would walk out the courtroom a free man. He asked his question.

"DC Maloney, in your evidence you suggest that my client made a reply to his caution and charge."

"That is correct."

"You suggest that you charged my client with housebreaking, and as soon as you finished he stated:-

'Smooth and creamy Galaxee,
That's the only chocolate bar for me.'"

"That is correct."

"For goodness sake DC Maloney, why on earth would my client make such a reply to a charge of housebreaking?"

The clear inference being that Tony had made this up.

"Your honour," Tony turned to address the judge in as deadpan a manner as he could muster. "I have absolutely no idea. Can I suggest that the council for the accused should have asked his client that question before attendance at court."

The courtroom erupted once more.

Once the laughter died down, Michael Savage stood in the middle of the court, his face red, and his shoulders hunched. Smaller and less daunting than he had been before. He was speechless. The judge, once again, annoyed by the silence, adjusted his spectacles down to the bridge of his nose and peered over them looking directly at Michael Savage, "Well?" he said.

"No more questions, your honour," and Michael Savage slumped into his chair.

After a quick summation by the Procurator Fiscal, the judge asked Ben Brown to stand up.

"I find you guilty of the charge against you. Have you anything to say before I pass sentence?"

Ben Brown looked across at the gallery where his friends and family sat. With a mischievous smile on his face, he turned towards the judge and stated,

"Smooth and creamy Galaxee,
That's the only chocolate bar for me."

The judge, not without a sense of humour himself, retorted:-

"You may like chocolate, Mr Brown
But in my court, you're going down
Because you can't mend your ways
You're going to prison for sixty days."

THE MICHAEL PARKINSON TELEVISION INTERVIEW

Parky: Going to prison for sixty days, ha ha, that's funny.

Malky: I know. Nice to know judges have a sense of humour too.

Parky: Were you ever frustrated with the sentences that judges gave? Did you think they were too lenient?

Malky: I can't say I was one to bother much about the sentences people received.

Parky: Is that because your job was to put them in front of the court? You took a professional attitude to your work and it wasn't your concern? You had done your bit and what happened after that was the remit of the court to decide, your job was only to present the evidence in an unbiased fashion? That it was the responsibility of the court to make any conclusions as to innocence or guilt and after that mete out appropriate punishment with magisterial wisdom? Is the sentence, therefore, of no concern to you?

Malky: Nah, I was just apathetic.

Parky: Um, yes, well, I'd like to ask you about some of the people you caught and put to court. It seems a difficult task to catch people with all the constraints that the law puts on police officers as regards evidence gathering. Do you feel that the rules of law hinder police officers in the execution of their duty?

Malky: It isn't the rules of law that hinder the police the most.

Chapter 6

AS STUPID AS

It was a surprise we caught anyone at all - what with all the silly things police officers got up to (and I include myself in that). I mean, I invited my colleague PC Uncle Sylvester to join my *Whatsapp* group, and it was three years before I realised that it was the wrong Sylvester. The Sylvester who joined was, in fact, a ten-year-old kid. I didn't notice. The immature conversations I had with this kid were pretty much what I expected from the real Uncle Sylvester. It wasn't until the kid turned thirteen and matured I realised he was the wrong Sylvester. I'll miss that kid. I'm now back having immature *Whatsapp* conversations with the real Uncle Sylvester.

As stupid as the police can be, I was forever astonished at the even greater stupidity shown by the criminals. We have all heard stories of criminals trying to rob banks with balaclavas on back to front so they couldn't see anything or the guy wearing a see-through stocking over his head, making him easy to identify. There was the guy who handed over a ransom note to a bank teller - on which he had signed his name. There was the robber who couldn't get out the bank because he pushed the door instead of pulling it, despite the sign on the door saying 'pull'. Crimes that were stupid things to do in the first place and even more brainless in their execution.

Some crimes made us scratch our heads but then we would make a little enquiry, and it didn't come as a shock when the guy got caught. One particular crime looked like it would be a major enquiry - for all of five seconds.

A taxi driver phoned us to report being robbed. A young man, with a large green army holdall, got into his taxi in the town centre and gave an address on the outskirts of town. The taxi driver took him to the address. No sooner did they arrive, the young man removed a broken Samurai sword from his holdall and threatened to kill the taxi driver if he didn't give him all his money. The top third of the sword missing so it could fit in the holdall.

The taxi driver was no pushover; not inclined to hand over his hard-earned cash. He grabbed the sword by the blade and struggled with him. Fortunately, the blade wasn't too sharp. They struggled for ages, and both ended up outside the vehicle where the taxi driver got the better of his assailant and wrestled the Samurai sword from his grip. The guy ran off leaving his bag behind.

The taxi driver went home and only reported the incident to us because his wife told him to (even taxi drivers obey their wives). Our call taker took details over the phone, then passed the description of the young man over the radio. His age, height, dress and the fact he had been carrying a large green army type holdall. Seconds later my office clerk popped through to see me.

"Did you hear that radio message," he asked.

"Yes," I replied, "I've sent two cops to speak to the taxi driver."

"About fifteen minutes ago Tommy Muggeridge was in the office to sign on as part of his bail conditions. He is the same age and height and he was carrying a large green army type holdall with him."

"What is he on bail for?"

"Robbing a taxi driver three weeks ago."

I called the CCTV office and asked them to check the recordings covering the office.

"Yes, we can see Tommy Muggeridge leaving the office walking to the corner then on the taxi rank and getting into a cab."

"Where does he stay?"

"45 Redmount Avenue."

"Where did the taxi driver say the robbery happened?"

"Where the guy wanted dropped off - outside 43 Redmount Avenue."

We had Tommy Muggeridge in custody before the cops even spoke to the taxi driver.

A fraudster called into a large clothing store and tried to hand back a pair of jeans, requesting a full refund.

"Do you have a receipt?"

"No, I threw it away."

"When did you buy these jeans?"

"A couple of weeks ago."

"Have you worn them?"

"Um, no."

"Can I see them?"

The store assistant took the jeans and found that they were not even a brand that the store stocked.

"Did you buy these jeans here?"

"Yes."

"Well, I don't know how because we don't stock this brand of jeans.

"You must do because I bought them here."

"I'm sorry I can't give you a refund, store policy."

"I want to speak to a manager."

"Certainly, sir."

The manager arrived and the assistant explained the situation to her.

"Can I help you, sir?"

"I want a refund for those jeans."

"Sir, as my assistant explained, store policy states we have to have a receipt to issue a monetary refund. If there is no receipt, we can issue a store credit if we are happy that the item is in an unused condition and you purchased it here. You have no receipt, and we have never stocked this brand of jeans, so you didn't purchase them here. I'm sorry we can't issue you a refund for something we didn't sell."

The fraudster went on the offensive.

"If you don't give me a refund, I am going to call the police."

"You will only waste your time, the police won't be able to do anything."

"Right, that's it. I'm calling the police."

The fraudster pulled out his mobile phone and dialled the emergency number.

"I NEED THE POLICE HERE NOW, THEY ARE REFUSING TO GIVE ME A REFUND."

All the time the fraudster kept his eyes on the manager, expecting to intimidate her into caving-in and provide him with a refund.

Normally, the police would advise the caller it wasn't a police matter, but the call-handler suspected something was amiss. The fraudster seemed angry and raised his voice. He decided it prudent to send a crew to investigate.

At that moment, I was in the town centre wrestling with the decision to have a ham salad sandwich on white or brown bread. My radio sparked into life and asked if anyone was near the store in question. As I was next door, I delayed my decision (and lunch) and trotted into the store.

I recognised the fraudster as a local man, I'd seen him around town before, but I couldn't put a name to him. He had the glassy eyes and distant look that takes over someone who has imbibed illegal substances for too long. The look that most members of the public perceive as dangerous. The fact is most long-term drug users become desperate and it is that desperation that can make them dangerous. This desperate stoned specimen was chancing his arm.

"Can I help you?" I asked.

"I want a refund for these jeans, and they are not giving me it."

The manager stepped in to explain.

"He didn't buy these jeans here. We don't stock that brand. He has no receipt, and that doesn't conform with store policy," she turned to look at him, "you can't expect us to give you money for nothing, can you?"

By the look on his face, I gathered that he did. I had a look at the jeans. They were not even nearly new. I initially suspected he had shoplifted them from another store, but the jeans looked as if they had been used to clean windows. The ends were frayed, and the zipper broken.

"When did you buy these?" I asked.

"About four weeks ago."

"They look as if they have been on the go for four years."

"Well, it might have been a little over four weeks."

"How long?"

"About four years."

The manager and I rolled our eyes in unison.

"Did you stock this brand four years ago?" I asked her.

"No. We have never stocked that brand. In any case, we wouldn't provide a refund for a garment that has been worn for four years."

"I wouldn't expect you to."

I turned to the fraudster and asked him to provide his full name.

"Angus McNally."

"Angus, you can't get a refund for these jeans. They weren't purchased here, and nobody in their right mind would give you money back for goods that have been worn for four years. It doesn't work like that."

"I'm not leaving until I get a refund. You better get the Chief Constable here as well."

"I don't think the Chief Constable would appreciate being dragged away from his desk for something like this, would he?"

"He will. I'm going to make a complaint about you. You can kiss your job goodbye. You can't tell me I'm not getting a refund."

"Excuse me a minute," I said and toddled off to get a check on the name he provided.

Ten minutes later two of my cops joined me and we arrested Angus on his fourteen outstanding arrest warrants. Stupid is, as stupid does.

But you don't have to be a criminal to do stupid things.

Have ever been driving along with a marked police car following you? No matter how innocent you may be, you might still feel a little apprehension. You check your speed to make sure you are keeping to the limits, double check you have your seatbelt on, and you will drive as safely and as smoothly as your skills allow. You might even put your mobile phone down and stop texting your girlfriend (but not always). When that blue light flashes behind you and the marked police car signals you to pull over, your apprehension will turn to trepidation. Sometimes, when that happens, people's brains don't quite function as they should. That is perhaps the only explanation for the story Big Bob related and had me in stitches.

Big Bob was driving behind a nice new BMW motor car. One of the rear lights wasn't working so he decided that it would be a good idea for his young probationer, Constable McFungus, to issue a V. Rec (Vehicle Defect Rectification Scheme). The V. Rec is a slip of paper which details a minor fault a driver must get fixed to avoid a fine. It serves the purpose of ensuring the fault gets repaired and that the car is roadworthy. It also ensures the driver or owner doesn't end up with a ticket.

Big Bob activated his blue lights and flashed the BMW indicating for it to pull over. As expected, it came to a stop in a safe place by the side of the road. Bob sent Constable McFungus to tell the driver to join him in his car so they could go through the process of issuing the V. Rec.

Constable McFungus alighted from the police car approached the driver sitting in his BMW spoke to him and then returned to the police car. As Constable McFungus walked back to the police car, Bob watched the driver of the BMW get out of his car, open the rear door of his BMW and climb in. The driver was now sat down in the rear seat of his car.

Bob looked at Constable McFungus as he entered the police car and asked him what he had told the driver.

Constable McFungus furrowed his brow in confusion, "I asked him to have a seat in the back of our car."

"Well, he has just got out of his driver's seat and sat in the back of his own car."

Bob instructed Constable McFungus to go back and tell the driver to come and sit in the back of the police car. The young cop returned to the BMW. He shouted to the driver and pointed towards the police car parked behind the

BMW. Constable McFungus about turned and returned to the front passenger seat beside Bob.

There was no movement from the driver of the BMW.

Once again Bob asked Constable McFungus what he had told the driver. Constable McFungus was adamant he had told the BMW driver to come and sit in the back of the police car. Bob waited, but there was still no movement from the driver of the BMW, other than he was looking back at the police car with a kind of anguished expression on his face.

'Strange behaviour,' thought Bob.

Why on earth would he sit in the backseat of his car in the first place? Was he just was anxious? What was he anxious about? Had he committed a crime? Had he been drinking or on drugs? Maybe he had murdered his wife, and she was lying dead in the boot? That would certainly have made him apprehensive.

Bob got out to speak to him.

As Bob reached the BMW, the driver looked up at him, a sheepish look on his face, "I can't get out. The child lock is on," he explained.

THE MICHAEL PARKINSON TELEVISION INTERVIEW

Parky: (laughing) That's very silly, however, if I could be serious for a minute. I know you have a serious message for us?

Malky: I'm not sure I know to what you are referring?

Parky: The one about the plagiarist superintendent.

Malky: How did you know about that story?

Parky: I have my sources.

Malky: Well, I had no intention of telling it. It was one of those things I wrote as a cathartic exercise. Once I had it off my chest, I didn't feel the need to put in any of my books. I don't think it will interest anyone.

Parky: I'm not so sure, perhaps it will open the public's eyes to what goes on in the police - behind closed doors?

Malky: There are so many more interesting characters than him and much more silly stories.

Parky: Yes, but the plagiarist superintendent story might serve as a warning for other cops.

Malky: There are other funnier incidents.

Parky: Which stories did you have in mind?

Malky: I have stories about probationers, detective constables as well as a plagiarist superintendent.

Parky: Perhaps you might like to tell us them all?

Chapter 7

VISSZA VAGY PEDIG

It sometimes pays to fight your corner, but be careful the corner you are fighting for is where you want to be. When bosses think you have twelve cops on your shift strength, they expect miracles to happen.

"Inspector McEwan, I want door-to-door enquiries carried out for the robbery last night. I want your officers to visit all houses within a mile radius of the locus. We will also need reassurance patrols in the town centre. I want road checks set up from 6 p.m. for the cruisers; we are getting a lot of complaints from the council about them racing in the car park at Tesco. I want the backlog of arrest warrants cleared up. I want all late reports submitted by tomorrow morning. I want…"

I interrupted Chief Inspector MacSever before he could want anymore, "No problem, sir. Is there a budget for the catering?"

"Catering, what catering?"

"Well, the robbery last night was at Ali's Convenience Store on the south side of town. That is a heavily populated area. The nearest block of flats has about two hundred residents. If it takes ten minutes to visit and interview everyone in each flat, then that will take a team of twenty officers a whole shift to complete, that assumes they get everyone in when they call. There are twelve blocks of flats so that means a team of twenty officers working for twelve nights on the blocks of flats alone. I would estimate there to be another four thousand houses in that mile radius so that will keep whoever it is you assign to organise the door-to-door enquiry busy for the next four months."

"I'm asking you to organise it."

"I can't."

"Why not?"

"Because my job is to manage critical incidents, which I will have to do while I am out on the reassurance patrols."

"I am not asking you to do the reassurance patrols; you can get your cops to do that."

"I need them for the road checks and the warrant operation. And we will need a budget for the overtime."

"What overtime?"

"Once they finish the road checks and the warrant operation, we will need to get them to stay on to complete their reports, that will incur overtime."

"There isn't any money for overtime," Chief Inspector MacSever sat back and folded his arms.

"No problem, sir. When are the extra officers arriving?"

"I haven't organised extra officers."

"Okay! I'll organise them. Where have they to come from?"

"We can't get officers from anywhere else. Everywhere else is short."

"Okay, sir. Which of the tasks you allocated do you want us to drop?"

"I want them all completed; you have twelve officers on your shift strength. You will have to manage it with them."

"As I pointed out yesterday, and the day before yesterday and the day before that - I have twelve officers showing on my group strength. One is currently re-assigned to the RMU, two are assigned to the major CID operation, one is off long-term sick, one has duties in the custody suite, and two are on holiday. That leaves me five officers with little service and experience to cover an area that routinely has a dozen emergency calls per shift. They all have their own enquiries to follow up; they already have the calls to attend that the previous shifts didn't manage to get to and they have paperwork sticking out their rear ends. We can't do it all. I need more officers on the group. My group has fewer officers than any other group at the station."

I began to fold my arms, then realised what I was doing. I didn't want to appear defensive or mirror Chief Inspector MacSever's pose, so I stopped as they were halfway up to my chest and held them out in front of me. My fists clenched as natural, and my right arm stretched out a little further.

Oh my God!

I faced Chief Inspector MacSever like a boxer in the ring.

What was I doing?

It looked like I was challenging him to a fight.

I wondered if the next words out of my mouth would be, "put em up, put em up!"

It was the first time I ever saw Chief Inspector MacSever look alarmed. He put his head down and shuffled the papers on his desk before mumbling, "Well, I have a new probationer coming to the station next week. I was going to put him into group two, but you can have him instead."
It worked!
There's a tip for everyone. If you want to win an argument with a Chief Inspector? Just put your fists up and challenge him to a fight.
"Who is it?"
"Tomas Kovacs, an older guy. He has an English degree, so he is a smart cookie."
"Fantastic, thank you, sir."

Broken leg - sticking plaster! I was seven cops short of my group strength, and Chief Inspector MacSever thought a new probationer would sort it!

My new start was an immigrant.
Tomas Kovacs moved to Scotland from Hungary. He had upped sticks with his whole family to seek a better life for themselves. MacSever was correct, Tomas was a bright man. He had an English degree, and before moving to Scotland, he had been teaching English as a private tutor in his small Hungarian town. Initially, it had been a good

enough living; he had been the only English teacher in his area, so his services were in big demand.

He did such a good job that the pupils he taught also got English degrees, and they too became private English tutors. The market for English tutors became saturated, and Tomas ended up being one of over twenty private English tutors in a five-mile radius. The economics of such a situation dictated his family up sticks and emigrate. They chose Scotland.

Tomas arrived in Scotland and thought he could teach English to all the Hungarians that had also moved to Scotland. He set up business, but the demand wasn't enough to scrape a living. After a while he decided to join the police. He sat the entrance exams, passed with flying colours and, because I had grumbled to Chief Inspector MacSever about being short staffed, Tomas found himself posted to my shift.

We designated PC Jane McSweggan as his tutor, and I hoped Tomas would be quick to settle in and become a useful member of the group.

Alas, there was a problem.

Tomas Kovacs was indeed bright, he had a good grasp of English, alas, he did not have such a good grasp of 'Scottish'. He couldn't quite comprehend the accent. It was a new language to him altogether. For example: In Scotland 'aye' means 'yes' not 'eye', 'ken' means 'know' and 'It's a braw, bricht, moonlicht nicht the nicht' was just a cognitive step too far.

*It's a braw, bricht, moonlicht nicht the nicht is a well known Scottish saying meaning 'I'm bored and I wish I was inside watching the telly'. The literal translation is 'It is a beautiful moonlight night tonight'.

Speaking to Tomas was not dissimilar to being on a delayed satellite link. First, Tomas had to translate the Scottish vernacular to English and then from English to Hungarian. Tomas had to formulate an answer and then translate it back to English. This satellite delay was pronounced enough to raise an eyebrow with Sergeant Dougieson and question his suitability to efficiently perform his duties.

"I think we need to evidence everything with Tomas," Sergeant Dougieson suggested. I got the distinct impression he didn't think there was much hope for Tomas. He might struggle to get through his probation. I decided not to make any assumptions. If I could help him become a good police officer, I would try my best. I took Tomas out on patrol with me to see for myself.

On our first day together I took the keys to a marked Ford Escort van, and we went out on our tour of duty.

"So Tomas," I said, "what made you join the police?"

In his broad Hungarian accent Tomas was candid with his answer.

"Umm ay wase on my way bauck from the shopps wone day and ay got stuck en a trauffic jam. Thure vase an accidunt up ahead. It wase quite a bad accidunt and we had to wait for about an hour before it was clearing for us."

I presumed he would tell me he watched the police officers deal with the accident and was so impressed that he had applied.

"So were you impressed with the way the police dealt with it?"

"No, ay vase sitting directly behund a bus that display a poleece recruitment advert on the bauck." (Part of a national campaign). "So after an hour of having nothink to do, I phoned the noomber. And here ay am."

I drove out of the office turned right behind a hatchback car. I suspected the driver was moving house because it carried a three piece suite. No furniture removal van required. The settee poked out the rear of the hatchback, stuffed in only as far as it could go, which left a good third still sticking out the back. The tailgate would therefore not shut and pointed up to the sky. Two armchairs sat on the roof, secured to the car using a clothes line. The clothes line wrapped over the armchairs and underneath the car, over and over until it had run out.

Before I could pull it over, it came to a stop. Arrived at its destination. I told Tomas to deal with the driver as he saw fit, but hinted that it wasn't the crime of the century. A bit of road safety advice might be the appropriate, in the circumstances.

Tomas got out of our vehicle and, as he did so, a teenager alighted from the hatchback and made his way to the rear of the car where he undid the clothes line. Tomas approached him and remonstrated with him over the unsafe load. I also alighted and listened while Tomas gave the teenager a lengthy and detailed lecture as to the danger his unsafe load posed to other road users. All in all, it wasn't a bad lecture - as lectures about stuffing sofas into the rear of hatchbacks go. Tomas covered the safety aspect to others, the safety aspect to the teenager himself and detailed that there were offences that could cost him a ticket.

Once he had finished, Tomas looked at me for confirmation he had said the right things.

"Anything else?" he asked me.

I smiled and reassured Tomas that what he had said was appropriate and acceptable as a resolution to the situation under the circumstances. But… and this was a big but.

"Do you not think you would be better speaking to the driver?"

The teenager had alighted from the front passenger seat while the middle-aged driver remained ensconced in the driver's seat. We all had a laugh, and the tension eased. I left the teenager to pass on Tomas's safety message.

As soon as Tomas was back with me in our car, he explained that they drive on the right in Hungary and the steering wheel is therefore on the left, hence his mistake.

I asked Tomas what enquiries he had on his plate. He produced an arrest warrant the sergeant had allocated to him. Brian S. McNutt was named on the warrant for non payment of a fine. We headed off to Brian's address. I parked the car and followed Tomas to a flat situated around the back of a row of shops. Tomas knocked on the door but received no reply; he explained that he had been at the address several times and had always received no reply. I had a look through the window and saw that the flat was bare and uninhabited. I then checked the warrant and discovered the address we were at was the wrong number. No points for guessing why he hadn't got his warrant sorted on two counts.

We called at the proper address, an upstairs flat, with the entry door on the ground floor. Tomas pressed the bell. It rang once, and he waited a few seconds for an answer, but no-one came.

"Nobody in," he said before giving up and walking away.

"Wait a minute," I said, experience telling me that the occupants of this particular flat might not be inclined to answer to a single ring. I pushed the bell and could hear the buzzer ringing upstairs. I kept my finger on it for a full minute before a bleary-eyed female answered the door.

Tomas asked the bleary-eyed female if Brian stayed there and she replied, "No."

Again Tomas looked at me shrugged and was about to walk away. I intervened, "You won't mind if I come in and speak to you then?" I asked the bleary-eyed female and walked past her into the flat. A cursory look into a bedroom on the way to the kitchen was enough to see that there was someone hiding under the covers in the bed. You can guess the rest.

After locking up our prisoner on a warrant, we went back out on patrol. A little while later, we stopped a car for only having one brake light working. After checking out the driver, we also discovered he also had no insurance. A basic case that required Tomas to note the driver's details and charge him. The satellite delay kicked in, Tomas took an endless time to get all the details he required and go through the process of charging him. I waited patiently but had to intervene several times when Tomas got procedures wrong. I was beginning to wonder if Tomas was all that suited to life in a uniform. It was not a great example of how to deal with a simple case.

Eventually, we got back out on patrol, and within a short time, I saw Peter Reid standing at a bus stop. His name reminded me of the time I was driving to work and heard a prank call by a local radio show host called Robin Galloway. Robin phoned a North East of Scotland newspaper and asked for the obituary column. The call went like this:-

Robin: Hello, it's Hector Brocklebank here from HB fish, I'm looking for the obituary column.

Lady: Oh right yeah, what was it you wanted to put in?

Robin: Just a price. Ye see we lost our dear brother-in-law there. Just at the weekend and I just wanted a price.

Lady: Is it a death notice?

Robin: Uh huh.

Lady: It goes by the line. So it just depends on how long it is.

Robin: Oh I see.

Lady: You can do it through your undertaker as well because if you do it privately, we have to get the name and address of the undertaker to confirm it.

Robin: Oh, well, Aye. It's no bother I can do that.

Lady: We can do it privately for you. I think it is about £2.60 a line.

Robin: Let me see. One, two, three… seven, eight, nine. Yes, it's just nine words.

Lady: It depends on the size of the words then.

Robin: Uh huh.

Lady: We can certainly do that for you. You can pre-pay it over the phone, or you can do it through your undertaker.

Robin: Uh huh. Well, if you could write it down for me just now, you can let me know, and we can get it pre-paid.

Lady: Okay, you want me to take it down for you just now?

Robin: Okay, I've written it down here what I was wanting to say if that is going to help.

Lady: Give me a second. Now, usually, it's 'peacefully' or 'suddenly'.

Robin: Oh aye. I wasn't going to go into that you see.

Lady: Right, what's the name of the deceased person?

Robin: Peter Reid.

Lady: Right, we will start with Reid, what did you want to put after that?

Robin: It's straight to the point you know.

Lady: Uh huh?
Robin: I didn't want anything too fancy.
Lady: No. What do you want to say?
Robin: Peter Reid, fae Peterheed, is deed.
Lady: (laughs) Uh huh. I can try that. I don't know if I will be allowed to do that, but I will certainly ask. What else did you want to say?
Robin: Volvo for sale.
Lady: (hangs up)
Robin: Not to worry. I'll try *Auto Trader.*

I arrived at work with tears of laughter running down my leg.

The Peter Reid I saw at the bus stop was about sixty years old and a nice old fellow. Nice, that is with one exception, that exception being when he was drunk. When Peter Reid was drunk, he was a pain in the backside. All too regular Peter Reid got drunk and then made a bloody nuisance of himself.

He was standing at the bus stop swearing at passersby and pretending to step out onto the roadway in front of passing cars. In the interests of his safety, and to prevent him causing a car to swerve into oncoming traffic, I offered him a lift home. Peter Reid was happy to accept and save himself a bus fare.

As soon as we ensconced Peter in the back of our car, he burst into song. I wouldn't mind, normally, but he was rather too loud and totally out of tune. He sat in the middle of the back seats, leaned forward and serenaded the two of us with a dubious sectarian chant. Then he stretched his arms around both of us in an attempt at a cuddle. His gratefulness was a little too heart-warming for my liking. I'm not averse to a bit of gratitude, but a one-hundred-decibel rendition of *'We are the Billy Boys'* and being grabbed around the neck as I am driving is a step too far.

I asked him to sit back and put on his seatbelt, at which point Peter Reid changed from being a singing, happy to be your pal, drunkard into a screaming, vitriolic and abusive drunk. He did not have a good word to say about

Tomas or myself. His venomous outburst was unexpected considering our generosity in giving him a free lift home. It was a tirade of threats and abuse that is unrepeatable here. Peter Reid then threw himself forward and tried to grab the steering wheel. I was travelling at fifty miles per hour on a two-lane undivided carriageway, with preceding, oncoming and following traffic. (That's police speak for 'it was busy'). That it was busy made his actions all the more dangerous.

But Peter Reid didn't get to grab the steering wheel and wrench it this way or that. At the very second, he was about to touch it Tomas sprung into action. He didn't need to translate Hungarian into English, then English into Scottish. He shouted in Hungarian, "VISSZA VAGY PEDIG!"

At the same moment, he grabbed Peter Reid's arms, turned one-hundred and eighty degrees in his seat and threw himself through the gap in the front seats landing on top of our passenger. Within a flash, he had wrapped a seatbelt around Peter Reid's body and arms and pinned him to the back seat.

Peter Reid hadn't a clue what had happened to him. He sat wrapped up in his seatbelt with Tomas sitting on top of him ready to act if he did anything else. Peter Reid was the quietest I had ever seen him, drunk or sober.

Slowly Tomas formulated his next words to Peter, "Now behave."

At that moment I knew Tomas would do just fine as a police officer, no matter what misgivings anyone had.

Tomas, I am pleased to say, completed his probation. He is careful about getting the right addresses; he is persistent when pursuing lines of inquiry and he remains completely unflustered when dealing with drunken louts. His ability to translate Hungarian has proved to be another wonderful asset for the police.

Oh, and he always speaks to the driver now when stopping cars.

It is a varied life in the police; you never know what is coming next. Anything can happen at any time. A serious road accident, a murder or a cat stuck up a tree. We drop everything and deal with it. So if we know when a big event will take place, perhaps an Old Firm game, an Orange Walk or even a Royal Visit, we like we can plan for it.

Royal visits are nice. No matter which Royal deigned to visit our area, the royalists would turn up in numbers, wave their Union Jack and cheer. It is all very pleasant and civilised. There is no drink involved, non-royalists just don't bother to turn up. Unlike some sporting events or orange walks there is no drinking culture associated with a royal visit. Young and old alike just turn up with their families and cheer in happy celebration they can see their king, queen, prince or princess. Yes, royal visits are nice.

While the royals themselves get a distorted view of the fresh painted town or city, they are in; it is also true their loyal subjects get a distorted view of the fresh decorated Royals as they pass by waving and smiling. For the police a royal visit is always a pain in the backside. No senior police officer wants anything untoward to happen to any of the Royals when they visit their area. Therefore months of planning, bomb searches, staffing issues, protection patrols, etc., precede a royal visit.

On the day of the royal visit we set up a control room, exclusive to the event, to manage the running. Staffed by experienced officers under the charge of a senior event commander, who will worry his fingernails away until the visiting Royals are out of his jurisdiction and safe. The control room will have various other senior officers in attendance, various specialist advisers (firearms, public order, dog handlers, traffic control, etc.).

Out on the route, there will be a preponderance of uniformed cops. Every junction, every building, every temporary barrier will have a uniform cop. We use every CCTV camera in the area to monitor the crowd, and eyes are everywhere to ensure that no rogue troublemaker can cause a nuisance or worse. We do everything to ensure the safe passage for the royal visitor. The primary aim, hammered home by the senior event commander at every pre-event meeting, is "Don't dare feck this up!"

Woe betide anyone who does anything that will cause the senior event commander embarrassment. During most major events that would hold true, but during a royal visit, the Royals also have their own permanent security staff appointed to overlook the arrangements. They follow the Royals all around the country and delve into the arrangements made by each force. Senior event commanders know that they do this all the time and they will comment on anything not in keeping with their security risk and that they will compare each force's efforts. Thus senior event commanders worry more about the potential for humiliation and shame than they do about the actual safety of the royal in question.

So when they announced a Royal visit to our big city all the royalists cheered, and all the police rolled their eyes and groaned. Chief Inspector MacSever announced it to us at the morning meeting.

"The Queen is coming to see the castle," he said, quite matter-of-fact.

The one royalist sitting in on the morning meeting was a Community Sergeant called Rupert Wentworth Hamilton. As his name would suggest, he was English, born and bred in a royalist borough of Hampshire. On hearing the news, Rupert clasped his hands together in unconcealed delight. The rest of us rolled our eyes and groaned. There was a slight pause then I asked the important question.

"Who is the event commander?"

"Chief Superintendent Cribber!"

We rolled our eyes and groaned again, even Rupert Wentworth Hamilton unclasped his hands and hunched his shoulders at this additional news.

Chief Superintendent Cribber wasn't anyone's favourite event commander. He was one of those ambitious senior officers who avoided getting into any situations where he might end up embarrassed or found out. Thus when he got one of these gigs (which he only did when he had exhausted all schemes to get out of it), he would go out of his way to ensure that he used every single person he could get involved in the organisation. He made specific officers responsible for every single minutiae of planning and made it clear that if anything went wrong, it would be their responsibility. The technical police term is 'slopey shoulders'.

Gentleman George warned about Cribber. I trusted George, he knew Cribber well. He described Cribber as a plagiarist who had got to where he was through deceit and deviousness. Cops often exaggerate perceived wrongdoings against them. I listen and nod then move on to the next story, always assuming that there might be a little embellishment. You know, one of those stories that get told after a few pints and the topic turns towards work. As soon as someone relates a grievance, the next person tries to trump it.

George trumped everyone when he related a story about Cribber. George worked for him for a short while. He prepared a report and submitted to him (when he was Detective Sergeant Cribber). Cribber changed Gentleman George's name on the cover and submitted the report as his own work. None too pleased, George challenged him about it. Cribber brazened it out, arguing that he had made significant changes to George's report and was therefore justified in changing George's name to his as the author. There was a lot more to it than that, but that was the part of his story that stuck in my mind. Anyone else telling the story would have caused me to raise an eyebrow, but Gentleman George is beyond reproach. I received further confirmation of Cribber's character when it happened to me.

Cribber worked his way up the ranks and transferred to my station as a superintendent. We had a serious court case in the offing involving potential terrorists; there would be big security issues. As it was on his patch, Cribber got the call and they told him to make contingency plans. These contingency plans had to cover every eventuality, including, if necessary, moving the trial from the courthouse to somewhere else. As soon as Cribber put down the phone, he picked it up again and invited me up to his office. I suspect he chose me for no other reason than the fact I was the nearest to his office. He dumped the job of coming up with the contingency plan unceremoniously on my lap. The only instruction Cribber felt necessary was to say, "It had better be right, or you will get the blame."

I tried to clarify a few points. Basic information: when, where, what? That sort of thing.

"You decide," he said, "but remember if something goes wrong it will be your fault."

The buck, it would appear, would stop with me. I had to admit as slopey shouldering goes Cribber did it with some flair. I went into my pocket and pulled out fourteen super strong elastic bands I kept especially for this kind of situation and stretched each one out individually between my thumb and forefinger before pinging them as hard as I could at Cribber's head.

Okay, I didn't do that, I just imagined myself doing it; I don't like to say 'you can feck right off' to superintendents, so I sidled off to get on with it. I threw myself into the task deciding to make sure that what I did I did to the best of my ability. I made enquiries with other forces to see if there was anything similar they had done, I checked with the local prison and obtained details of their contingency plans for running a court within their walls. I consulted with the court, the firearms tactical advisor, the sheriff clerk's office, the Procurator Fiscal's office and even the Scottish Government.

In due course, I prepared a comprehensive report and operational order (this was a 'just in case' remember) to cover the eventuality that we might need to run a court case somewhere other than the court building.

Security and safety were the prime goals, and I think I achieved it. I was proud of my exhaustive report, and when I printed it off, it ran to dozens of pages. A thick tome of work that covered every aspect of the contingency plan down to the last detail. At any stage, no matter what the cause for concern, you would only need to look at my report and find the course of action to follow. I had guidelines laid out for every possible occurrence.

I submitted it to Cribber.

A week later Cribber phoned me in my office, "Malky, can you send me an electronic copy of that report please."

"Why is that sir? Is there something wrong with it?" I knew there wasn't.

"No. No. It's fine. I just need to make a couple of changes."

A month later Cribber called his team of senior officers together, including me, for a meeting. The topic of the meeting was - My contingency plan.

No sooner had we sat down Cribber handed out printed copies of MY contingency plan. I skipped through the pages of the report I had spent weeks researching, drafting, re-drafting and creating. The only thing I could find different was on the front page. Instead of 'Inspector McEwan' as the author, it read 'Superintendent Cribber'. I was dumbstruck. My jaw dropped, and my mouth opened and stayed like that for the next forty-five minutes as Cribber brazenly outlined 'his' contingency plans. I listened to him tell me what I might have to do with the contingency plans I had drafted. I went into my pocket and rummaged around looking for super strong elastic bands - fortunately for Cribber, there were none there. Yup, plagiarism works! At least it did for the new-promoted Assistant Chief Constable Cribber.

A lot of cops had experiences like that with Cribber, so we weren't best pleased to be informed that he was in command for the for the royal visit.

The usual things happened, he gave everyone tasks to organise various parts of the event. Complete an order, arrange staff, organise road closures, liaise with the council, etc. We made plans and put them in place. For things like that, the police are a well-oiled machine.

Cribber called a final meeting. He went through all our plans and read them out as if he had written every single one with a quill pen in his own blood. The plans covered the secure passage of the Royals as they entered our area, all the way to the castle where they were due to have lunch, and all the way back to the force boundary. There was only one change he asked for from all we had put together. For some bizarre reason, he decided that he wanted a detective constable on the roof of the castle. His request passed down the line, and Detective Constable Andy Lambert volunteered for the task but putting both his arms so far up his back so that his hands touched the nape of his neck.

Access to the roof of the castle was through a ladder up to a trapdoor that allowed the occasional inspection of the turrets. On the day of the royal visit Andy, knuckles white, climbed the ladder and through the trapdoor and onto the roof. There wasn't much room for him to wander around but he could look over one side of the battlements to see the main inner ward. Every other side only allowed him to stare off into the distance and admire the view.

Andy had came prepared. He had his heavy raincoat, just in case the forecast changed its mind. The forecast said glorious sunshine, but in Scotland, that could mean a slight peek of sunlight behind the clouds in between the hailstorms. Andy had his flask of coffee, three bottles of water, sandwiches, crisps, chocolate bars, biscuits and even a packet of wine gums to keep himself amused. He knew once he was up there; he was trapped until the royal visit had been and gone. He was the only one on the roof and control asked him for confirmation he was in place before ignoring him for the rest of the day.

Detective Constable Andy Lambert peered over the battlement overlooking the inner ward and saw many people scurrying about like ants. He couldn't make out anything they were doing and saw no point in making himself dizzy, so he settled himself into a corner of the flat roof and watched the clouds go by. After an hour his flask of coffee was empty, his sandwiches eaten, and a chocolate bar decimated. He was now chewing his way through his wine gums and before long they would be gone too. The heat of the sun and the saltiness of the crisps created a thirst, so he downed the bottles of water.

The royal visitor was late, not an unusual occurrence for a royal visit. Just another pain the backside for those of us that had to police such things. Andy stood up to have another look over the battlement, observed nothing untoward and settled back to look at the single wispy cloud in the far distance.

The sun blazed as predicted and Andy also drank the three bottles of water. The time passed slow. Andy hoped that the royal visitor wouldn't dally. He was now bursting for a pee. All that coffee and water was sloshing about in his bladder pressing against the seams and making him a tad uncomfortable. He tried to hold it in.

The royal visitors seemed to be taking a long time over their lunch. Andy felt an urgent need, he couldn't wait anymore. He went to the far corner of the turret and peed into a rain channel. It was perfectly safe; he thought. Nobody could see him. He was at the highest point in the city, and nobody was overlooking him. There wasn't even a bird in the sky. His bladder emptied into the rain channel for a full minute and a half. Andy shook the last drops away, sighed and closed his eyes in relief.

It wasn't until Andy opened them again, a full ten seconds later, that he saw the pee draining down the gutter towards the east side. The gutter met the wall and turned at a right angle towards the south; his pee followed the same course. It had travelled from the far side of the turret, turned two ninety-degree angles and had reached the inner ward.

By now the royal visitors had finished their lunch and were making their way back down from the castle. A crowd were present either side, and the Royals ambled by asking polite questions of their loyal subjects.

The pee flowed along the gutter and disappeared into the channel at the back of a gargoyle's head.

In the olden days, they didn't have drains that ran water down into gutter pipes and safely down the building. The channels simply directed the water into the back of a gargoyle's head and a hole allowed the rain to dispense from its mouth. It was a clever way of ensuring the water didn't run directly down the wall causing damage.

That is what happened to Andy's pee.

The royal visitors walked through the middle of the inner ward of the castle on a beautiful hot summer's day. Like a thunder-plump, pee spouted from the gargoyle's head and splattered to the ground dousing a group of VIPs who were in the process of clapping as the Royals walked past them.

Andy had a little apologising to do when he came down.

THE MICHAEL PARKINSON TELEVISION INTERVIEW

Parky: It is fortunate that you can laugh and find the funny side of the job because I know that the job of a police officer can be frustrating.

Malky: Frustrating, yes. More so nowadays with all the cuts. I salute those who are still on the job. They are having a much more difficult time. I consider myself lucky.

Parky: Lucky?

Malky: Yes, lucky. I joined at a time when they were taking on anybody (including me). The favourite saying I heard when I joined was 'The jobs fecked' - that was over three decades ago. The government had to improve pay and conditions, and I joined just at the right time.

Parky: So you think the conditions are much better now?

Malky: I think all the cuts regressed the service back to the state it was when I joined. The wages have been static for almost ten years. There are far fewer officers on the beat now than ten years ago, and this has had a detrimental effect on the service the public receives.

Parky: In what way?

Malky: Violent crime is up, officer morale is down, and good cops are leaving.

Parky: The Government might argue that they are making the police service more efficient?

Malky: I have no objection to improving efficiency. Improving efficiency is a good thing. There is a big difference between efficiency savings and cost-cutting. When I meet police officers still in the job they tell me that instead of there being a minimum of six covering an area, there is now just two. I look at the car they are driving, and I see the driver's seat has no stuffing in the back, worn away by overuse. Cars that we considered unroadworthy after 100,000 miles now do

150,000 miles. That is not safe for the police or the public. I called into our main Police Headquarters last Wednesday afternoon, and it was closed. That office that used to be open to the public twenty-four hours a day seven days per week.

Parky: The main headquarters was shut?

Malky: Well, there was a notice up saying the office was closed for lunch. The one time when most people are likely to pop in.

Parky: So what did you do?

Malky: I was about to walk away and not bother, then I saw two women on the inside of the glass doors trying to get out. I signalled to them I would help and I pressed the intercom on the outside. After a minute a voice asked if she could help me. I explained the situation, and she asked me which office I was at. It was only then I realised that the intercom had buzzed me through to the main control room for Scotland - an office forty miles away.

Parky: That's crazy.

Malky: I agree. I explained to her I was just about to go away, but two women were trying to get out. "Are they police officers?" She asked me.

Parky: Seriously?

Malky: Yes seriously. I wouldn't have bothered them because I was just handing something in and I knew the lady on the other end of the intercom would have to disturb the duty sergeant to come and deal with me and duty sergeants are busy enough. It is not efficiency when someone has to do a job that could pay someone half as much to do.

Parky: So what happened?

Malky: Well, it so happened that a senior officer was leaving the office and he opened the door and marched out. The two ladies followed, and I walked in the open door. There was no-one on reception, but I knew the lady on the other end of the intercom would contact the duty sergeant to attend, so I waited in the reception to explain to him what had happened and hand my stuff over. It might be someone I knew, and I could chew the fat. There was one of those cardboard cut-out police officers in the foyer so he could keep me company while I waited.

Parky: A cardboard cut out of a police officer?

Malky: Yeah. A lot of bargain basement shops put them in their windows to deter shoplifters. There is science behind it. Shops that have them have as much as fifty percent less stock going missing as those that don't. Some places in Australia go one step further and use cardboard cut-out police cars at the side of the road to reduce speeding - that works too. From a distance, people don't know if it is the real thing or not.

Parky: So the police should invest in more of these cardboard cut-outs instead of real officers?

Malky: Maybe they should, but they shouldn't put them in the front foyer of their main Police Headquarters.

Parky: Why not?

Malky: Because then it looks like there are police in and people turn up and find the doors locked and get frustrated. All the time a cardboard cut-out police officer is staring at them through the glass doors, mocking them with his big wide open eyes and pointy finger.

Parky: Ha ha. That would be annoying. So how long did it take for the sergeant to come and deal with you?

Malky: He didn't. No-one came. I waited for twenty-five minutes and never saw a single soul.

Parky: Did you complain?

Malky: Naw, they have enough to do. I picked up the cardboard cut-out police officer and made my escape with him.

Parky: Serves them right. So now you are out the job you still get frustrated by the police. I bet when you were in the job it was the public who frustrated you?

Malky: Not all the time.

Chapter 8

BOILING HEADS

There were lots of occasions I would go out into the community and end up coming back to the office shaking my head. I would despair at some of the sights I saw. There are people out there who just have different ideas to normal people. It stunned me at what squalor people can live in. Places where I have had an overwhelming urge to wipe my feet on the way out.

I have stood on a jobbie in a sitting-room. I have seen jobbies on every second step on the way upstairs. People have asked me to have a seat on a blood-stained duvet covering a settee and on lifting the duvet I found that the duvet was the better option (I remained standing). I have seen pots in a sink that were growing a variety of penicillin. I have wandered up a hallway wondering what the smell was and wished I hadn't discovered the cause. I have seen nappies full of excrement being scraped off and put back on the child.

You get the picture.

A common explanation for their unpleasant living circumstances was, "We're decorating!"

I often felt the need to raise an eyebrow at a mother who said, "We are in the middle of painting the house!" as an explanation for a jobbie lying on a bare floorboard. There was never any evidence of any decorating, at least none that used paint, wallpaper or paste. The most memorable house I attended, however, was this one:-

I attended at a council house in a poor part of the city. A place where the garden furniture comprised a of threadbare sofa plonked next to an inoperable fridge and a soot blackened cooker. An explosion of weeds blurred the boundary and covered a small rusted metal fence. The rubbish strewn drive led to a pile of rubble where a concrete garage had once been, but no more.

I manoeuvred my way through and knocked on a uPVC door that had more dents and scrapes than a car at the end of a demolition derby. The pink, hand-painted, foot high number fifteen on the door confirmed I was at the right address.

On being invited in, I had to clamber over a telegraph pole. The pole was now half its original length having been introduced to the house through the rear living-room window. It was now protruding only about seven feet out the window but crossed the entire length of the living room where it came to rest in the fireplace. The end of the telegraph pole was smouldering away nice, giving off a reasonable heat to counteract the draft from the open window. This telegraph pole appeared to be the only source of heat for the house and now and then the family congregated around the pole to help push it further into the fireplace as the end burned down.

My immediate concern was 'fire hazard' and as if telepathic the occupier stated that the bricks underneath the pole around the fire prevented any danger of sparks igniting the rest of the house or of it burning down the pole too quick. The bricks in question had come from the interior wall in the living room. Without regard to the effect on the wallpaper, a gaping hole presented itself. On the other side of the hole was a bedroom. In this bedroom was a bed and propped up in the bed was an elderly and infirm man. Grandad, a frail looking man with grey facial growth and a dribble running down the side of his mouth. Grandad's bed lay at an angle so he could look straight through the hole in the living room wall. The occupier saw the perplexed look on my face and explained.

"Grandad was finding it hard to get out of his bed. So we knocked the hole in the wall so he could see the telly."

Yup. We came across some real eye-opening sights.

However, nothing made me despair more than some of the bureaucratic nonsense that came my way within the office.

Since the time of William Pitt, governments had been promising to reduce the burden of police paperwork. We had a lot, even when I first started. We had Crime Reports, road accident reports, sudden death reports and even fire reports (a job you would think would be the remit of the fire services).

Every time a general election was in the offing, each political party would include details in their manifestos of how they would get the police out of their police stations and onto the street fighting crime. Then, no matter which party got into power, their promises never came to anything. Reducing the burden of paperwork for the Police is a difficult thing to do. Often even a minor change in the law impacted on the police by introducing additional matters to record.

"We need to free the police from inappropriate rules and regulations," said the politicians one week and slated them the next for not being able to provide exact figures for the number of holes in their socks.

Instead they introduced Crime Recording Standards. The rules of the Crime Recording Standards meant, no matter how minor a crime, full details had to be typed into a computer for reference. All very sensible you might think, but in reality, this happened:-

Before the introduction of the Crime Recording Standards, if a pint of milk went missing from your doorstep, you might phone the police. The office clerk would take a note of your call, record it on two or three lines in the book and then pass it down to the sergeants for their information. The sergeants realised that it would be almost impossible to detect the crime, so they devoted no effort whatsoever in either taking a complaint or carrying out investigations. Why devote two officers for two hours to carry out an inquiry for something that cost the householder pennies. The officers would go about their other duties, and that was it. Maybe (and this is a big maybe) the police found out who was responsible, the sergeant sent a cop to give him a warning and tell him not to do it again.

After introducing the Crime Recording Standards if you called the police to report the theft of your milk the call handler would take a note of your complaint and record it on the computer. This electronic document (or crime file) remains on record forever. The crime file gets allocated to a sergeant, and he asks a cop to investigate. The cop is obliged to do door-to-door enquiry, interview the complainer and obtain his statement. He also interviews the milk delivery boy and notes a statement from him to confirm that he left the pint of milk on the doorstep. He would go back to the office and record all this information on the electronic crime file system. The sergeant would read it and perhaps suggest other lines of enquiry. His inspector would read it and also suggest other lines of enquiry. The crime management unit (set up to review these crime files) would read it and they too suggest other lines of enquiry (you wouldn't believe what they came up with). The cop has to spend his time making all these enquiries. Fourteen days later he would re-interview the complainer, and record any further information on the crime file. Everyone in the management chain would have the opportunity to review everything he did to detect this crime.

Just maybe (and this is a big maybe) someone got information regarding who was responsible, the sergeant would send a cop to detain that person. The cop would have to take a corroborating officer, and in the process of bringing the person responsible back to the office he would involve parents (if it was a juvenile), the custody sergeant, the custody assistant and even a lawyer. He'd have to record the interview, fingerprint the lad and photograph him - and so it went on.

Once the cop completed all his enquiries, he would submit a report to the Procurator Fiscal or to the Children's Reporter. The process could take months and, in the end, the person responsible would get a warning.

Sometimes it was worse. If the Chief Constable was under pressure for not getting enough detections, he would insist on more effort. The instruction to do more would get passed on down the line. No matter how many other pressing matters there were, the department monitoring crimes will not allow us to file a crime report as undetected until each and every task was complete - no matter how injudicious a waste of resources it is. Under pressure to get the crime detected the sergeant might dedicate two officers to carry out a watch.

So for four nights, two cops in plain-clothes would set up a watch. They would be there when the milkman made his deliveries, and they would wait and watch. Four nights, two police officers, one pint of milk. If they were lucky enough to catch someone, let's say they saw the Paperboy stealing a pint of milk from another doorway, the police would have to go through the whole process of arresting him, interviewing, etcetera. A lot of work for a young lad who was just delivering papers and got thirsty. After much paperwork and palaver, the Paperboy would receive a warning. Everybody would be happy - except those that couldn't get the services of a police officer while the watch was going on.

These days the police have to create 'Ward Plans' to keep councillors happy and develop 'PACT' (Police and Communities Together) priorities that no one ever reads. They have to prepare 'Area Agendas' and 'Community Action Plans' that are different - but the same because no one pays any attention to them. A cop should pay heed to them but what do you think he does when he gets a call to a shoplifting? He deals with the shoplifting.

There are also 'Repeat Victim Action Plans', 'Intelligence Requirements', 'Pro-activity Logs', 'Divisional Improvement Plans', 'Performance Frameworks', 'Public Performance Reports', 'Single Outcome Agreements', 'Strategic Tasking and Coordinating', 'Tactical Tasking and Coordinating' and… I could go on.

So much for reducing the burden of police paperwork!

The police, as an organisation, is as rational and sensible as you will get. As much as I had frustrations over the amount of paperwork and red-tape, my police force prioritised the work in a level-headed manner. We followed employment procedures. If you weren't happy about something in the police, then you could raise the matter, and they took it seriously. The private sector, I know, can be brutal. If you weren't happy about something you could be out the door before the last burger you flipped hit the grill. Those that are self-employed have an even harder time. Fall ill, and you don't get paid!

With that in mind, I found I could suffer most things, (except Coronation Street), but I was always maddened by time spent preparing reports and plans that no-one read. There was only one thing that made me madder - people who like to make the job harder than it should be.

Like the inspector in the training department. One day I received an e-mail from him:-

Inspector McEwan,

The Training Department is currently looking to identify additional Diversity Awareness Trainers. Training comprises an initial five-day course at the Police College. After that, we would want the staff member to assist with the two-day training courses run throughout the year. Total commitment to assisting trainers would be a maximum of three courses in any calendar year.

We have identified, Constable Gillian Gentle, from your area as a potential candidate. I would be obliged if you could confirm her suitability to undertake this training and seek your authority to utilise her in this role.

Regards

Training Inspector

I had responsibility for the Community Safety Team, which consisted of a sergeant and three cops. PC Gillian Gentle worked at another station but they moved her, temporarily, off frontline duties to our Community Safety Team because she was pregnant.

I had a chat with the Community Safety Team sergeant before replying to the training inspector:-

Dear Training Inspector,

I have discussed your request with Constable Gillian Gentle's immediate line manager and can confirm that she would be a suitable candidate. Her line manager can see no difficulty in either making her available for the training course or indeed assisting with training in the future. Please feel free to place her on the course.

Regards.

Inspector McEwan.

I received a reply the same day:-

Inspector McEwan,

Thank you. Please complete the attached training needs analysis form regarding Constable Gentle's suitability to undertake the course.

Regards.

Training Inspector.

More paperwork! What an imposition. Here was the training department in need of candidates for their training course. They asked for a specific person, having identified her as suitable themselves, but I had to complete a 'training needs analysis form'. I was a tad miffed, but the better part of my nature is that I am an obliging fellow and I like to get things done. I duly sat down and filled out the form and sent it back to the training inspector less than an hour later:-

Dear Training Inspector,

Training needs analysis form completed and attached.

Regards.

Inspector McEwan.

I put all thoughts of Gillian Gentle, diversity awareness training, and forms to the back of my mind and got on with my work. Seven days later, another e-mail arrived:-

Inspector McEwan,

Thank you. Please complete the attached Training Impact Costs form regarding freeing Constable Gentle from her duties within the Community Safety Team.

Regards.

Training Inspector.

I had hardly been aware of the Training Needs Analysis form, far less the Training Impact Costs form. What kind of torture was that? Rather than just send it back with a curt note, I decided it prudent to acquaint myself with the requirements of the Training Impact Costs form. Working as an Inspector teaches that patience is a virtue. I researched what was required and completed as best as I saw fit. As much as the situation was now becoming a little exasperating, at least I now knew what a Training Impact

Costs form was and had practical experience completing it. Positive Malky Attitude (PMA).

I returned the form:-

Dear Training Inspector

Please find attached Training Impact Costs form. As stated in my last email, Constable Gentle's line manager is able to cope with her absence.

Regards

Inspector McEwan.

A further week passed, and all thoughts of the training inspector's irksome and time-consuming requests had faded. I am blessed with a bad memory, which allows life's little inconveniences to be quickly forgotten, leaving me with a 'glass half full' frame of mind. With my Positive Malky Attitude, my glass is generally half full of beer. Then the next email arrived to bugger it all up:-

Inspector McEwan,

I understand that Constable Gentle is only in the Community Safety Team temporarily as she is pregnant. Does this cause any issue for you or affect her suitability to undertake the said training.

Regards.

Training Inspector.

Eh! Why on earth would that make a difference? I thought. It was the training department that wanted her in the first place. I'd said 'yes', this was as much as I presumed was required (otherwise I might have said 'no' from the outset). First, it was a Training Needs Analysis form, then a Training Impact Costs form. What next?

I replied to the training inspector:-

Dear Training Inspector,

Constable Gentle is pregnant and has been placed on the Community Safety Team temporarily to relieve her of frontline duties while she is with child. I have no issues with her undertaking the said training and suspect we would be held to account if we declined a development opportunity based on the grounds of pregnancy

Regards

Inspector McEwan.

That would sort him out, I thought. Any suggestion of 'being held to account' for anything frightened pedantic pen pushers into submission. I believed I would hear no more of it. Isn't it astonishing that people you have had few dealings with can still hate you? The next e-mail arrived two days later:-

Inspector McEwan,

Please confirm with HRD that her present state of pregnancy does not affect her suitability to undertake the said training.

Regards.

Training Inspector.

So now I had to contact the Human Resources Department! Why couldn't he do that? Why on earth did I have to do it? Couldn't he just crawl away and get on with some training or something? I had better things to do with my time. As it turned out the things I had to get on with distracted me for a couple of hours, by which time I had calmed down. Blood pressure back to normal I conceded that he had said 'please' and I don't like to say 'no'. I forwarded the training inspector's email to HRD with a brief note:-

FWD: HRD

Dear HRD,

Can you confirm the above, please?

Regards

Inspector McEwan.

I hoped that they would take a quick look and agree that there were no issues and let us know within a day or so. My expectation was that they would sit on it for a week and throw another obstacle in my way. The Human Resources Department was another section of the police that seemed designed to fulfil the desires of every HR staff in placing obstacles in front of the ordinary police officer trying to get on with some work. I turned out to be wrong. It took two weeks for them to reply and throw two obstacles in my way.

Inspector McEwan,

We cannot deny an officer training or development opportunities on the grounds of pregnancy. To do so is gender discrimination. However, have you looked at her absence management record as she may not meet the criteria to undertake the course due to her poor absence record.

Regards

HRD

Absence record! No, I hadn't thought of looking at her absence record. I thought I might not live long enough to see my pension if this kept up. It didn't make a blind bit of difference to me. I wasn't looking to develop her for the role of diversity trainer. They asked if the training department could use her. I said 'yes', but now I was to look at her absence record because there was a rule about cops not being afforded training or development opportunities if their attendance was poor.

I checked Constable Gentle's attendance record. The absence management policy criteria stated that if an officer had more than three absences through sickness in any calendar year or a continuous absence over twelve days, then they should not be considered for additional training or development opportunities. Constable Gillian Gentle had four separate absences in the past calendar year.

Whoop de doo! What did I care?

I forwarded the reply to the training inspector with another note:-

Dear Training Inspector,

Please see above reply from HRD. I have no objections to her undertaking the training, her line manager has no objections, and HRD confirms we cannot deny her the training or development opportunity on the grounds of her pregnancy. Please go ahead and place her on the course.

Inspector McEwan.

As soon as I clicked the 'send' button I had this knotted feeling in the pit of my stomach that this would not be the end of the saga. The training inspector appeared to be practising embuggerance with such flair he could have won a talent showt. That fear was realised two days later when I received another e-mail:-

Inspector McEwan,

I have examined Constable Gentle's absence management record and note she has been absent from work on four separate occasions in the past year totalling 17 working days lost. As such she fails to meet the criteria of suitability for undertaking additional training or development (being absent on over three occasions in the past year). In order to overcome this obstacle, we will require a memo from you detailing why she should be allowed to undertake this training when she does not meet the criteria under the absence management policy.

Regards.

Training Inspector.

Wait a minute! Why do I need to do a memo? She is not even my officer; she is only here temporarily. It should be the Chief Inspector Operations dealing with this. After all, he will be the one that will lose her to the training courses once she is back working operationally.

I'm not just a pretty face you know. Time to send a smart reply:-

Dear Training Inspector,

I have no issues with Constable Gentles undertaking this training. Her current line manager has no issues with her undertaking this training. However, as she is only with me temporarily, I have forwarded this message to Chief Inspector Operations for him to complete said memo.

Regards

Inspector McEwan.

The response from the Chief Inspector Operations was immediate:-

Inspector McEwan,

Constable Gentle is currently your responsibility. I suggest that YOU complete the required memo.

Regards.

Chief Inspector Operations.

Dismissed and outranked in one short and snappy few lines. I had no other choice but to sit for two hours drafting a reasoned and logical argument to allow Constable Gentles the opportunity to undertake a diversity awareness training course despite not meeting the criteria under the absence management policy.

Dear Training Inspector,

Please find attached memo giving my full reasoned support allowing Constable Gentle to undergo the Diversity Awareness training.

Regards.

Inspector McEwan.

That should do it - I thought. Nope - one day later my inbox was assaulted from all directions:-

Inspector McEwan,

I have correspondence from Chief Inspector Operations who is unhappy that Constable Gentle will undergo developmental training when she does not meet the criteria under the absence management policy. Can I suggest you discuss the matter with him?

Regards.

Training Inspector.

The police is a disciplined service. One should be careful about how one goes about speaking to colleagues - especially if they are of a higher rank. I am always wary of being caught out by putting something on paper (or e-mail) that could be construed as controversial - far less disrespectful. But here I was, weeks in, still dealing with a request initiated by the Training Department to take an officer on a training course. They wanted her I said 'yes'. That was not sufficient. I had to complete two sets of forms, draft a memo and engage in a long winded e-mail correspondence to justify why the officer could go on a training course that the Training Department wanted her to go on in the first place.

I thought long and hard about my reply, and five seconds later I sent this:-

Dear Chief Inspector Operations,
Dear Training Inspector,
Dear HRD,

I suggest that you all go away and boil yer heeds!

Regards.

Inspector McEwan.

THE MICHAEL PARKINSON TELEVISION INTERVIEW

Parky: So it was other police inspectors that frustrated you the most.

Malky: Not just inspectors, cops could do that too.

Chapter 9

NEIL NEIL NEIL

That wasn't my only run-in with the Training Department. The new 'Officer Safety Training Programme' made me raise more than just an eyebrow.

Police officers are highly trained and proficient in officer safety techniques. Accomplished and skilful at safely securing a violent suspect. They undergo extensive initial training and years of constant drill and rigorous practice. Police officers thus have a high degree of self-discipline, they are superb physical specimens and are capable of superhuman feats. There is nothing that will detract an officer from his goal. They have an inbuilt strength and determination second to none. With this mindset and the relentless training they undergo, they become perfect examples of the human form.

Well, not exactly!

Police officers get initial officer safety training when they join. Two afternoons in the gym playing with plastic batons and dummy CS spray canisters. The dummy CS spray canisters only contain water. Some of the more childish officers take great delight in aiming for the crotch area instead of the face, leaving a slapstick wet patch on the front of their colleague's tracksuit bottoms. Of course, I was above such nonsense.

Once every couple of years we had to go through mandatory re-training. All sorts of shapes and sizes and ranks of officers turn up at the gym and sit around signing forms for about an hour. The officer safety instructors then lead the motley crew through a series of exercises designed as a warm up. It serves to identify those who aren't fit enough to plod their way around the gym three times without pulling a muscle or coughing up their lungs.

Most cops worn out from working taxing night shifts. Exhausted, they stand around paying lip service to the instructor's commands. The rest are desk jockeys whose only dexterity is being able to type nonsensical initiatives at eighty words per minute.

Following the 'warm up' the rest of the morning is spent doing the same training routine we did every year. Starting with the 'come-along hold' (which everyone remembers) and then going through a gamut of other holds and handcuff techniques (which everyone forgets). In the afternoon we watch a repeat of the same First Aid video they force us to sit through every year - the one where the chemistry teacher cuts his wrist on broken glass when he stuffs paper into a bin. If I had to watch it one more time, I'd have gladly volunteered my wrist for the same treatment. Officer safety training was the same dull, repetitive and pointless exercises year in year out.

That was until the training underwent a radical shake-up.

Some wag redesigned the tired old programme. This wag persuaded the bosses that his revamped training was the bees' knees. We had a new warm up and everything. No longer did we stand to face the instructor whirling our arms about in some mad belief that this would prevent injury. No longer did we plod in a circle around the gym, at a pitiful pace to ensure that the front runners didn't catch up with the pie eaters at the rear. We had a new warm up. This new warm-up introduced us to 'the crab'.

'The Crab' was an exercise that entailed pairing up with another officer and getting down on all fours. The pair then had to lock shoulders and push. Well named because with legs splayed out and bodies locked together pushing against each other resulted in a sideways motion - not dissimilar to the movements of a decapod crustacean with a missing claw.

While the new programme relieved the monotony of years of doing the same thing; I wondered who designed 'the crab'. It is not an exercise I had seen practised anywhere else. I'm sure if I watched every single workout video from the dawn of the video machine, I'd bet my handcuffs and baton you would not find a similar such exercise. Where in the world of policing would we ever end up on all fours, locking shoulders with a suspect and pushing? Would our three minute warm up really prepare us for that eventuality? I'm serious - when was I ever going to end up in that position with a member of the public?

What 'the crab' did do was cause merriment. We invariably got up from 'the crab' with a smile on our face as we laughed off our embarrassment. I couldn't help thinking there will be a prankster somewhere (not unlike myself) gleefully giggling away in utter delight that the bosses had fallen for it. Every time he walked into an officer safety training day he would smile to himself knowing they had adopted his prank warm-up exercise. I wonder if there are officers on their officer safety training still pairing up, getting down on all fours and performing 'the crab?'

Attending mandatory courses, such as Officer Safety Training was an unwelcome disruption most of the time. On the odd occasion, however, they fell into the category of 'welcome diversion'.

If you read *'The really FUNNY thing about being a COP'*, you may recall Neil, the tall, ginger-haired young probationer who joined me to preserve a scene-of-crime after Brian S. Nutt had discharged a revolver into his television. Neil and I got instructions to guard his house until morning. Posted on the door, we had to stay there all night to prevent unauthorised entry and any contamination of the scene.

I knew Neil to say hello to, but that was all. I hadn't worked with him before. As we would be there all night, I thought I had better get to know Neil a little better and sparked up a conversation. It helps pass the time quicker.

"What's your name and where do you come from?" I said in my best Cilla Black, *Blind Date* voice.

"Neil."

"What's your favourite film?"

"I don't really watch films."

"What would be in your top ten desert island discs then?"

"I'm not really into music."

"What would you say is the funniest sitcom that has ever been on the telly?"

"I don't really watch television."

"Football team?"

"I'm not really into football."

"What is the most inspiring book you have ever read?"

"I don't really read books."

"Favourite holiday destination?"

"We always just go to her mum's cottage in Wales."

"Who would be your dream date?"

"I'm married."

"Did you see the news tonight?"

"I never watch the news."

"Do you play any sport?"

"I'm not really into sport."

"For goodness' sake Neil. You don't watch films, and you don't listen to music. You don't watch telly, either for the comedy or the news, you don't play sports, you have no thoughts about women, you don't read books, and you go to the same cottage every year to live with your in-laws. What on earth do you do?"

"I told you," he said in all seriousness, "I'm married."

Neil ended up in the traffic department.

"Better to be interested in something than nothing at all," my Dad used to say as he counted the toenails in his toenail collection (come to think of it, perhaps that is a bad example).

Many years later I found myself on the same officer safety course as Neil. I had spent the previous six weeks auditing productions. I used to think standing about guarding a locus was the most soul-destroying job in the police - not so. Working your way through a production store, marrying entries on a production register with the actual production is on a par with it. But what sucks the life out of you is when you approach cops and tell them they have a week to sort a problem you have discovered - before they find themselves in bother - and they doggedly avoid all cajoling in preference for a bollocking. The stupid thing is that once bollocked; they still have to sort out their production.

It was with some delight then when I left the production store and went on my Officer Safety Training course.

I arrived nice and early, keen to get started. I took part in the warm-up - including getting down on all fours, locking shoulders with Neil and scuttling about like a crab. I joined in in the mock exercises and squirted Neil in the crotch with the dummy CS spray (turns out I wasn't above such nonsense). I even watched the First Aid video making no sarcastic comments like; "I wonder what happens next?" or screaming "DON'T PUT YOUR HAND IN THE BIN."

The morning sped by in a flurry of frolicking fun, and before I knew it, the instructor allowed us to escape for lunch.

I walked into the canteen and took my place in the queue. There was the usual boiler suit brigade in first, waiting on their bacon rolls being prepared. The shirt sleeve delegation arrived behind them to get their tea and scones and disappear back up the staircase, all purchases eaten and drunk at their desk.

I shuffled in line behind them until I caught the eye of the canteen lady.

"A roll and sausage with brown sauce please."

"We don't do brown sauce."

"No brown sauce?"

"No brown sauce," she repeated without a single iota of sympathy for having run out of the stuff.

"Have you run out of the stuff?" I smiled, wondering if I should settle for tomato sauce or just double it up with a runny egg.

"No. We don't do brown sauce."

"No brown sauce," I said, surprised, I leant forward and whispered: " Why not? Would that make it too tasty?"

Her face a stony glower.

"I'll have a roll and bacon then please."

"How de ye want it?"

Oh! I have a choice.

"Can I have it crispy please?"

"No. I mean do you want it in a bag or on a plate? Are you taking it away or sitting in?"

"I'll sit in, thank you. What kind of coffee do you do?"

"Nescafe."

"No cappuccino?"

"Nescafe, black or Nescafe white."

"I'll take it white please."

She presented my bacon roll flattened on a tiny plate and handed me a mug of black coffee. I looked at her and was about to bring up the lack of milkiness, but before I could say anything she pointed at a jug sitting on a milk-stained table at the far side of the cash register, "Milk's in the jug!".

I took my coffee and bacon roll and sat down at an empty table. Neil joined me; no-one else sat down beside us, stuck, once again, in a position where I had to make conversation with him.

I think I was a much more considerate person by then. Over the years I had learned to tolerance of others, and as Neil sat down, I wondered if all those years ago I had done him a disservice. Certainly, my predictions had not come true. Neil had worked with other officers for over three weeks, and none of them had found suicide necessary. I wasn't even aware that any of his partners had resigned or even asked for a transfer - so much for my powers of prophecy.

I thought back to my old self, I assumed, back then, that to be interesting one had to take an interest in films, music, television, football, books, holidays, the opposite sex, the news or sport. Neil had expressed no form of curiosity about any of those subjects, and I had immediately and prejudicially assumed him to be devoid of all ability to be an entertaining or engaging conversationalist. There were plenty other topics I hadn't chosen to ask him about.

I hadn't asked if he was into dancing, martial arts, crosswords, Sudoku, yoga, pottery or any number of other hobbies. I hadn't thought it through. I hadn't played the game like a true sportsman. It was time to explore other avenues that might spark a fascinating conversation with him.

"How are you, Neil?"

"Okay."

"How is work?"

"Okay."

"How is family life?"

"Okay."

"What did you think of the officer safety training this morning?"

"It was okay."

At this I paused, cocked my head to the side and looked at him, expectant, waiting to see if I could elicit a little more. Neil looked at me. Uncomfortable. He didn't say a word. After a short while, I gave up.

"Do you like dancing?"

"I don't dance."

"Have you ever done martial arts?"

"No."

"Do you like crosswords?"

"Not really."

"What about number games, do you do Sudoku?"

"Never heard of it."

"Yoga? Pottery?"

"No."

Now I was losing my patience. The tolerant nature I had adopted over the years grated away, and I contemplated a merciful death. I just wasn't sure if it was Neil or me I'd shoot.

Then it struck me. How stupid I was. Neil had joined the Traffic Department. I hadn't considered this with any of my attempts to kick off an absorbing discussion. I had been picking topics at random. Why hadn't I picked a subject bound to excite him? Suddenly it was obvious. Time to engage him in a topic which interested him. I could have a pleasant post lunch tête-à-tête before going back to the officer safety training.

"Neil, you have been in the Traffic Department for a few years now."

"Yes."

I hit him with the question, convinced it would elicit an animated conversation.

"Do you have a favourite car?"

Neil's eyes looked up and left, a sure sign he was thinking, as he searched his brain for an answer.

"No. Not really," was all Neil could come up with.

The exasperation on my face must have shown. My tolerant disposition crumbled. My face contorted into that of an anguished soul. The camaraderie I had sought to while away a pleasant lunch break was well and truly out of my grasp. Destined to sit at the lunch table, with Neil, in agonising tedium. Sitting alone would have been preferable to the stilted dullness of sharing a table with him. Neil must have sensed my anguish; I could see him searching the left side of his brain again, desperate to come up with something that resembled dialogue between two sentient beings.

And then, shock, surprise, disbelief - he did!

There was an extended pregnant and embarrassing pause, but Neil recognised the need to placate my obvious desire to have a scintillating conversation. He did it by asking me the same question.

"Do you have a favourite car?"

"Aye," I replied as I stood up from the table to make my escape, "Jimmy, he is so much funnier than Alan."

THE MICHAEL PARKINSON TELEVISION INTERVIEW

Parky: So you were frustrated by cops, inspectors, chief inspectors and superintendents?

Malky: Only a small minority. Most police officers were a pleasure to work with, and I had the honour of working with some of the best.

Parky: What about civilian staff?

Malky: Likewise, I had the honour of working with some of the best civilian staff too.

Parky: All of them?

Malky: Well, there was the rare exception.

Parky: Would I be correct in saying that there was one in particular, a retired police officer in fact, that caused you some grief?

Malky: Ah! I see what you are getting at, Michael. The person you are referring to retired as a police sergeant and took up a civilian role in the office. He wasn't the most helpful of people. Cops would walk into the front office to get a vehicle check or an enquiry done and see he was on, about turn and walk out again knowing he would be difficult about doing it. He seemed to rub people up the wrong way.

Parky: So, what was the story?

Malky: You know what, I think I'd rather tell you about Betty, our other civilian office clerk.

Chapter 10

WE NEED MORE LIKE BETTY

It may come as a surprise, but it wasn't uncommon for people to make up things and lie to the police. People make things up about many things for all sorts of reasons. Malicious complaints about police officers, fraudulent claims to scam insurers and they even reported crimes that never happened.

Malicious complaints about police officers were often just smoke screens to cover up their wrongdoings. Most were easy to disprove and put the person at risk of being charged.

Insurance companies instruct their customers, first and foremost, to report crimes to the police. They will not accept something as stolen or vandalised if they haven't made the police aware. It is an easy way for the insurance companies to avoid having to do any enquiries themselves.

People who invent crimes do so for various reasons. Mostly it was because of the way the welfare system works. The welfare system is there to assist needy individuals and families. It is right and proper we look after each other and our system does exactly that for the majority of people. Unfortunately, there are some who try to take advantage.

One of the most overused methods to extract additional funds from the Department of Work and Pensions (DWP formally the DSS) is to allege you have been the victim of a robbery. Being robbed, you can qualify for an emergency loan. Of course, you don't just walk into a DWP office, tell them you have been robbed and walk out with a couple of hundred quid in your pocket. The DWP will not accept your claim for an emergency loan if you don't have a crime reference number. To get a crime reference number you have to call into a Police Office and report the crime.

The police are obliged to take a statement, investigate the matter and go to great lengths, time and effort to detect this robbery. Robbery is a crime of violence and treated seriously. Even if there is a suspicion that the person was there to scam the DWP out of money, they still investigate. The first clue that the robbery might not have happened is when the alleged victim walks in and says, "I need a crime reference number." Or, "The dole office sent me."

I mean who gets robbed and goes straight to the dole office before calling the police?

However, even in those situations, the police treat the allegation as a serious crime. They are professional in making enquiry. It is in everybody's interest to catch the perpetrator of such a crime. The police can't just assume that the robbery didn't take place. They have to look into it and take every possible step to detect it, no matter how much they suspect it may be a lot of bunkum. The police don't stop investigating it until they get the person responsible or, in the course of their enquiries, can prove that it didn't happen. Investigating any serious crime, like a robbery, is a time-consuming, labour intensive and a costly business for the police, even if it turns out the crime didn't happen.

There was one exception.

Betty McMaster was born and brought up in the same town she worked. She had various unskilled jobs for years and ended up with the important job as our police office cleaner. Despite the boring nature of the job she worked away, always cheery and with a pleasant word for everyone. Hardworking, contented, friendly, kind and funny she was a delight to see every morning. She always had a smile on her face and a little glint of mischief in her eye. She was quick witted and happy to wind up a cop as she would a senior officer. There were no airs and graces about her. What you saw was what you got whether you were a prince or a pauper Betty would treat you the same. With kind-heartedness, a bit of teasing repartee and after chatting with Betty you walked away feeling that the world was a better place.

Then one day the job of civilian office clerk became available. An astute chief inspector suggested to Betty that she should apply for it.

"Oh I've no experience of that kind of thing."

With a little persuasion, she did apply, had a great interview and got the job. Betty stepped into the role and was an instant success. With her knowledge of the locals, hard work and common sense approach she solved a lot of problems before they even got reported to the police. Her no nonsense approach was refreshing - albeit somewhat unorthodox.

One day I wandered into the front office to ask Betty to make a small enquiry for me. Betty was just getting up to answer a caller at the front counter, and I waited for her. I had a look through the glass and saw that the caller was Mickey Devlin. Mickey was one of our local criminals, a drug user, thief and, by all accounts, a very naughty boy. I was curious. What did he want? Under normal circumstances, Mickey had to be dragged into a police station. I moved around to the front counter door where I could listen but remained out of sight.

"I need a crime reference number," Mickey informed Betty.

"What for?"

"I have been sent by the dole office."

"Oh aye. And what exactly do you need this crime reference number for?"

"I've been robbed."

That grabbed my full attention as the mention of a serious crime always does. It would mean tying up lots of officers to investigate it, identifying the locus and securing it so we could carry out a full scene of crime examination. I immediately had visions of the entire shift getting tied up. The CID would have to get involved; we might have to set up a major incident enquiry room. We were busy enough without having to drop everything and concentrate on this. I pushed my ear up against the gap in the door.

"Away tae fuck," Betty told him.

Interesting response from Betty.

There was a pregnant pause as Mickey considered what to say next.

"I have to report it cause the dole office told me I had to."

"Haud oan! Let me get this right. Someone robbed you, and the only reason you want to report it to the police is that the dole office told you to?"

"Well, I want to get my money back."

"Really Fannybaws? Was it the dole office that robbed you?"

"No, it was a big guy."

"Oh aye, so where was this alleged robbery supposed to have taken place?" Betty couldn't have been more scornful in her tone or have a more disbelieving look on her face.

"Um, Rose Street about an hour ago."

"Away ya glaikit bastard! Rose Street an hour ago? So to get to the dole office, you would have to walk right past this police office. Why didn't you report it here?"

"I needed an emergency loan."

"An emergency loan! How much of a loan did you want?"

"He stole a hundred and fifty quid from me, and I wanted it back."

"A hundred and fifty quid!" Betty's sceptical tone reached new heights, "Away tae fuck! I work for a living, and I have never had one hundred and fifty quid in my pocket. How did you get that when you don't even work?"

"I saved it up."

"Away tae fuck! You've never saved up any mair than you need tae score a tenner bag."

Mickey Devlin's best-laid plan to skin the dole office out of an emergency loan had unravelled, scuppered at the first hurdle. Desperate, he added more information to make his story sound a little more believable.

"They took my jacket as well."

"Away tae fuck! It wouldnae be a working jacket would it, cos ye huvnae done a day's work in yer life ya wee shite."

I had to push my jaw back up. Mickey Devlin was trying to report a serious crime (and we always take these things seriously). We scrutinise every possible shred of evidence before we make any conclusions. Here was Betty circumventing all that hard work with an insightful piece of cynicism and it seemed to be working.

Unconvincingly Mickey tried once more, "Um, it's true, they hit me with a stick, robbed me and shot off on their scooters."

"What kind of stick?"

"A big stick."

"Where about?"

"In Rose Street."

"Naw, I mean where on your body did they hit you?"

"On my head."

"Aye, ye might huv got battered wi the ugly stick when you were a bairn, but you huvnae got a mark on you the noo."

"I'll probably get a bruise later."

"Aye, when I gie ye a slap."

"I have. I have been robbed." Bolshy.

"How many people supposedly robbed you?"

"About three or four."

"Away tae fuck! First, it was just one guy; now it's three or four, can you no count?"

"It was four of them I think."

"Tell me again where did they hit you?"

"On my head, I got knocked to the ground."

"Away tae fuck! How are they going to get yer jacket off when you are on the ground and who the hell robs someone and runs off on a scooter, wis it the Ant Hill Mob?"

"Um, can I not get a crime reference number then."

"Away tae fuck before I lock you up for the weekend."

Mickey Devlin got the message, his face flushed with embarrassment and he about turned and walked out the office. One expletive filled interrogation from Betty had circumvented a whole lot of hard work, time and investigation.

I dodged back into the office and pretended to be reading a poster on the wall. Betty came back and asked if she could help me.

"Could you oblige and do a PNC check for me please?"

"No problem at all."

"Who was that at the counter?" I inquired.

"Jist a guy looking fur directions."

Betty didn't even look up from her computer. She printed off the details I wanted and handed the sheet to me.

"Good job Betty!"

"Anytime," she smiled.

I think we could do with more Betty's in our front office.

THE MICHAEL PARKINSON TELEVISION INTERVIEW

Parky: Did Mickey Devlin come back in to complain?

Malky: Nope. I think he realised that he would just get himself into trouble for making a false allegation of crime.

Parky: Did you have a lot of complaints about the police to deal with?

Malky: Yes, I had my fair share.

Parky: Were these difficult enquiries for you?

Malky: There were some that took a lot of work, others I was able to resolve pretty quickly.

Parky: Did they always involve a lot of paperwork?

Malky: Oh yes. Paperwork was a nightmare. That was why I always liked to resolve problems before they became complaints.

Chapter 11

JAKEY'S COMPLAINT ABOUT THE POLIS

I popped into the custody suite one night. As an Inspector it was my job to check on the welfare of the prisoners. My usual routine was to read through their custody records, checking what they were in for, etc., before visiting them in their cells to make sure:

1. They were alive.
2. They hadn't escaped and
3. Both No. 1 and 2 weren't likely to happen.

On looking down the list on the computer, I came across a prisoner locked up for drunk driving. He'd crashed his car into a car being driven by an off duty cop and drove off without stopping. A hit and run. When caught he failed the Breathalyser (a device that measures how much alcohol is on someone's breath). The custody sergeant seemed delighted to inform me the prisoner had in fact blown a count on the approved Breathalyser machine of 212 microgrammes of alcohol per 100 millilitres of breath.

Another occasion for my jaw to drop. The legal limit for driving was 35 microgrammes of alcohol per 100 millilitres of breath (reduced to 22ug in 2014 in Scotland). This guy had blown over six times the legal limit.

Over the years I had come across a lot of drunk drivers. When you get to over 100 microgrammes of alcohol per 100 millilitres of breath, they struggle to blow into the Breathalyser device because they are so drunk. In fact, the highest count I had ever seen was 145 microgrammes of alcohol per 100 millilitres of breath. We had to help that guy stand up.

The highest count I had ever heard of, until that day, was 158 microgrammes of alcohol per 100 millilitres of breath. The story is that the guy was so drunk they couldn't get him to court the next day because he was comatose. They had to keep him another day for him to sober up.

I had to see the guy that had blown 212. What kind of state would he be in? I had a real concern for his well-being. With so much alcohol in his system, he might be in danger of breaching reason No. 1 for my visit. Despite my worries, I also had a large dose of morbid curiosity.

I left the computer, marched down to his cell and opened his cell hatch. There he was sitting on the edge of his bed reading a newspaper. He looked up and nodded at me and nonchalant, "Hi," he said.

I nodded back, more than a little confused. I looked around his cell in case our drunk driver was doubled up and lying in a corner somewhere but no. The guy reading the newspaper was the only guy in the cell.

I went back to the computer and checked that I had been looking in the right cell. The computer confirmed I had the correct cell. I went back down and spoke to the drunk driver.

I got him to confirm his name. He had the same name. He admitted that he had been drinking and had blown 212 microgrammes of alcohol per 100 millilitres of breath. He didn't know any better but was a little worried as the cops that dealt with him had told him it was the highest reading they had seen.

He seemed lucid, and although I detected a slight slur in his voice that didn't equate to a count of 212. Either he had the constitution of an ox or something wasn't right. My left eyebrow raised itself involuntarily, and I always listen to my raised left eyebrow. I decided to investigate further.

I called the arresting officers down to the custody suite and went through the case. The off duty cop phoned on his mobile, explained what had happened and followed the guy for half a mile before these two cops caught up with him. They stopped him and required him to provide a roadside breath test, which he failed. They arrested him and brought back to the station where he underwent the statutory second test on the approved Breathalyser device. He blew 212 microgrammes of alcohol per 100 millilitres of breath. The printout from the Breathalyser device attested to the validity of what they told me.

"Was there anything strange or unusual about the test?" I asked.

"No," was the reply. The cops reassured me they had carried out the test to the book.

"You see, I expected to see your prisoner comatose on the floor with a count of 212, but that isn't the case. He is sitting up reading a newspaper and is perfectly coherent. Are you sure there wasn't anything you did that was out of the ordinary?"

"Well," one cop said hesitant, "he had a little trouble blowing into the Breathalyser at first due to his asthma."

"Asthma, mm hm. Did you let him use his inhaler?" I asked.

"Yes."

I went to the prisoner's property and picked up the inhaler. A quick look at the contents resolved my curiosity. I turned to the cops, "Do either of you have any idea what 'ethanol' is?"

I could picture the court case:-

"So you say he blew a count of 212?"

"Yes."

"Did you let him use his inhaler?"

"Yes."

"Do you know it contains ethanol?"

"Duh!"

"CASE DISMISSED."

In fairness to the drunk driver, I arranged for the officers to complete the Breathalyser test again. This time, without the use of his alcohol infused inhaler, he blew just over the limit. He was charged and appeared in court the next day but at least this time the case had a chance of succeeding. It was all part of the job of the inspector. I had to ensure that the cops did their job and in cases like that, it kept them out of trouble.

It was also part of my job to investigate complaints about the police. Some were serious, most were minor, and a lot of them were frivolous or even malicious. Police officers are subjected to a lot of hostility. The people they deal with sometimes vent their ill feeling by making complaints.

We took complaints about the police seriously. Every investigation results in a report being written and submitted through the chain of command before ending up on the desk of the Professional Standards Department. Each report scrutinised by ever more distrustful senior ranks as it made its way up the tree. And we did get it wrong sometimes. In those situations people deserve an explanation and apology. The police strive to be as professional as they can.

It was sometimes difficult to show sympathy to some of those who complained though.

Now and then we come across people who defy the theory of evolution. How on earth did their ancestors survive long enough to pass on their genes?

One of those defying just evolution was 'Jakey' who had somehow made it all the way to forty-five years of age, despite his seriously flawed gene pool.

Jakey was a male who had sponged his way through his life, never once lifting a hand to contribute to society in any way, shape or form. A man who had failed at school failed to work and failed at life. He had to rely on others to support him; Jakey was effectively a ward of the state. The state provided him with a house and furnishings. The welfare state supplied him with his television, his television licence, his gas and electricity. His everyday living costs were no burden to him, it all came from the taxpayer.

The only sign that old Jakey could do anything for himself was his ability to dupe doctors into registering him disabled, thus providing him with additional benefits. This extra money funded his drinking. You could say drinking was a hobby of his, maybe even a passion. An uncontrollable urge that made him stay up all night so he can pursue it. A passion that consumed him from the moment he woke until the moment he lay down in a comatose heap on the floor. Jakey's enthusiasm for the drink knew no bounds. Buckfast, White Lightning Cider, Tenants Super Lager - you name it Jakey would drink it. I even saw him drink a Bulgarian Merlot. Geez!

So one day I ended up sitting in his dirty little house on a dirty duvet on a dirty settee noting his complaint about the police..

Jakey had phoned in asking for a police inspector so he could make a complaint about the police. He complained that while he had been in the hospital (because he'd been shot in the face by an air-pistol), police had searched his house and left it as if a 'bomb' had gone off.

He also complained that police had taken a curtain from his house and he wanted this back. Jakey further stated that the officers in attendance had damaged his stereo, emptied his washing machine on to the floor and left his clothes strewn around the place. According to 'Jakey', it had taken him an age to tidy up.

My first question was, "You've tidied up?"

I asked this of him with a raised eyebrow as I scanned the scene. If you can imagine letting thirty teenagers loose in a house with thirty cases of beer, thirty bottles of Buckfast, thirty bottles of extra strong cider and a stereo for an evening, thirty days later it would look like that.

"Aye," Jakey replied without the slightest trace of irony or even embarrassment, "it took me ages."

It was 10.30 a.m. and his pal, Wee Davey, who was there to support him in his time of need, kept nipping out the room to fill up his cracked and tea stained mug with some high octane cider fuel.

I listened to Jakey's side of the story.

About four years previous Jakey was in a relationship. As is the way with Jakey's relationships, his partner wasn't the best of catches. She would put any normal fisherman off fishing for good. I suspected that at birth the midwife had slapped her face, several times, with a hard wooden bat. Wait - that's not fair - it might have been a metal bat. A woman who had fallen out of the ugly tree and smacked every branch on the way down. Anyway, not even a parent could have shown her any love. The absence of nurturing as a child resulted in her lacking anything loosely described as a personality. Unable to call upon the use of any charm whatsoever she was best described as a 'vile, foul mouthed witch' - but only if she was sober. She was worse with a drink in her. Her one endeavour at prettying herself up was when she considered tooth whitening. So she stole a small tub of Tippex and painted her solitary incisor with it.

Stand back guys - I saw her first!

When she had a few drinks (and there wasn't a day went by when her income support didn't stretch to the minimum 8.5% proof truth drug), she tended towards the downright nauseating. Hence, the relationship between Jakey and his girlfriend was a little tense.

Jakey hit the bottle, and his girlfriend hit him. She hit the bottle, and he hid in fear of what would happen. The y called the police on an almost on a daily basis. It got to the stage that advice was no longer an option and every time one or both were arrested.

One day, during this relationship they, were sitting in their house drinking. Mrs Jakey on the couch, a glass in one hand and a pie in the other. They argued. She became abusive, and he reacted by shouting back at her.

Whether through drink or simply because he is an idiot, Jakey gave his girlfriend a look. Not just any look, this was a look of complete and utter distaste.

"Right. You want to see something?" He asked her.

"What ur ye gonnae dae, ya prick!"

"Right. I'll show you something!" Almost spitting the words at her.

He bent down and picked up his air pistol from the table beside his chair and placed it against his temple.

"I'll show you something!" he repeated and pulled the trigger shooting himself in the head.

The air pistol was a 0.177 pellet gun, loaded with a soft snub metal pellet. The pellet exited the barrel with a force of 30lbs per square inch and a speed of 255 miles per hour. There was no distance between the end of the barrel and the side of Jakey's temple, so it entered the soft flesh tissue of his temple, punching its way through the skin. It buried its way through some minor blood vessels and internal flesh before lodging itself firmly in the bone of his skull.

He bled.

Mrs Jakey called the police. The police contacted an ambulance, and they took Jakey to the hospital where he underwent an operation to remove the pellet. The officers kept the air weapon as a production. The investigation confirmed, to the satisfaction of all concerned, that the wound was self-inflicted.

Three years later (two weeks before I sat on his dirty little couch to get his complaint) Jakey received a letter from the Police Custodier. The Letter informed him they had an item belonging to him (the air pistol) and asked that he come and collect it.

The Police Custodier had carried out a large audit and found this weapon sitting at the back of their storage cupboard. The sensible thing to do might have been to destroy it, however, with there being a lack of disposal instructions, technically the owner may have it back. They lettered Jakey, and a few days later he popped by to collect it.

The same night Jakey and his friend were at his house drinking some strong cider. In the middle of god knows what kind of carry on the air-pistol appeared. Jakey once again found himself shot in the face. This time the pellet entered his cheek and lodged in the soft tissue of his mouth. There was a lot of blood.

Jakey's friend found a pair of tweezers and 'sterilised' them by swirling them about in his cracked and stained mug containing 8.5% proof cider. For twenty minutes he foraged around in Jakey's cheek trying to extricate the pellet. He only succeeded in pushing it deeper into his fleshy tissue and in the process he covered the place in blood. Inevitably, they had to call an ambulance.

Jakey and his pal decided not to relay the true story, the message they passed to the ambulance staff was that Jakey had been shot in the face with an air weapon. Because of the potential danger to themselves, ambulance personnel do not attend to such calls on their own; they asked the police to attend with them.

Because the information received was that a 'firearm' had been used, and that Jakey had been shot in the face by an unknown person, we sent an Armed Response Vehicle to the locus, along with every available cop. The sergeant and inspector dropped what they were doing and headed down too.

Jakey lied to the officers. He stated that he had been walking in the street outside his house when a youth stepped out in front of him and shot him in the face with an air pistol.

Being shot in the face is a serious allegation to make. The Police will do their utmost to catch this youth. In the process, they will tie up officers to guard the locus, carry out street searches involving the Traffic Department and Dog Section. The CID took on the enquiry, and everybody and even everybody's auntie ended up busying themselves with trying to detect this crime.

In the middle of it all, a smart young cop thought to himself that something didn't quite ring true. He passed on his doubts to his supervisor who in turn discussed it with his inspector. The inspector shared the concerns with the investigating detective officer.

Three hours later the hospital opened Jakey's cheek from the inside of his mouth and removed the pellet before sewing him back up again. It was three days before they released him from the hospital.

On the day he left the hospital, the CID took the opportunity to invite Jakey back to their office. Once there, they soon picked holes in his story, and Jakey admitted to making everything up. He'd simply shot himself again - this time in the face instead of his head. Jakey found himself charged with wasting police time.

Ten days later I sat in his dirty little house and continued to question him, "What exactly do you want to complain about?"

"The mess they made, they wrecked the place. I had to tidy it up. They broke my stereo too. I want compensation for that."

"What mess did they make?"

"They hauled the clothes out of my washing machine and just left them on the floor."

"Was this clean or dirty washing?"

"Dirty," Jakey admitted without blinking an eye.

"So you had to put it all back into the washing machine?" My patience was wearing as thin as custard - he genuinely saw this as a hardship.

"Aye. That's no right!" Jakey said, indignant, "and they took my curtain!"

"They took your curtain as a production because it had blood on it. You reported a serious crime, and the CID were only doing their job," I explained looking for some come and go.

"Aye. But that wisnae blood fae then that was another time."

"When?"

"About three years ago. When I shot myself in the heid."

"Why did you do that?"

"I wanted to show my wife something," he said as if it was the most logical thing in the world to do.

I changed the subject.

"You said your stereo was damaged?"

"That's it there." He pointed to a lidless, silver and black record player on the floor in the corner of the room. The top had been used as a beer mat on many occasions, and three buttons were missing off the front."

"When did you get that?"

"Ah canny mind. A while ago."

"Where did you get it?"

"Ah canny mind."

"What's wrong with it?"

"It's no working!"

"Why?"

"I think they kicked it."

I examined the record player. There was no needle on the stylus.

"There is no needle on the stylus!" I told him exasperated.

"No?" was all he could muster.

Slowly I looked around the room,

"Do you actually have any records at all?"

"Eh no."

"Did you get this from the dump?"

He hung his head and didn't answer confirming my suspicions.

"So are you looking for compensation?" I asked

"Aye."

"How much do you want?"

"I dunno."

"You must have an idea?"

"I dunno."

"Would a hundred thousand pounds do?"

At this Jakey realised he would not get a single penny from us. He looked at me, disgruntled, and tried a different tack.

"Well it is your fault that this has happened," he said looking to apportion all blame on me.

"Wait a minute," I replied, "You get yourself drunk, shoot yourself in the face, try to get your mate to remove the pellet but he can't. So you call the ambulance and tell them someone in the street shot you. We tie up twenty officers, send in a team of forensic examiners and involve the CID for days investigating this, and it turns out it is all lies. In fact, you shot yourself, again. During of our investigation, before you admitted to making it up, we go about our business as professional as ever. Carry out a thorough search of the area and a scene of crime examination of your house. We take the necessary productions, photograph your injuries and the locus. All of this at no little cost and then find out you have lied to us. How is it my fault?"

"Well if you hadnae given me the gun back in the first instance I couldnae huv have shot myself again!"

"Mr Jakey. You can go and boil yer heed."

…and that, Dear Superintendent, is what you should put in your final letter to close the complaint.

THE MICHAEL PARKINSON TELEVISION INTERVIEW

Parky: So was dealing with complaints the most frustrating part of being an inspector?

Malky: Complaints about the police could be difficult because the people we dealt with were difficult. I wouldn't say they were the most frustrating. Ultimately, if they were just being thorny for the sake of making things hard, then I could write a report with my findings and draft up a letter telling them to go and boil their heed - in a polite way.

Parky: So what did you find the most frustrating part of being an inspector?

Chapter 12

MEETINGS

"The 'two pizza rule' is a secret to productive meetings that helped Amazon CEO Jeff Bezos become one of the world's richest men." - Business Insider.

I read that from an article sent in a daily email I had solicited months ago and had done nothing with other than delete: According to the article, Jeff Bezos meets with Amazon investors for just six hours... a year. And he avoids early morning meetings at all costs. Personally, I wondered how he put up with the investors for six hours, but the next bit of his strategy had me confused. The 'two pizza rule', is simple. The theory is that the more people you pack into a meeting, the less productive the meeting will be. Bezos' solution? Never hold a meeting where two pizzas couldn't feed the entire group.

Perhaps you are now doing what I did at first, nodding your head in agreement? It makes sense, doesn't it? Maybe that is just one of the little bits of wisdom we all need to do our jobs better. Using that one little gem could see us propel ourselves from mediocre to meritorious.

Ahem! Can I stop you there? The 'two pizza rule' is absolute bonkers. What does it even mean? Are they big pizzas or small pizzas? Can you cut them into twelve slices (12 slices x 2 = 24 people)? How dainty!

Let's be honest about it; I could eat two pizzas on my own - in fact I have - that would make meetings quicker. Any meeting would only last as long as it took for me to eat the two pizzas. I could have them with a beer and watch repeats of *Frazier* or *Friends*.

Maybe the 'two pizza rule' means just two people like a romantic dinner and a nice glass of wine. I mean cmon 'two pizza rule', does that mean two, four, six or twenty-four people? Just tell us and stop dicking around with pizza metaphors.

It doesn't even consider the flavour of the pizza. If covered in pineapple or anchovies, what I'd do is stuff them back in the box and then get on with some real work.

The basic message, without all the pizza metaphors, is if you want to have a productive meeting keep the attendees down to those that need to be there. Anyone who doesn't need to be there is wasting their time and will ultimately waste everyone else's time. The smaller the meeting, the more productive it will be.

So what did the police do? We went and got ourselves linked up to TV conference calling. Instead of a chief inspector running a meeting for their area with their staff, a superintendent ran the meeting for the entire force. It meant three chief inspectors piping their meetings electronically to everyone else, with the superintendent as chair. I groaned when I heard the news. A morning meeting that took half an hour to forty-five minutes would now take three times as long. Fortunately, at the time the new TV conference calling came into being I was working with a particularly astute chief inspector.

Chief Inspector Rab McRabbitson was exceptionally competent. Courteous, conscientious and intelligent. A boss who placed trust in his staff and showed a genuine interest in them. He never felt the need to micro-manage, and as a result, he got the best out of people. I learned a great deal and held the deepest respect for him. On the day the TV conferencing started, Chief Inspector McRabbitson was chairing our side. The usual suspects were sitting in attendance at our meeting, and at the end of our table, our television screen showed the other two meetings in our force. The C division chief inspector sat with a massive entourage, and on the split screen, the superintendent sat with the F division chief inspector and an even larger group. Two pizzas wouldn't feed this lot; you would need Jamie Oliver and a couple of hog roasts to keep this lot happy.

"Who would like to start?" asked the superintendent.

Before the words were out of his mouth, Chief Inspector McRabbitson volunteered.

"We will go first, if that suits you, sir."

Chief Inspector McRabbitson expertly ran through our area's business. The superintendent nodded his way through everything he said. At the conclusion, before anyone had the chance to move on to another area he said, "Superintendent if there are no more questions regarding our area I'll just sign off."

It was a brilliant gamble. The superintendent had no more questions; he had no choice but to agree. It meant that we didn't have to sit through the business from two other areas. I switched off the conference feed, and the TV screen went blank. We then set about congratulating Chief Inspector McRabbitson on his ploy to get in first, and that was the way it remained until Chief Inspector McRabbitson retired.

When Chief Inspector McRabbitson went on holiday, it became my responsibility to run the morning meeting. I tried starting our meeting half an hour early, sped through our business and dismissed everyone so they could get back to work. When the TV conference started, I looked at my split screen and saw the superintendent sitting with the F division chief inspector and all his entourage, the C division chief inspector and all his entourage, they all looked at their screens and saw little old me, all on my own.

"Where is everyone, Inspector McEwan?" the superintendent asked.

"Sir, we have concluded our business, I have tasked them all up, and I have dismissed them to get on with those jobs. I can answer any questions you have."

"Right, okay, um, let's get on with it then."

I suspect the superintendent wasn't happy about it, but I stuck to my guns. It made sense. Why have ten officers sit for an hour listening to things they didn't need to listen to?

Progress isn't about being able to crowd forty or fifty people into a meeting via TV conferencing. Progress is about freeing up those forty or fifty people to get on with some work. Meetings drag the life and soul out of people. The effects of sitting for an hour or two listening to people who like the sound of their voice, criticising others for what they did or didn't do can empty the spirit. You watch the next time you leave a large meeting; everyone scurries off as fast as they can, not to get on with the jobs tasked to them but to get caffeine into their system. It is a good forty-five minutes before people can function properly again.

Latterly, the daily morning meeting started at nine o'clock on the dot. The official title was 'tasking and coordinating' meeting. To prepare for it, I had to get in early and read up all the logs, the crime reports and the incidents of note. I needed to know all that had happened since I had last been on duty. Everyone attending the meeting did the same. Nobody liked to get caught out. Before the meeting, everyone printed off all the information to take in with them. Sometimes up to a dozen people would attend the meeting, each and every one with their own copies of everything they had read on the computer. There wouldn't be much left of a tree with all that duplicated information churning out of the printer.

I did something about it. I barred everyone from printing a copy; from now on we'd work from my documents alone. Nobody liked that. It was as if their brains had been severed at the base. Their bodies couldn't operate without screeds of paperwork to touch, see and smell. I only saved one or two trees before I had to avert a mutiny by allowing them to print all the stuff off again.

I realised I was just as bad. One morning I switched on my computer, found the logs, crime reports and other information I was looking for and set it all to print. The printer was in my secretaries office, so I had to get up off my chair cross the foyer to her room, passing the shredder which some wag had posted the words 'SUGGESTION BOX' in bold letters on the front. The printer was at the back of her office. The screeds of paper still churned out, so I had to wait a minute for it to finish.

All of a sudden my secretary, Rosie, burst out laughing. I checked my trousers, but the zipper was firmly in the up position.

"What are you laughing at?" I enquired.

She went bright red with embarrassment and tried to brush it off as nothing. I pressed her, and she eventually admitted to laughing at a statement she was typing and acknowledged she really shouldn't be laughing at it as it was tragic. I read the passage:-

"...I knew there was something not quite right with my wife because when we had sex she always kind of held back or something. I don't know what it was. I just couldn't put my finger on it."

Maybe that was the problem.

I grabbed my printouts and headed into the meeting room. Chief Inspector Chumley sat at the head of the table. A man whose motto was 'If you can't beat them, your stick isn't long enough'. He seemed to find it easier to belittle than praise.

Sitting at the table were the duty sergeant, the community sergeant, a co-inspector, the analyst, the detective inspector, the detective sergeant, the intelligence officer and the community safety sergeant. It was a wonder that there was anyone left to patrol the street.

I took my seat, Chief Inspector Chumley started on the days business. First the crime return. He cogitated over every single crime that had occurred in the last twenty-four hours. Why didn't they do this? Why didn't they do that? What on earth were they thinking? Everything scrutinised in microscopic detail. Every decision questioned. Nothing left untouched by the scorn around the table.

In hindsight, everything anyone did in the past twenty-four hours could and would come under criticism. It was easy, in the cold light of day they could find fault with anything. It didn't matter that the cops were juggling a dozen different things when it happened. It didn't matter they were exhausted. It didn't matter that the people they were dealing with didn't 'play the game'. It didn't matter if they were short staffed or even if they had done a good job. It was just all too easy, in hindsight, to find fault.

Chief Inspector Chumley began the meeting. His first concern was our missing person. The previous day we had got word of a vulnerable missing person. A forty-year-old painter and decorator had walked into Accident and Emergency and reported he had taken an overdose of Viagra and Amphetamine.

Viagra comes in a little blue pill (I'm told) that keeps you up all night. Instead of taking a single pill, our painter and decorator had deemed it necessary to take the full packet of twelve. Amphetamine (also known as 'speed') effects users by making them feel wide awake, excited and chatty. Clubbers take 'speed' because they think it gives them the energy to dance away for hours. A single pill is sufficient for most who partake of them. Our painter and decorator had taken a potentially lethal dose of six.

After being booked in, but before seeing a doctor, our painter and decorator left the hospital. Spotted on CCTV entering his car and driving off, hospital staff were concerned enough to report it, as he could be a danger to himself or other road users. There were a few sniggers around the table, but Chief Inspector Chumley remained as professional as ever. With concern in his voice, he asked if we had found him.

The duty sergeant piped up, "Yes, but they couldn't get him out the car until the swelling went down!"

Ignoring the flippant comment Chief Inspector Chumley continued to show his concern, "Will he be all right? Will there be after effects for him? Why did he do it?"

The duty sergeant smiled and said, "He was fine, it was just a rush of blood to the head."

There were several other comments and much hilarity. The Chief Inspector tried, and spectacularly failed, to bring it to a professional conclusion when, in all innocence, he told everyone he was just worried that this man might 'come again'.

The next item on the agenda was a concern for an elderly male. At 2320hrs last night, Mrs Saunders called in concerned about the welfare of her husband (Mr Saunders, ninety-four years of age). He had left the house two hours earlier and hadn't returned. The last time this happened, we found him drunk in a park and he had to be admitted to hospital. Checks at all hospitals proved negative.

About 0300hrs we traced Mr Saunders at his home address. He'd just returned from the 'dancing'. Mr Saunders was annoyed with his wife for being forgetful as he had informed her, before going out, that he was going to the dancing.

There was a bit of discussion about what actual disco had let him in and question marks over his actual ability to dance. I felt that Mr Saunders was to be admired, and I secretly hoped that if I get to that age, I too would feel the need to go dancing.

Chief Inspector Chumley continued with the rest of the meeting, pausing only to criticise the actions of others. Rarely did he allow room for humour and any attempts at humour spurred him to rein in the meeting. He followed the agenda to the letter. He progressed the business, meting out his instructions for each task and set our priorities for the day. To conclude, he clearly wanted to re-establish his authority.

"Now I know you are meant to praise in public and reprimand in private and all that but... " he eyed the Community Sergeant, "when am I going to get that report on the I.T. system?"

"All the ingredients are there, sir. I just need to get the right mix and put it all together - you will have your cake in a couple of weeks."

"Well, see if you can cook it in the microwave rather than the slow cooker, eh!"

He went on to chastise one of the other sergeants for a problem that was an I.T. fault and nothing to do with him. Chumley worked his way around the table taking a swipe at everyone. He was not in a good mood. Nothing pleased him. I looked at my colleagues and could feel the tension. Which one of us would he berate next? Could I get through this meeting without being the target of Chief Inspector Chumley's wrath?

Then he hit the Jackpot!

He turned to the Intelligence Development Officer (IDO), a cynical ex-detective, and listed tasks he wanted him to do that day. Tommy, the IDO, picked up two pens put both in his right hand and made notes with both pens on his notepad at the same time. The notes he made thus been written in duplicate as the two pens scribed side by side over his notepad. Chumley paused as he saw what he was doing. With a stern look, he eyed him up and down, "I don't know why you are noting it down twice," he rebuked, "You don't do it the first time."

Comedy gold!

Before the meeting finished, Chief Inspector Chumley advised us we were to have the privilege of a visit from the Chief Constable that afternoon.

"Can you make sure that everyone is out and about on patrol," he instructed.

"I have a thought..."

"A thought!" said Chumley, "You've been thinking? We can't have that, what have I told you all about thinking for yourselves?"

I ignored him.

"What if they have paperwork to do?" A sensible question I thought.

"It doesn't matter, everyone out walking the streets, full uniform and make sure they have their hats on."

"Is that because the Chief Constable likes empty offices or because he prefers his staff to dick around wasting their time when they have important reports to get submitted?"

He ignored me. The meeting finished and everyone, including myself, got up to leave.

"Where are you going, McEwan?" Chumley asked.

"Back to work, sir."

"Not yet," he said with a wry smile, "I need you to attend the next meeting for me."

I felt the hairs on the back of my neck rise, and gut instinct kicked the walls in the pit of my belly.

Get out - run! Go now.

"What meeting, sir?"

Chumley licked his lips as his sadistic nature savoured my reaction to his next bombshell.

"It's a partners meeting for the 'No Knives Better Lives' campaign." He said as his wry grin changed to a full blown smile before he made a guttural sound I interpreted as an evil guffaw.

I slumped back down into my chair, despondent.

The 'No Knives Better Lives' campaign was an initiative being rolled out to the most violent areas of Scotland. Now it was coming here. There had been an initial advance party to see if our area deserved their attention. I sat in on the first meeting expecting to pass a pleasant twenty minutes before everyone accepted we didn't have a knife problem. The meeting lasted for four hours, and I had contributed every fifteen minutes by saying, "We don't have a knife problem here."

After three hours and fifty-five minutes talking it through they all agreed we didn't have a knife problem in the area.

"Why don't we try it, anyway?" someone said.

And that was what they did. They were going to experiment with it in our area. What nonsense. We didn't have a knife problem, but they were going waste time and money on an initiative, anyway.

The partners included a local councillor who liked the sound of his own voice. A head social worker who liked the sound of her own voice. A deputy head social worker who liked the sound of his own voice. A community worker who liked the sound of her own voice. A member of the neighbourhood watch who liked the sound of his own voice. A community sergeant who liked the sound of his own voice. The head of the neighbourhood planning forum who liked the sound of his own voice. I think I might have missed a couple, but you get the picture.

So there I was stuck again. Instructed to sit through another excruciatingly mundane and endless meeting. If there is one thing that impedes work - it's a meeting.

"Who is chairing the meeting?" I asked in the desperate hope it wasn't Chief Inspector Maurice Minor. Chief Inspector Maurice Minor was the single most practised person I knew in the art of 'Management speak'. However simple the point he was making, it came out of his mouth in the most convoluted, overly elaborate and ridiculous phrase you could imagine.

"Chief Inspector Maurice Minor,"
I formed my fingers into the shape of a gun, stuck my hand to the roof of my mouth and pulled the trigger. Chumley rubbed his hands together with glee.

The meeting was due to start in ten minutes. I headed off to find a kettle to make the strongest coffee, strong enough to stand a spoon upright. I would need it.

Perhaps it was the coffee, but by the time I had made my way back to the meeting room, I'd had an idea. Chief Inspector Minor was already there, sitting at the head of the table. I pulled up a chair to the left of him and sat down. I got out my large A4 pad of paper and pointedly scribed a large heading in the centre of my page:-

'W. SPEAK'

Then I drew two columns. At the top of the first column, I wrote,

'CHIEF INSPECTOR MINOR'

and at the top of the second column, I wrote:-

'EVERYONE ELSE'

Chief Inspector Maurice Minor looked up from his paperwork, and his eyes landed on my handiwork.

"What's that mean?" he asked.

"Oh, nothing!"

The rest of the attendees dribbled in and took a seat. Chief Inspector Minor got the meeting under way.

"Okay, thank you for coming. It is good to see we have the right people on the bus, everyone is sitting in the front seats, and we are ready to push the accelerator."

Animatedly I picked up my pen and put a large tick in the left column under the heading 'CHIEF INSPECTOR MINOR'.

He continued, "As you are all aware there is a piece of work ongoing at the moment around the 'No Knives Better Lives' campaign but we don't want to have paralysis by analysis. There is no I in TEAM, so I'd like you all to run your ideas up the flagpole and kick off the game. There is light at the end of the tunnel in the life-cycle of our partnership."

I returned to his column and gave it another five ticks. Chief Inspector Minor saw the ticks mounting up in his column. He had a flustered breather before carrying on.

"Perhaps I will pause there and let everyone around the table give their input; I'm always open to feedback."

I notched another two ticks in his column.

There was a cacophony of voices from the partners as every one of the 'like the sound of their own voice' brigade tried to get in first. The result was just a rabble that continued until Chief Inspector Minor brought them to order with the suggestion they give everyone a chance by going round the table in a clockwise direction.

The local councillor was first. For the next fifteen minutes, he waffled on about nothing. The gist of his long winded dialogue was that he had given the campaign 'priority thought' which was to say he had not done diddly squat since the last meeting. Maybe he had thought about it, but even that was debatable. The local councillor achieved the first tick in the 'EVERYONE ELSE' column.

Chief Inspector Minor listened intently and summarised his contribution with, "That's great. Clearly there is a bit of work still going on, and that is a positive step in the right direction for everyone."

I gave him another two ticks in his column.

Next up was the head social worker. She went on at great length as to the benefits of the 'No Knives Better Lives' campaign and gushed over how the campaign will have a positive effect on her clientele.

She earned two ticks in the 'EVERYONE ELSE' column.

Chief Inspector Minor was as impressed with her as the councillor, quick to praise her efforts when she finished.

"That's wonderful. We get the picture that this was just meant to be. It is a case of working smarter not harder."

The CHIEF INSPECTOR MINOR column received a further two ticks, and that was enough to put him right off his next thought.

"I can't think when you do that!" he said to me, and then to everyone else he explained, "He is noting down every time I say something wankery. Oh my god! I can't think."

I struggled to hold myself together. I had to purse my lips and pinch my leg under the table to prevent myself from bursting into laughter.

This just might be a worthwhile meeting after all.

It didn't stop him, though, or any of the others. The meeting continued for another two hours. The upshot of the whole thing; they decided to daub the towns pavements with chalked stencils that said, 'No Knives Better Lives'.

I wonder how much of a difference it made? What self-respecting knife wielding youth would come across a stencil on the pavement and think, 'shit, I better get rid of this blade in my pocket?'

The meeting wasn't an entire waste of my time. At the end, I had notes regarding the meanings of some of the management speak used. This is what I now understood the phrases to mean:-

"In terms of..." means, "I don't know what to say, so I will just repeat what someone else has said so it looks as if I know what I am talking about."

"We need to drill down the figures," actually means, "We need to pretend that we will look at the figures and draw some conclusions but I will do nothing until I get promoted or transferred and then it will all get forgotten about."

"The crux of the matter is," means, "I don't know what to say but what I say next will not be the crux of the matter."

"Obviously," means, "This isn't obvious unless you listened to my w.speak at some other obscure meeting."

"We need to link in with our partners," means, "I need to speak to someone at the Social Work Department, but I won't because I am waiting to get promoted or transferred then I won't need to speak to anyone."

"There is a piece of work on going at present," means, "We agreed I would do some work after the last meeting, but I did nothing and will continue to avoid doing the work I agreed to do until I get promoted or transferred."

"In terms of drilling down on the figures, the crux of the matter is that obviously we need to link in with our partners to drill down the figures in terms of the piece of work that is ongoing at the present….." means, "I definitely think I should be promoted."

As the attendees spilled from the meeting room and headed off to do nothing more than forget about what they were supposed to do for the next meeting, I sighed with relief; now I could get back to work. My relief was short lived as I headed for the door Chief Inspector Chumley pushed his way back in.

"Ah, McEwan, sit back down again!"

"But, but!"

"No buts! Sit down. I need you here for the strategic planning meeting for the town fair."

Dejected, I sat down, opened my notepad and turned to a fresh page. My fate sealed. I would have to sit through another long winded meeting, but this time I wouldn't just be ticking columns, he would task me with organising anything that needed organising. The clue was the word 'strategic' a word that meant for Chief Inspector Chumley that he needed to think about things. Doing them would be my responsibility.

Several pages later we had gone through the whole catalogue of 'strategic' thought processes that a chief inspector can invent. I had a long list of organisational tasks to be getting on with and still had done nothing other than attend meetings that day. With everything covered I closed my notepad.

"Wait," said Chumley, "one more thing. What if we could get the mounted police to attend the town fair too?"

"Well, that is what they are for," I replied.

"See if they can supply two horses and riders then. That should do it."

I toddled off. Later, I contacted the mounted section, they couldn't have been more helpful; they'd supply two horses and two riders, no problem. Town fairs were just the thing they were good at.

The next day I sat in on the hindsight meeting, and at the end, Chief Inspector Chumley asked, "How did you get on with the horsey section?"

"The mounted division is more than happy to assist. They put the event in their diary and will send two horses and riders for high viz patrols through the town."

It was in mid-sentence that the little mischievous imp that lives in my brain decided to have a bit of fun.

"The only thing is, Chief Inspector, they require a sweeper supplied by our division."

"A sweeper?"

"Yes. Someone to follow the horses with a brush and shovel to pick up the horse manure. They can't supply one on that day."

"You are kidding!"

"I know it is an imposition, but according to them, they can't do it for us unless we supply a sweeper. Too many complaints from the public if they don't."

"Do you have someone in mind?"

"No, sir. Everyone has a job. I could ask the resource management unit to see if they can get someone."

"Good, we won't get if we don't ask."

He moved the topic on.

The next morning at the end of the hindsight meeting Chumley asked, "How did you get on with arranging the sweeper?"

"Ah. We have a problem. Resource management says they can't get someone for that. It is not the best of jobs, and nobody is willing to do it."

"What are we going to do?"

"Well, we could offer it to someone as an overtime shift, sir."

"Well, just do that. I suppose they deserve the overtime pay for such a job."

The next morning it was the first thing he asked me, "Did you get a sweeper for the horsey section?"

"It is against the overtime policy, sir; Resource Management has strict guidelines about what they can ask the cops to do on overtime and sweeping up horse dung all day doesn't fall into that category."

"Oh for God's sake! That is unbelievable. You know what I'll bloody well go down there and do it myself!"

I stood up and made my way to the door, trying not to laugh.

"Where are you going?" Chumley asked.

"I'm just heading down to the garage to see if we have a pair of wellies that will fit you, sir!"

THE MICHAEL PARKINSON TELEVISION INTERVIEW

Parky: Ha ha, 'wellies that will fit you', that's so funny, ha ha ha.

Malky: He didn't think so.

Parky: No, I imagine not. Did you play many pranks on your bosses?

Malky: I used to steal my chief inspector's car keys and move his car one spot to the left in the car park.

Parky: How did you do that?

Malky: His locker was next to mine in the changing room, and he left his keys hanging on a hook on the inside of his door, but he always left it open. One lunchtime I took them and moved his car from his chief inspector's parking bay to the left, which was the inspector's parking bay. Then I put his keys back.

Parky: What did he do when he went out to it?

Malky: He didn't notice. At least he didn't notice the first few times I did it. He just marched up to his car and drove off.

Parky: Was he stupid?

Malky: I didn't always get to see him going out to his car, often I was dealing with other things. I tried moving it to the right a few times, into the superintendent's parking bay and I even turned it around so that it was facing the other way.

Parky: He must have noticed?

Malky: He did eventually. One week I moved it one extra space every day so by the Thursday it was four parking bays away from his spot. On Friday his locker was locked.

Parky: Maybe not that stupid then?

Malky: Maybe not. But talking about stupid people…

Chapter 13

INTERVIEW TECHNIQUES

President Donald Trump has said many things that have made normal; level-headed people drop their jaw in disbelief. I'm flabbergasted at his stance on climate change, immigration, and torture. While I will leave the argument for action on climate change and immigration to those in a better position than me to argue the case, I felt that my thirty years plus working in the police has given me an insight into the best way to interview someone.

Donald Trump said torture is okay. He said, *'Does it work? Does torture work? And the answer was yes. Absolutely'*. Speaking about the people at the highest level of intelligence, he added: *'If they want to do it, I will work toward that end. I want to do everything within the bounds of what you're allowed to do legally. But I do feel it works? Absolutely I feel it works.'*

No, it doesn't Donald. Not unless you want to terrorise someone into saying something he doesn't believe or deny something he believes. There has been some pretty scathing analysis of 'enhanced interrogation techniques' (a polite way to describe 'waterboarding').

'We have to fight fire with fire,' said Trump - when have you ever seen a fireman arrive at a fire and attack it with a flamethrower?

There is no evidence that waterboarding works. Not a shred of evidence. All it does is allow prejudiced interrogators to intimidate a subject into conforming to their preconceived ideas. You get the answer you want to get, not the truth. Any manner of torture fails to find consistent, replicable and provable information. Torture is the worst possible way of getting to the genuine truth. It is not reliable, it is not dependable, and it is ethically wrong. Neuroscientists, who have spent many years studying the subject, confirm that torture of any kind degrades the quality of information that an interviewee provides. They can offer incontrovertible evidence that waterboarding, or any other form of suffering inflicted on an interviewee, will hurt the reliability of what they tell the interrogator.

So what is the best way to interview someone?

It might be a surprise to you, but people like to talk. Ask anyone what their favourite thing to do is and they will spout off several choices, sex, eating, drinking, skiing, reading, playing poker, watching a good film or whatever it is. The act of telling is, in fact, their most favourite thing. People like talking about themselves. I know I do. Talking about ourselves triggers our brain's reward system.

Good investigators know people like to talk. They never use threats or bullying. Good interviewers let people talk. They never ask a direct question. They pay no special attention to the answers they get. They listen and verify the information provided. It was a skill I learned too. Without using these skills, I might never have learned Doris's secret.

About 4 a.m. one night shift Doris, the cleaner, came in to start her work. I had just returned to the office having completed my rounds across the force and sat at my desk doing paperwork. Doris made me a coffee, placing it carefully on top of my notebook on my desk. A handy little coaster she must have thought. I lifted it off and saw the wet ring of coffee now staining my notebook. I gave Doris one of those withering looks I normally save for murderers, rapists and the worst of humanity. Doris was oblivious. She had made herself a coffee too and with no invitation sat on the chair on the other side of my desk.

"Thank you, Doris," the underlying meaning of which was 'leave me alone'

"What's been happening?" She asked, keen to be the first to get any gossip.

"Oh, this and that," I said, "thankfully it has quietened down, and I can now get on with my paperwork." (Hint hint).

"Aye, I must get on too, the floors won't buff themselves you know," but she didn't move, she just sat there thinking up her next question. There was a long pause as I looked at my computer and Doris sipped her coffee. Doris had a modus operandi; Doris came into the office, made coffee, started a conversation and made it last as long as she could. She would then shuffle some cleaning materials around pretending to work and half an hour later be back with another brew.

"Mind when you worked with Scotty? He was some boy, wasn't he?"

Of course, I remembered Scotty Boy. How could I forget him? I had the honour of doing his eulogy at his funeral. There were always things that reminded me of him. Whenever I heard Rangers supporters singing, whenever I saw a WWII pilots helmet, if I came across an abandoned football lying in the street and, sadly, whenever I crossed from the 4th green to the 5th tee at my local golf club, passing by the place where he died.

We missed it. Behind the façade of smiles, behind the bravado, behind the mischief, the pranks and the shenanigans lay someone troubled. Buried in his mind. Wounds he concealed, sadness masquerading as dry wit, demons that snagged his thoughts. For all the love, the life, the hope in his heart some things still drew blood and elicited screams. There was no cry for help, no outward signs of mental anguish. He didn't talk about it; he did the unimaginable and extinguished his ache.

Yes, I 'minded' him, I remembered him a lot.

"What do you mean he was some boy?"

Doris didn't need to tell me he was some boy. I knew him well enough to know he was some boy - I've even written about some of the nonsense he got up to in my previous books. He was some boy because he was full of nonsense, silly and the most loyal a person could be to his friends. Doris had mentioned his name out of the blue. I surmised she had recalled a story about him; I knew most of them - like the time he pulled a Marigold glove over his head and blew it up and the Chief Constable walked in on him. There were lots of stories.

"Oh, ye ken," she said, "jist that he was some boy."

Doris had a story to tell. If I was too direct, she might not let me in on it. I decided my best bet was to feign indifference.

"Yup," I said and turned back to look at my computer.

Doris sat silent for a moment.

"Aye, he wis some boy wis Scotty," she said, reflective.

Further confirmation there was something she was concealing from me.

"What do you mean?"

"Oh, you know, he was an awfy man at times."

"An awfy man at times?"

"Aye, he got up to some nonsense."

"Some nonsense?"

"Ye ken, aw the things he got up to."

"Aye."

I continued to look at my computer and tap the occasional key. Doris was swithering about whether or not she should tell me her story. My apparent lack of interest was a void she had to fill. There was another long pause.

"Aye, he could persuade us to dae some daft things ye ken."

Now we were getting somewhere. Scotty Boy had persuaded her to do something daft. The natural response to that would be to pay attention and ask questions, probe her until she came clean. I remained silent, concentrating on my computer screen, ignoring Doris. It was too much for her.

"Dae ye ken he broke the floor buffer?"

Breaking the floor buffer was one I hadn't heard. The floor buffers were the big machines like lawn mowers that had pads on the bottom. The cleaners used them first thing in the morning, plugged them in and vibrated them up and down the corridors until the floors were sparkling clean and once again ready to be trodden on with muddy size ten police boots.

"Floor buffer?"

"Och, I may as well tell you, it was nearly twenty years ago", and Doris went on to relate the story of Scotty Boy and the floor buffer race.

Doris started work, as usual, 3 a.m. She worked beside another cleaner called Alice. Scotty Boy was on night shift, and as soon as Alice and Doris appeared in, he engaged them in his usual kidology and banter.

"Aye, you two are in early, problems at home?"

Within a couple of minutes, Scotty Boy had persuaded both cleaners to assist him in a race. Alice and Doris plugged in their floor buffers, Scotty Boy and his colleague climbed on top, one each. Under Scotty Boy's instruction, the cleaners were to race them from the front office to the canteen.

"On your marks, get set, GO!" Shouted Scotty Boy, and they were off.

There was much bumping, giggling and hilarity. The buffers vibrated away as Scotty Boy stood on top of one, his colleague on the other.

"Faster Doris, faster - YEE HAH!"

Halfway to the canteen, Doris had pushed Scotty Boy out into a small lead.

"Faster Doris, faster," Scotty Boy demanded.

Then the inevitable happened, there was an almighty crack. The floor buffer Scotty Boy was standing on came to a sudden stop.

The entire casing had cracked in two. It wasn't designed to carry the weight of a cop in full uniform on an impromptu race through a police office. Alice and Doris scurried away to shred their buffer-racing taxi licences, worried that they would get into trouble.

Scotty Boy disappeared to his office and emerged an hour later with a memo in his hand and a big smile on his face. The memo detailed (not quite truthfully) how the damage to the buffer was accidental. He submitted the memo, and a couple of days later a new floor buffer arrived at the office. There were no questions asked. None of the protagonists said another word about it. A secret Doris kept for twenty years until she fell for the old interrogator trick and admitted what happened. Yup, people like to talk.

THE MICHAEL PARKINSON TELEVISION INTERVIEW

Parky: You are giving away my secrets.

Malky: Parky, you are the master interrogator.

Parky: Well, thank you. Let me try it out on you. Do you have any secrets?

Malky: I have loads of secrets.

Parky: Mm hm?

Malky: Ah! I see what you are doing there.

Parky: Mm hm?

Malky: I'd like some of my secrets to stay a secret.

Parky: Mm hm?

Malky: I'm not falling for it.

Parky: Okay then, can you tell me what was the most exciting time you had in your career?

Chapter 14

THE LONGEST POLICE PURSUIT IN SCOTLAND (EVER)

Who doesn't love a car chase?

In the iconic 1968 film 'Bullitt' we saw a car chase that lasted a full eleven minutes. In cinematic terms this is a long time. The film itself lasted one hour fifty minutes, so ten percent of the film taken up with one chase scene. It was a chase that lasted far longer than in any film that had gone before. It set the bar pretty high, but it paved the way for some films which were nothing more than one pursuit after another. In the film 'Gone in 60 seconds', for example, the final car chase lasted forty minutes. Nothing but burning rubber, screeching tyres and crash after crash.

Contrary to what you see in films and television, police pursuits don't normally last that long. Drivers trying to evade arrest have to contend with the fact that police are everywhere and we can direct officers to intercept. We can call upon the services of a police helicopter, and we get highly trained drivers on the case. When the Traffic Department turn up in their powerful vehicles people tend to give up, bail out or simply panic and crash.

High-speed pursuits are therefore rare. Nowadays a lot of training is about ensuring that public safety comes first. Officers are not allowed to get involved in a pursuit if they haven't had the relevant training. A high-speed chase can get the adrenalin pumping and adrenalin fuelled decisions may not be the best. Thus the overall control of a pursuit becomes the responsibility of an experienced senior officer in the control room.

The Control Room Inspector, distanced from the pursuit, bases his decisions on the information fed back to him. He will put the safety of the police officers, the public and even the perpetrator first. In certain circumstances, he will call off the pursuit and stand all cars down if he considers it too dangerous to continue. Each pursuit is risk assessed and if there is too much risk, the pursuit is abandoned even if it means that a perpetrator will get away.

Early in my service, PC Prim and I got ourselves involved in the longest police pursuit there has ever been in Scotland. It was the most exciting and most scary thing all wrapped into one. A crazy mad pursuit that lasted even longer than the forty minutes 'Gone in 60 seconds' car chase. We were lucky that the only injury was a broken arm.

We were night shift and out on patrol in a built up area on the outskirts of the town. It was about 1 a.m., we had been dealing with calls for the first three hours of our shift before heading back to the office for a coffee. PC Prim was driving, and I was sitting shotgun. PC Prim stopped at a junction intending to turn left. A truck passed in front of us, heading in the opposite direction from where we were going. It was a 'Scania' 16-tonne tipper-truck, about the size of a bus. Thundering past at a great rate of knots.

PC Prim commented "That was going a bit fast, wasn't it?"

"Not only that," I replied, "It's halfway across the other side of the road, and it didn't have any lights on. I think you better get after it."

Now at this stage, I think we both thought it would be a shame to miss our coffee, but duty beckoned. Stopping a lorry to give the driver a warning wouldn't take that long, though. PC Prim turned our marked police car and followed the truck. I switched on our blue flashing lights. The truck drove on.

The truck headed straight out of town. It wasn't clear that the driver had seen our blue flashing lights, and we didn't want to blare our two-tone horns in a built up area in the middle of the night. People were sleeping. The truck headed to a T junction and PC Prim saw this as an opportunity to pull across to the centre of the road as the truck slowed for the corner and thus he would be sure to see our flashing lights - indicating him to stop. But the truck didn't stop; it didn't even slow down, it veered across the roadway in front of us as it turned left at the T junction. It was going too fast as it took the corner and had to take a wide line crossing to the wrong carriageway. Any innocent vehicle travelling westwards at that part of the road would have been crushed. Luckily there was no traffic.

The truck swerved back across the roadway and drove on up the by-pass and out of town. I got on the radio to let control know what was happening, starting a running commentary.

"We are in pursuit of a Scania lorry type tipper-truck heading up the by-pass. It is travelling between fifty and sixty miles per hour and is straddling the white lines. It is not displaying lights. It is a serious danger to oncoming traffic."

I passed the registration number, and they came back with an owner. It belonged to a local quarry business. Control dispatched a crew to contact the owner of the quarry and establish who was driving or if it had been stolen.

"We have come to the end of the by-pass, and it has gone straight over the roundabout. And when I say straight over, I mean right through the middle. It flattened a signpost and the flower bed. It is now continuing straight on. It is heading towards the bridge."

The control room alerted all adjacent forces, and told us that assistance, in the form of traffic crews, were on their way. I continued to give a running commentary as PC Prim followed it at a reasonably safe distance. We switched on our two-tone horns, and they blared away in companion to our flashing blue lights. I hoped they might alert oncoming cars to the danger coming their way.

The truck went through a small town, still travelling at 50 mph and continued to head towards the bridge. A traffic car was waiting at the bridge, parked nose-in to the lay-by, but its rear end was protruding out onto the roadway. It too was flashing all its available lights. It was a clear sign for the driver to stop. But he didn't. He tried to swerve around the traffic car but clipped the rear bumper and sent it spinning. The traffic car now had a big dent in its rear end but still managed to recover and follow us. A local patrol car raced up behind us. Now there were three vehicles in pursuit.

The next roundabout gave the truck driver a choice of three exits. He could turn left and head towards the nearest big town. If he turned right, it would take him out into the country and straight on would take him onto the motorway to Glasgow. He surprised us all when he crossed the road before the roundabout, went round the roundabout anti-clockwise and entered the motorway in the wrong direction. The truck joined the northbound carriageway of the motorway driving southbound. We were in serious trouble. The truck was now heading directly towards vehicles travelling northbound at motorway speeds. It was dangerous before, but this upped the stakes.

PC Prim made a snap decision. If he followed it onto the wrong carriageway, then we would put ourselves in real danger, but if we didn't, there would be nothing to alert northbound traffic they had a sixteen-tonne truck heading towards them. At least if we were behind it, vehicles might see our flashing blue lights, and that just might be enough to warn them. PC Prim followed the truck onto the wrong carriageway. The traffic car and the other local patrol car also followed us. We moved into a single file on the hard shoulder and kept a reasonable distance behind the truck. It was frightening to think of what might happen.

I continued with my running commentary on the radio to control and they arranged for roadblocks to prevent further vehicles from entering the northbound carriageway. That would take time to get everyone in place, but at least attempts were being made to protect the public. Another two traffic cars, joined us on the northbound carriageway. They went ahead of the truck with blue lights flashing to provide an earlier warning to oncoming traffic.

We had a few near misses. A BMW rocketed towards us. The driver was not expecting an unlit sixteen-tonne truck to come towards him headfirst. He rounded the bend in the distance and saw the blue lights but must have assumed that they were on the opposite carriageway. It concerned him enough to drop his speed from about 95 mph, but he continued at the motorway speed limit of seventy. By the time he realised there was a truck heading towards him, there was not a great deal of time to brake or take avoiding action, the gap closed at a combined speed of 140 mph. He slammed on his anchors and slewed to the outside lane. The truck just kept going on the inside lane oblivious. If the BMW driver hadn't swerved out of the way, the result would have been catastrophic.

We passed several other cars that had pulled onto the hard shoulder and sat hoping the truck would avoid them.

After eight miles we came to the end of the motorway in the form of another roundabout. Because he had been on the wrong carriageway, we had been heading away from Glasgow. The truck entered the roundabout and proceeded around it in an anti-clockwise direction. This time an inspector in an unmarked car had to swerve out the way. He mounted the kerb and missed the truck by inches. The inspector kept going over the kerb and down an embankment before coming to a stop in a small copse of willow trees. Fortunately, he suffered nothing more than bruised pride.

The truck continued oblivious or at least unconcerned and entered the northbound carriageway in the wrong direction. We were now heading back to Glasgow southbound. We were joined by two other marked cars. Five vehicles all flashing blue lights as we sat behind the truck. The two traffic cars on the opposite carriageway reformed and headed southbound on the opposite carriageway to us. Joined by another two marked police cars both flashing blue lights.

Control got back to us.

"The owner of the truck has confirmed that it has been stolen. A crew are taking details just now."

PC Prim and I looked at each other and nodded. We both knew it. Drivers don't drive off from the police in a prolonged chase if they know at the end they will get caught, not unless drunk. We suspected that our truck driver must be drunk too from the erratic manner of his driving.

We continued to follow the truck heading south on the northbound carriageway. Travelling at varying speeds between fifty and sixty mph. Luckily, the traffic was fairly light at that time of the morning, and police road blocks at the entrance ramps to the motorway did their job in preventing more cars coming into the path of our stolen lorry. The few cars that came towards us slewed into the side of the road, wary of the mass of blue lights heading towards them. We crossed our force boundary and a further four traffic crews and another four general police patrol vehicles joined in the pursuit.

As I continued my commentary, I looked back and saw about twenty police vehicles in total all flashing their blue lights. Half of us on the wrong carriageway and the other half in front, alongside and behind us. It reminded me of a scene from the film 'The Blues Brothers'. Exciting and frightening all at the same time. Whether it was the prolonged adrenalin rush or just relief we hadn't crashed yet, I am not sure, but I started laughing. PC Prim looked at me puzzled, then he too smiled, his face cracked open, and he too laughed. It was a scene we would remember for the rest of our lives.

Then the truck in front of us slammed on its brakes. PC Prim saw it late due to us laughing. He slammed on his brakes in the fiercest emergency stop and shot out his left arm across my chest to prevent me from going through the windscreen. A moment before we impacted with the rear end of the truck it swerved left and sped up heading up the exit ramp and off the motorway.

Our laughing ceased, and training took over again. PC Prim followed the truck, and I radioed in our new direction to control.

"You are now out with our force area," came the reply. "Stand down, stand down, I repeat, stand down."

I looked at PC Prim, and he looked at me, distraught. This was our pursuit. Our capture. Our arrest. We were being told to leave it and return to our area. It was against all of our natural instincts.

I said as much to control.

"It is no longer your pursuit. Stand down."

PC Prim slowed and allowed the Strathclyde traffic cars to take over, but he didn't turn around.

"I can't see anywhere to turn," he winked.

We kept going, but the adrenalin rush was over. We were deflated, and as the truck entered the first big town, we decided that we had better stay on the right side of our control room inspector and at the next roundabout PC Prim went all the way around it, and we headed back to our area, albeit at a more sedate pace.

Moments later the radio blared an update

"The truck has entered the car park of a shopping mall. All exits are blocked. It is driving around in circles."

"Turn around - let's get back there," I shouted at PC Prim.

"It has come to a halt," was the next radio message, just as PC Prim about-turned and headed back through the same roundabout.

"The driver has fallen out of the cab and has broken his arm."

This time we did turn back and head home. The driver may have been our arrest, but we didn't want to have the job of escorting him to the hospital and sitting with him all night. We weren't that stupid.

I looked at my watch. From start to finish the pursuit lasted one hour and five minutes. Some twenty-five minutes longer than the 'Gone in 60 seconds' car chase and certainly longer than any other pursuit in Scotland that I had ever heard. I'm happy to be informed otherwise, but I still haven't heard of there being a longer pursuit. It was perhaps as not as thrilling as the 'Gone in 60 seconds car chase', but it was potentially as dangerous.

The best thing about it was only the truck driver was injured. The worst thing about it was I had to write the police report. It took ten times as long to write as the car chase lasted. The longest police pursuit in Scotland was a devil of a job to put on paper. So if any police officer gets upset at having to abandon a pursuit for safety reasons, they should think of the paperwork.

THE MICHAEL PARKINSON TELEVISION INTERVIEW

Parky: Exciting chase.

Malky: Then boring.

Parky: Writing the report?

Malky: Exactly.

Parky: Odd then that you decided to become a writer when you retired?

Malky: I know, come to think of it that is a bit strange.

Parky: When did you decide that you wanted to write books?

Chapter 15

THE PRE-RETIREMENT COURSE

A couple of years before I retired I went on a two-day pre-retirement course. It was quite useful. The main message was, 'start saving for your retirement'. A course that would have been a lot more help at the start of my career. I would advise all young cops (or anybody) to think about their 'exit strategy' now and not leave it until the last minute.

The Police Mutual Assurance Society (PMAS) offer pre-retirement courses for free. A pleasant lady from the PMAS, called Shiela, ran my course. Sheila was there to provide a comprehensive overview of what we could expect from our retirement, and to enlighten us as to the financial products available from them. One product being life insurance.

"For only £26.95 per month, serving members can get £120,000 life insurance; this includes critical illness cover, legal expenses, worldwide travel insurance, motoring breakdown cover and even mobile phone cover, " Shiela explained.

Sitting to my left was PC Gary Gorman. His ears perked up at the mention of a £120k payout. He pulled out his notepad and pen and did arithmetic on the paper. I peered over his shoulder trying to make sense of his calculations. He worked away for a few minutes, chewed on his pen, thinking, then suddenly his hand shot up.

"Excuse me. Can I ask a question about the figures you gave?"

"Certainly, what do you want to know?

"The payout is £120k, is that right?

"Yes, that's correct."

"Yet we only pay a small amount of money every month."

"Yes, that's correct."

"I've just worked out what we pay compared to what the payout is and was just wondering…"

"Yes."

"What's the catch?"

Everybody in the class turned round to look at PC Gary Gorman.

"The catch?" Said the nice PMAS lady.

"Yes, what's the catch? Over thirty years I'd only be paying in £26.95 per month which works out at under £10,000. What's the catch?"

Sheila, the nice lady from the PMAS, furrowed her brow and tried to figure out what PC Gorman was getting at. All eyes were on him. Then it clicked, I understood.

"Gary, the catch is, to get your £120k... you need to die!"

Shiela changed the subject. To break the ice she went round the room asking us all our names, what service we had and what our plans were for the future. A traffic cop sitting at the front enlightened her to his name and that he had twenty-nine and three quarters years service (twenty-six and three-quarters of which he had spent in the traffic department). He also told her he intended to do nothing, nada, not a jot when he retired.

Some wag at the back of the room (who wrote this book) made a comment, "No change there then," much to the hilarity from the rest of the cops on the course.

When it was my turn, I introduced myself and stated that I intended to write a book when I retired. Sheila was kind enough to enquire what my book was about. I explained that the working title was 'Stupid things I did in the Police'.

The traffic officer was first to respond with, "Ho ho that will be a big book then," all much to the agreement and merriment from the rest of the cops on the course.

Touche!

The nice lady from the PMAS pressed me further.

"Writing books doesn't pay the bills, you only make money when you sell them. Will you do anything else to earn money while you write your book and if you do how will you find the time to write it?"

"Oh yes," I assured her, "I plan to rejoin the police, work my way into the traffic department... then I will have all the time in the world to write my book!"

Touche back!

THE MICHAEL PARKINSON TELEVISION INTERVIEW

Parky: You had this idea to write a book about your time in the police for some time?

Malky: Yes, I had it in my head from about five years service.

Parky: Is that because you had a lot of silly things happen to you?

Malky: It is the nature of the job. Police officers deal with the strangest things, some are awful, some are exciting, some are sad, and some are hilarious.

Parky: I gather you think it a good idea for all cops to keep a personal note of the silly incidents that happen so they can write a book too?

Malky: There is no doubt that every cop could come up with a book or two. They don't have to write a book, though. Even if it is just a personal diary, I guarantee they will take something from it.

Parky: So when they get home they should record what happened that day?

Malky: Not even when they get home. If any cop wants to get on in the job, they should keep a professional diary - evidence of the good work and skills they have. There is no way their bosses will know everything for appraisal time. Everyone should write their own appraisals.

Parky: Secondly, you suggest that everyone should think about what they will do after they retire?

Malky: Absolutely, from day one they should think about it. Not two years before they retire - or even like me, leaving it until six months after I retired. You can't save for a retirement in six months. Start saving when you join or have an exit strategy.

Parky: Good advice. If you are over fifty and need a funeral plan, I know a company that will give you a free pen just for a quote.

Malky: Um, yes, thanks for all those adverts, Parky.

Parky: Moving on. You have mentioned that you used to work with the nicest guy in the world?

Malky: I worked with a lot of nice people, guys and gals.

Parky: What about the one who was really unlucky?

Malky: PC Penfold?

Parky: No the other one, the one who used to lose his phone all the time?

Malky: Oh yes, he used to lose it when he went drinking so as a precaution he never took it with him. He was the nicest guy in the world.

Chapter 16

THE NICEST GUY IN THE WORLD

Plumpish, blond-haired, always smiling and willing to do anything for you. The nicest guy in the world is an adorable chap, a shame then he is so unlucky.

Two weeks before he was due to be married he heard a knock at his door. Standing on his doorstep was a young lady holding hands with a young boy and a young girl. The children, aged about four years, looked remarkably similar to each other. He couldn't quite place where he had met the young lady before.

"Can I help you?" he asked.

"Do you remember that rugby trip you had to Wales about five years ago?" She asked him with a pronounced Welsh accent.

"Er… yes," he said, wondering where she was going with her line of questioning.

"Well," she continued, "I'd like you to meet Derwen and Dafina."

"Derwen and Dafina?"

"Yes, Derwen and Dafina… your children."

It all flooded back to him. He had met the young lady five years previously on a weekend rugby trip to Wales. A drunken weekend, the highlight of which had been a one-night-stand.

A DNA test cost him £500, but he didn't need it to know the kids were his. He needed only look at them. They too were blond, smiley and nice. Despite having two unexpected mouths to feed, the wedding went ahead, and he married his fiancee. Albeit, she kept close tabs on him.

One cold Friday night in December my shift decided to have a Christmas night out. I stayed at home, being an old fuddy-duddy. It was that or my wife wouldn't let me - I can't quite remember. In any case, they probably didn't want their inspector tagging along and spoiling their fun. On the shift at the time was the nicest guy in the world. Unlike me, the nicest guy in the world's wife did give him licence to join his shift on their Christmas night out.

The shift met up at Barry's flat before going out. Barry was a single guy and didn't mind having everyone come round. It was the kind of single man's flat that looked tidier after a party than it did before. They consumed alcohol in its various colours and brews as a precursor to the evening's revelries.

At 10 p.m. they headed on into town. Two taxis dropped them off in the town centre. On alighting, they trooped into the hippest pub in town, the nicest guy in the world bringing up the rear. As they all squeezed past the two bouncers on the door, the nicest guy in the world had an unfortunate trip on the kerb and landed at the feet of the bouncers. This unfortunate trip went unnoticed by his colleagues who had all passed inspection by the bouncers and gained entry to the pub.

The nicest guy in the world stood up, shook himself down and headed for the door of the pub to join his colleagues. The bouncers, however, had a different idea. Here was a guy who had clearly been drinking and couldn't even negotiate a four-inch kerb. They didn't know he was the nicest guy in the world and they didn't know he was a cop. They assumed he'd had one or two drinks too many.

Bouncing rule No. 1. *Do not let drunk people into the pub.*

The nicest guy in the world was refused entry. He protested his soberness and appealed their decision.

Bouncing rule No. 2. *Do not let argumentative people into the pub.*

The nicest guy in the world realised the bouncers weren't interested in joining a debate. Bouncers refuse to listen to anything that a drunk argumentative person will tell them. Therefore they simply refused him entry and ignored anything he said.

***Bouncing rule No. 3**. Do not talk to anyone who breaks rule 1 or 2.*

The nicest guy in the world was in the habit of losing his mobile phone when on a night out (I said he was the nicest guy in the world, not the luckiest). Due to this, he left his mobile phone at home whenever he was out drinking. Inconveniently, this was where it was on this occasion, and thus he could not phone his colleagues to come back out. He waited to see if his colleagues popped back to find him. He sat on a wall opposite the pub and waited. Inside the pub, the rest of the shift chipped in for a kitty and determined to get through it as quickly as their throats would allow. None of them had seen him trip and fall outside.

"Where's the nicest guy in the world?"
"Dunno,"
"Must have gone home."
And with that, they never gave him another thought.

With no sign of his colleagues, the nicest guy in the world yawned and realised that he was tired. He had had a busy week at work, and the few drinks he had consumed at Barry's flat had taken their toll. Nobody inside had missed him, so he decided that he would save money and just make his way home. A good night's sleep wouldn't go amiss.

He walked down to the train station. He arrived just in time to see his train home pulling out of the platform as it began its journey without him. The timetable showed another hour before the next one. He stood and waited in the cold. An hour later the next train arrived. He was glad to enter the warm carriage and snuggle into a comfy seat. As soon as the train took off, his tiredness and the reassuring clickety-clack sent him off to sleep.

The nicest guy in the world slept for half an hour. He woke when it stopped. He realised he had missed his station, and now the train was sitting four miles further north of his destination. He looked across the platform and saw a train on the opposite track. He needed to be on that train, so he jumped up, exited his train and ran across the bridge. He made the train with seconds to spare, entering just as the doors shut. The train tooted and pulled off.

Alas, the train he got on took off in a northerly direction taking him even further away from his home.

The nicest guy in the world got off the train at the next stop, an unmanned single platform station. It was now midnight, and he was the only person there. He waited in the hope of another train coming to take him back but after two hours in the cold and no sign of any train he walked into the village to find a phone box. The nearest one he discovered was a half hour walk away but once found he phoned for a taxi.

The taxi journey home cost him £45, and he arrived home at 3 a.m. By coincidence, this was exactly the same time that his colleagues made it home from their night out. However, they had had a better time and had spent less money.

The nicest guy in the world didn't have much luck on any night out. On another occasion, a group of his friends went into town for a few beers. Unfortunately, a week before the night out, the nicest guy in the world fell off a quad bike and broke his leg. Not to be beaten, with the help of a stookie and a crutch he made the night out. They tried a few pubs before ending up in a licenced bowling club. They had a rather nice night quaffing beer and swapping stories.

At closing time they got up to leave and first out the door was the nicest guy in the world. The combination of his leg in a stookie, using a crutch and drink made him a little unsteady on his feet. As the door of the bowling club closed behind him, he tripped on the steps leading down to the street causing him to fall. He tumbled uncontrollably towards the pavement.

Fortunately for the nicest guy in the world, a passerby with quick reflexes put his arms out and grabbed him, preventing him from smacking his head off the ground. However, in preventing him from hitting the road, he also lost his balance, and the two of them fell to the pavement in a tangled embrace. At that precise moment, the rest of the entourage emerged from the bowling club. They wrongly interpreted the situation. It looked to them as if their pal, the nicest guy in the world, was getting assaulted in some unprovoked attack. The passerby found himself subjected to a rain of punches and kicks by the group all intent on retribution.

The nicest guy in the world brought them all to their senses by shouting and pulling them off.

"He was just trying to help me," he pleaded.

As the bruised and beaten passer-by stood up, indignant, he threatened to call the Police and have them all arrested.

The barmaid from the bowling club, who had been locking the club door, instructed all to come back into the club. Including the passerby. She then ordered every one of them to buy the passerby a drink. The lads continued drinking in a closed door session for another two hours. After that, the passerby may have sported a black eye, and a bloodied nose, but he also had six new best friends.

Problem solved by the barmaid.

THE MICHAEL PARKINSON TELEVISION INTERVIEW

Parky: The nicest guy in the world was unlucky, wasn't he?

Malky: Not so much these days, still nice but doing well for himself.

Parky: What about the other unlucky guy?

Malky: PC Penfold?

Parky: Yes, PC Penfold. You always have a new story about him?

Chapter 17

CAREER DEVILMENT

I qualified for the Scottish Police Golf Championships in the year that the much-anticipated Millennium Bridge opened to the public and quickly closed again after it swayed uncontrollably as soon as people walked across. I smile when I see the engineer who designed it (an in-law) and it never fails to amuse me to sway back and forth whenever I am in his company.

They should have left it to sway. People pay for less excitement.

We headed to the North East to play the golf. Our hotel was a flophouse out by the Airport. There were rooms within the hotel but also a row of chalets on the other side of the car park. It was first come first served, so I got a room in the hotel. PC Penfold and his golfing buddy, Big Al, arrived a little later and got a chalet.

After unpacking, we had a light bite and toddled off to bed nice and early to prepare for the following day's joust with irons and woods.

On the day of the competition PC Penfold had an early tee off time so by lunchtime, game complete, he was back in the clubhouse downing beer. Gradually the bar filled up as others finished their rounds. When Big Al finished playing, he and PC Penfold toddled off to their chalet to get ready for an evening out on the bevvy.

The chalet PC Penfold and Big Al were sharing was a twin with a toilet and a small shower. Big Al went to shower first. PC Penfold found an ironing board and a basic iron, deciding it was a good idea to press his trousers.

As Big Al soaped himself in the shower, PC Penfold thought it would be a good idea to have a little quiz.

"Big Al," he shouted. "See if you can name this tune," he then proceeded to whistle *Yankee Doodle Dandy*. Big Al shouted the correct answer through the door within a few beats.

"Okay. Your turn," PC Penfold shouted.

At that exact moment a little bird perched on a tree right outside the open bathroom window and whistled away a tune that might have meant something to another bird of the same species but to the human ear, it was just a random series of high-pitched notes.

"Is it the theme tune to 'Star Trek'?" shouted PC Penfold in all seriousness. At which point Big Al nearly fell out the shower laughing.

Once ready they headed back to the bar. By early evening PC Penfold had had enough liquid sustenance and retired to bed. Big Al, who had been a little more sensible with the early drinking, lasted a little longer before retiring for the night.

The next day I woke at nine. I got up and opened the curtains. At the same time, across the car park, the middle chalet door opened and out stepped PC Penfold. PC Penfold was sporting nothing but his birthday suit. As his eyes adjusted to the light, he bared his rotund and hairy body to the world. He stretched, yawned and scratched his balls. Slowly he came to the realisation he was standing stark naked in a car park right in front of the hotel. The car park was busy with patrons who had breakfasted and were now leaving. The patrons forced to view the naked sight of a plump, hirsute forty-five-year-old man who hadn't quite sobered up yet.

The chalet door was on a spring hinge and had closed shut behind him. PC Penfold turned around and battered on the door with his fists, shouting on Big Al to come and open up. In doing so, he attracted more attention to himself. Now he was subjecting myself and the other patrons to the sight of his hairy bum. It was almost enough to put me off my breakfast.

Eventually, his comatose room-mate roused himself from his drunken sleep and opened the door. PC Penfold disappeared back inside his chalet.

I showered, dressed and went down for breakfast. PC Penfold and Big Al joined me at my table afterwards. There was something odd about PC Penfold; he seemed a little unsteady and, as he sat down, he knocked his cutlery and sent it crashing to the floor, clumsy. He wasn't quite his usual self. I enquired as to his well-being.

"I'm fine, but you will never believe what happened to me this morning," he said.

"I think I can guess," I replied smiling.

"I need some glasses," PC Penfold continued.

"Eh?"

"It's his fault!" he said pointing at Big Al.

I was a little confused but probed further asking why.

"'Cos I was thirsty in the middle of the night," Big Al piped in.

"Eh?"

"I had a bit of a drooch. You know sometimes drinking too much can make you thirsty? So I got up in the middle of the night and had a glass of water in the bathroom."

PC Penfold interjected at this point clarifying the whole story, "Aye, but he drank the glass of water I had my contact lenses in!"

So that's why he needed glasses.

We play the Scottish Golf Championship over two days. After the first round, the evening entertainment is determined by how well we did. Those in with a good score and a chance of winning a prize have a conservative night out with others in the same boat. A nice meal, a glass of non-alcoholic fruit juice and then take themselves off to bed nice and early. They then wake up refreshed and ready for the next day's competition.

Those that have had a bad round on the first day (that's me by-the-way) make the most of the new surroundings they find themselves in. New pubs sought; new drinks tried and tested. No thought given to the next day and not a care if one plays well.

Constable Charlie McFarley fell into the first category. His impressive first round saw him top the leaderboard by two shots. A sensible round on the second day would give him a great chance of a first, second or third place. His eye was on first prize, he wanted to take home the impressive Scottish trophy.

"Shall we just have a wee bite at the clubhouse and head back to our digs," he suggested.

Unfortunately for Charlie, there was no-one else in our group who fell into the first category. Every single one of us had resolutely failed to play any form of decent golf. We all fell into the second group.

"Naw, let's head down the town and get pissed," was the consensus.

Charlie, faced with an evening on his own or accompanying us to the town, deciding that it was too early to be retiring. We bundled into a taxi and headed for the delights of the city.

About 2 a.m. we bundled out of our taxi back to our digs. It wasn't until we arrived in the foyer that Big Al did a head count.

"Where's Charlie?"

All of us scratched our heads. Too tired or too drunk to care. Not Big Al. Big Al was still sober enough to muster up some concern.

"We had better report him missing," he suggested.

"He'll turn up."

"He'll be fine."

"He'll be all right."

Big Al had a different opinion, "No, I think we better report him missing. What if something has happened to him?"

I remembered that Big Al was last to tee off the next day.

"Okay, if we report him missing, it would be sensible if the person who is last to tee off tomorrow stayed up to do it."

After a bit of discussion, Big Al took on the responsibility. The taxi that dropped us off was just about to leave, Big Al waved it down, climbed into the back and asked the driver to take him to the city police office. He headed off back into town. We waved at Big Al as he peered out the back window.

"Why didn't he just use the phone?" PC Penfold suggested, and with that, we all trooped off to bed.

It turned out that Constable Charlie McFarley wasn't so much missing as comatose. The rest of us were so drunk we couldn't remember where we had put him. Charlie woke up under a swing in the local play park. He sat up and banged the front of his head on the swing. His efforts to push his assailant away resulted in the swing shooting off then returning under the powers of gravity. It swung back and struck him with even more force to the back of his head. Give Charlie his due, he extricated himself from the play park and made his way back to the flophouse. He grabbed his clubs and arrived on the course with seconds to spare. Charlie went to work intent on setting a new Scottish Golf Championship record.

Constable Charlie McFarley now holds the Scottish Championship record for the largest disparity between the two rounds of golf ever played. His second round saw him hit the little white ball one-hundred and twenty-seven blows. He went from first place to fifth from last - he wasn't last because two players failed to submit a card, one player didn't turn up and another abandoned the game half way through after throwing up on the ninth green.

I went back to work a day later, having failed once again to impress on the golf course but happy to have pipped Charlie into sixth from last place. It was always great to get back to work and relate all the antics that went on.

Then it was back to work. One of the most important tasks I had to do was appraisals. I always felt that staff were our most important resource and conducting proper appraisals were key in maintaining morale. Unfortunately, there were others who had different ideas. Everyone from a cop to Chief Constable had different ideas. That meant there was no consistency.

When I first started out, there was a simple process to assess probationers. If your sergeant liked you, you got through your probation. If he didn't like you, you didn't.

Nowadays there is a more evidence based approach. Probationers have to achieve competency in all the facets of the job, and their tutor has to record these competencies on a purpose made form. If a probationer fails to meet any criteria, then a process of remedial training is instigated. He or she is monitored and their progress discussed at case conferences. It is all designed to give people the best chance of making it through their probation. Of course, it also provides evidence to support any decision to let someone go. A necessary precaution in today's litigation friendly society.

Once an officer completes his probation, his line manager has to complete a yearly assessment. It depended on who was giving you your appraisal how good it was or even if it went ahead. Sometimes three or four years could go by without me ever receiving an appraisal. Even when I received an appraisal, the value of the process depended on whether my line manager was trained, interested or competent.

Early in my service, I experienced line managers who didn't know how the system was supposed to work, some who were indifferent and the occasional one who was not really very good at anything. My favourite quote for that particular sergeant was; *'His men would follow him anywhere, but only out of morbid curiosity.'* Google cannot enlighten me who first used that phrase, but it seems to crop up in a lot of different occupations.

Criticism is hard to swallow for anybody. I have been on the end, and I know it is what sticks in my mind. You have to be a 'Dunker' not to give a toss. It is even more galling when force fed that criticism by a manager who doesn't follow the proper procedures, isn't interested or competent.

It is different now, but good practice for a sergeant (or any manager) engaged in doing an appraisal is first of all alert the appraisee that the process is underway. The appraisee should be given time to collate and present evidence of his or her performance. The manager should then take time to discuss his appraisal with the appraisee and afford the opportunity to read and sign the final submission. Nothing should be a surprise.

If the first time an appraisee knows that his appraisal has been completed is when his chief inspector mentions it in the passing, then the system hasn't been followed. That happened to me:

"I've got your appraisal McEwan," my chief inspector said as he passed me in the corridor, making no indication whether it was good, bad or indifferent. He carried on into his office.

I was interested enough to about turn and chap his door.

"Will you be going over it with me?" I asked, "Only I wasn't aware it had been completed.

"Uh. Oh well if you must," he replied.

He raked around his desk found a folder and handed me my appraisal, "You can have a seat and read it."

I hadn't gone far before I questioned some bland remarks, typical of an unimaginative manager regurgitating his standard phrases. That feeling remained with me throughout my service and was one reason I took great care over appraisals when it became my job to complete them. I felt they were important in acknowledging people for their efforts and that a good appraisal could motivate people to do their best.

"Can I ask that I get the chance to discuss this with my sergeant before you submit it, sir?"

"Yes. Yes. Just take it away with you. I thought you might want to do that."

I drove straight to his office to see him.

"Sergeant, can I see you regarding my appraisal?

"Oh! I did that. It's submitted," he said.

"Yes. That's the problem."

"Problem?"

I had a long conversation with Sergeant Napoleon. It was a conversation we should have had at the start of the process and certainly not after my appraisal had made its way from him, through my inspector to my chief inspector. Our conversation finished with me asking:

"How many sergeants does it take to change a light bulb?"

"Um, I don't know."

"Only one, except in your case you need two?"

He looked at me somewhat confused.

I explained, "Since you would be happy sitting in the dark, you would need someone else to come in and change it for you."

I retired on a Friday, had a party on Saturday and turned fifty on Sunday. It was quite a weekend. A few months later I was basking in the glorious sunshine as I walked up the second hole of my golf course and crossed to the fourteenth fairway to play my wayward ball. A group of men were coming down towards me as they played down the fourteenth. A gregarious chap out in front regaled me with, "What a fantastic day."

I agreed.

"Wonderful, yes. Just a shame about the golf," referring to my wayward shot, but I was unperturbed, it was sunny, and I was retired, and I was playing golf. I smiled my cheeriest smile.

It was only then I noticed that playing with the gregarious chap was the ex-Sergeant Napoleon. He was a little way behind and was duffing his way down the fourteenth, cursing each sclaff of his ball. He glowered at me.

Bugger. I hope he didn't think I was referring to him.

I started another job. Winter came, and nine months after I retired I felt a searing pain in my lower back. NHS 24 diagnosed me over the phone as having sciatica and recommended gentle stretching. Over the next eight days, a series of doctors attending the house persisted with that diagnosis and prescribed ever stronger pain killers. On the eighth day, my sister called and took one look at my jaundiced eyes and rushed me to hospital.

The emergency room doctors had me in an induced coma within an hour. All my organs had shut down. They discovered that the pain I was suffering was down to an abscess in my lower back. It was in such a dangerous position they couldn't operate. The abscess had poisoned my system. Meningitis was attacking my body and septicemia had caused my immune system to malfunction and infect every part of my body. They linked me up to every conceivable machine, pumped my veins with broad spectrum antibiotics. I remained in a coma, dangerously unwell and unaware of my plight for ten days. The skill, dedication and perseverance of the Intensive Care staff saved my life.

When I came out of my coma, I was a wasted, pain ridden shell. I remained in the hospital for six weeks, and even when I got home, I had to return every day for a further six weeks to receive a daily dose of intravenous antibiotics. At first, I couldn't get out of my bed on my own. It took months before I could even walk my dog a hundred yards. In time I got better, for therapy I wrote books. It was two years before I played another round of golf. I was proud of myself when I finished that round. It was an achievement. I walked through the car park to put my clubs away. I saw ex-Sergeant Napoleon standing at the boot of his car. I had to walk past him to get to my vehicle. I pretended not to notice him.

"Malcolm, can I have a word with you?"

"Yes, what is it?"

"See about two years ago, you were playing up the second fairway, and I was playing down the fourteenth, and you made a comment about my golf. Well, after what has happened to you, I think you should keep those comments to yourself."

Seriously? Two years ago? I struggled to recall the incident. How do you reply to that? My first thought was to tell him to go to hell. But I didn't. I consoled myself with the thought if he had to live with himself his whole life, I could put up with him for a minute or two. I find this worth remembering when I meet thorny people. I took the high road.

"Aye, nae bother," I said, and I walked on to my car.

The thing is, I had those stories about Sergeant Napoleon in my head. I had decided not to put them in my first book *'The really funny thing about being a COP'*. That short conversation with him changed my mind. My perspective had changed. Life is far too short to hold grudges. Being bitter about life or people will eat you up. I now go out of my way to avoid people who are bitter or twisted. I would rather remember the good times and spend time with people who make me laugh.

Towards the end of my service, there was a push to doing appraisals a little more professionally. A task force of senior officers got the job of reviewing the set-up. After months of sitting in an office thinking about it, they came up with a new format based on what another Force was doing. It took a year or two to train up everyone and implement the new appraisal system.

It wouldn't be long before someone would point out that the Force that we had copied it from abandoned it in preference for yet another process. Through lack of interest and any cohesive strategy, the appraisal system fell by the wayside. Some officers got feedback others went several years with no assessment whatsoever.

My viewpoint remained the same; people are the police service's most important resource. Recognition of their efforts hangs an essential part of good management and spending the time with someone, talking with them about them, is a worthwhile exercise - more than that, it is essential for making an organisation great.

As an inspector, it was my job to complete appraisals for my sergeants. I had the job of assessing a good temporary support sergeant. The role meant that he didn't have a permanent group to cover but did all the odd jobs around the station and covered the other sergeant's groups when they were on holiday, at court or ill. I thought it prudent to seek the opinions of other supervisors. Sergeant Gates had completed six months in the role and had worked with various other sergeants in the station. I deemed it wise to get the best evaluation of his performance before sitting down with him and going over his appraisal. I sent out a questionnaire to all the other supervisors that worked with him. I asked that they supply any evidence they had as regards Temporary Sergeant Gates' performance under the approved headings.

A (plumpish) sergeant who had recently been done out of overtime by Temporary Sergeant Gates, sent me back:-

COMMUNICATION

"Likes overtime"

SELF MOTIVATION

"Loves overtime"

RELATIONSHIPS WITH COLLEAGUES

"Truly really loves overtime"

RELATIONSHIPS WITH THE PUBLIC

"Truly really really adores overtime"

DECISION MAKING

"Decides to work all the overtime"

SELF MANAGEMENT

"Manages his overtime well"

CREATIVITY AND INNOVATION

"Creates his own innovative overtime opportunities"

LEADERSHIP

"Guess"

MANAGING AND DEVELOPING STAFF

"Yawn"

APPRAISER'S COMMENTS

"ZZZZZZZZZZZ"

I considered it so funny that I gave Temporary Sergeant Gates the opportunity to respond:-

"You come to your work, do your best, you feel obliged to do all that you are asked (including 2 x overtime shifts), and he's having a go. He mentions nothing of "loves doing his weekend night shifts to cover while he is off gallivanting at some party, he must have a huge family with the number of weddings, funerals, engagements, etc. he has to attend... that's a lot of buffets hmmm might explain his girth!"

After more work, the appraisal system transformed again. This time it they computerised it, and the name changed to 'Performance Review' system. Once a year an officer had to input his work related personal objectives into the system. Then he had to identify his personal development needs before sending it on electronically to his supervisor. The supervisor had the job of ticking boxes in relation to the officer's core skills and commenting on the officer's objectives and development needs.

The electronic submission introduced automated reminders for cops and sergeants to submit them in time. That seemed to work for them, but a little further up the tree, there was the usual indifference shown with reminders, electronic or otherwise. Chief Superintendent Amnesiac retired with thirty-six performance reviews sitting in his in-box. He had had over five hundred automatic reminders emailed to him, and he had studiously deleted each and every one without doing diddly squat about them. The irony was that the performance review system required him only to tick a box. A simple electronic tick would complete the thing. He didn't even have to read it. The fact that he didn't tick the box meant that he got a further reminder emailed to him every two weeks and thus there was more work in having to delete his emails.

I know this because the inspector in charge of the system had tried to speak to him about it.

"Sir, regarding the performance reviews sitting in your in-box, we need you to tick them to ensure that they are complete. Only then can they be retrieved on the computer system. Right now they are just sitting in cyberspace."

"I haven't received any reminders," he told the inspector making it clear he was not responsible.

"Sir, there is an electronic log showing they are sitting in your in-box and that they require you to tick them before we can file them. It is just the way the system works."

"I haven't received any reminders," he told the inspector again.

"Sir, we can see from the email history the date and time the reminders are sent and received."

"I have received no reminders," he told the inspector a third time.

"Sir, the reminders have a 'read receipt' and show the date and time that you received them, the date and time you opened them up and read them and the date and time you deleted them."

This time Chief Superintendent Amnesiac stood up, looked the inspector in the eye, sternly and without batting an eyelid said, "I have received no reminders!"

The inspector got the message, he about turned and walked out scuppered by rank. Chief Superintendent Amnesiac continued to delete every single email for every single performance review reminder until he retired. I understand the thirty-six performance reviews, sitting with him, were irretrievable.

Three months before I was due to retire I got my appraisal to complete. I perused the form and deliberated over my response to my work related personal objectives and put:-

"Well, there is probably not much you could do with me now."

My appraisal made it all the way to my chief superintendent who sent it back with the suggestion that he detected a little devilment in my response. I was gently reprimanded to, 'behave at least until you retire'.

However, my little bit of devilment paled into insignificance when I received PC Wally Walker's performance review. First a little background.

Before the Scottish Police Forces amalgamated only Strathclyde Police had a police helicopter. The two largest forces, Lothian & Borders and Strathclyde Police, had a mounted section. In the thirty years of working with my small force, I could only think of one occasion when we had asked for or required the services of our mounted colleagues. To be fair, even if we required them, whatever we were dealing with would probably have been all over by the time they had galloped to our assistance. I could think of the odd occasion when we had requested the help of the police helicopter. Mainly, to assist in the search for persons lost in the hills.

PC Wally Walker had ten years service. A beat cop who had no intention of ever applying for promotion and had one rule, 'never volunteer for anything'. While he was a capable individual, he was inclined to mock of every new process or dictum. Much of the time he was funny with it, for he was quick with his wit, although he was not very forthcoming with any better suggestions.

Wally completed the self-assessment and 'development needs' section of his performance review and submitted it to his sergeant. His sergeant paid attention to what Wally had requested and dutifully commented. He then passed it on. I read it and had tears rolling down my cheeks by the end. Here is what it said:-

Development need 1:-

"As we move forward into the new dawn of Police Scotland and the different opportunities that are now available to Police officers, I request an attachment with the Air Support Unit. I feel that this would raise my awareness, give me a more rounded view of Police Scotland and provide me with new ideas on how different areas work and in turn, would make me a better officer."

His sergeant added his comments:-

"I am always keen to support an individual who looks to develop their career and enhance their knowledge and learning within the organisation. I will endeavour to ensure that he is given an attachment to the Air Support Unit thus ensuring he is given a certain elevation to heighten his overall view to policing Scotland. This attachment should give him a lift and a better all-round view. It is good to see him aiming so high."

Development need 2:-

"An attachment with the Mounted Division would also be of benefit as this would allow me to gain experience within an area of policing that was not available previously."

His sergeant added his comments:-

"I have discussed this attachment with the officer. I can see that he is seriously looking for a change in his current role. The equestrian demands placed on an officer within the Mounted Branch I don't believe are any greater than that of a patrol officer. However, the partnership between rider and mount I don't doubt will take a little longer to sit in. But this is

not wholly insurmountable for this officer to achieve. I am sure he could manage such an attachment at a canter, and such an attachment would hand over the reins to him to take charge of his own career development. He would, however, have to work on his BMI before I would fully support an attachment to this area of police work. To this end, he has to work on the physical aspect and requirement needs that such a posting would demand."

Aye, a trip up in a helicopter or a ride on a horse would certainly give him a different viewpoint. I also gathered his sergeant thought him too fat to ride a horse!

What a chuckle! I was paralysed with tears reading it. I wondered if it started with Wally and his sergeant picked up from there or were the two of them in cahoots and sent it to me as a test. I like to think I have a good sense of humour; I wasn't going to take offence or berate them for it. It was just good clean fun, hilarious even. I genuinely cried tears laughing at it. Rather than send it straight back for amendment, I decided to call in PC Wally Walker for his appraisal counselling and tell him how much I appreciated his humour.

An hour later Wally knocked on my door.

"Come in, Wally," I said smiling, "have a seat, and we'll go over your appraisal."

"Thank you, Inspector."

"Wally, can I just say that I haven't laughed so much since the first episode of *You've Been Framed*."

"What do you mean, sir?"

"Your development needs - just brilliant."

PC Wally Walker remained stony faced. An ex-rugby player, his battered phizog showed none of the delights that I expected from praising his prank development needs.

"What's wrong with them, sir?"

"Nothing is wrong with them; they cheered me up no end. I was in tears with it and with your sergeant's comments."

"I was perfectly serious, sir."

PC Wally Walker was deadpan. There was no indication he had been joking. There was no crease around his eyes to show he was trying to suppress a smile. On the contrary, he looked concerned and solemn.

Shit! Did I make a mistake? Was he really serious about wanting a secondment to the Air Support Unit? Did he really want to work a week with the horsey section? Had I dashed all his hopes? Would he consider me to be completely unprofessional? I suppose I had been a little unprofessional. I had laughed out loud at his development needs. I had told him I thought it was a joke. Here he was, genuinely wanting to expand his knowledge. What if he wanted to submit a grievance against me?

"Wally, I'm sorry. I haven't taken this seriously, and for that I apologise. Can we start again?"

"I suppose so, sir."

"Okay, as regards the Air Support Unit, what do you think you will get out of that?"

"Well, I think it will raise my awareness of… um, er, well, I might see the bigger picture."

"You don't just want a flight in a helicopter?"

"No, sir, I think it would be a good thing for my development."

"Have you done any flying before?"

"I've been on a plane to Lanzarote."

"I mean, have you shown any interest in flying before? Have you taken lessons? Have you been up in a helicopter? Do you know if you suffer from air sickness or not?"

"I was sick on the plane back from Lanzarote, but that was just because I had too many vodkas."

"Have you done any research into the Air Support Unit?"

"Er, um, not really."

"Do you have any idea what is required of an officer in that unit?"

"Er, um not really, but I could learn. You never know I could become a pilot."

"The pilots in the Air Support Unit are all civilians. The police officers are there to navigate, maintain communications and gather evidence from the thermal imaging cameras. They have to read maps and carry out the majority of radio exchanges. There will be an extensive training course to go on before anyone can join that unit."

"Oh!"

"Have you done any research at all to see if they accommodate secondments from officers or even if they allow untrained officers to go up in the air?"

"No, sir."

"Well, maybe you should do that first?"

"Yes, sir."

"I take it you have an interest in horses?"

"I like to have a bet on the Grand National every year."

"Have you ever ridden a horse?"

"Er, um, no."

"Do you know anything about the horsey unit?"

"Er, um, no."

"Well, maybe you should do a bit of research and see if they do secondments too."

"Yes, sir."

"If it is any consolation, I don't think your sergeant was fair when he mentioned your BMI as a reason for not supporting you."

"Aye, he's got a cheek."

"If you come back with valid reasons and interests and a plan for going to these units and it is not just something you could learn all about by giving them a phone call, then I'll endorse it, okay."

"That's great, thank you, sir."

PC Wally Walker got up from his chair and headed for the door.

"Oh, and by-the-way," I said, "I wish I'd put those things down on my last appraisal for my development needs."

PC Wally Walker smiled for the first time.
"Aye, that would have been funny."

THE MICHAEL PARKINSON TELEVISION INTERVIEW

Parky: Did he go away and do his research?

Malky: Of course not, that would have been too much work.

Parky: So he didn't follow up his request to go to those units?

Malky: Wally just needed a break. Anything would do. It happens, cops get burned out after a while and a change of scene, a different role or even just a holiday is enough to recharge their batteries.

Parky: So did he move somewhere else?

Malky: Naw, he had a week in Lanzarote and came back all refreshed.

Parky: He didn't put in a grievance for you laughing at his request then?

Malky: No, my apology was enough, I think. Although Wally wasn't the only person in the job that I had to apologise to.

Chapter 18

FOOT AND MOUTH

I've had to do a little bit of apologising in my time.

One morning I was sitting having my morning coffee with my colleague Ken. Ken is a nice fellow, and we got on well. The conversation started off with the weather, then the previous night's football and on to whether or not monkeys can eat chocolate. We crossed off all the important topics before discussing what we had to do that day. There was a pause before Ken seemed to have an idle thought.

"What do you think about Barbie?" he asked.

Barbie Bradshaw worked as an office clerk in another station. She was particular about her appearance, no matter what shift she was working or what job she had to do she was always immaculately turned out. She liked to apply makeup - a lot of makeup. There are buildings in Pompei that have less foundation. She is a petite girl with a reserved smile and a professional manner, occasionally mistaken for aloofness. It made her even more attractive to the opposite sex, yet few men made any moves to ask her out because it was the generally held view she was unobtainable. To be fair - she was to most.

Without thinking, I lifted my size eight police boot and stuck it firmly in my gob - metaphorically speaking. What I actually did was launch into a diatribe of what I perceived to be wrong with Barbie, "Oh No!" I said at one point. "Can you imagine waking up in the morning with all that makeup spread all over the duvet?"

Ken did not pursue the subject any further.

Despite still working with Ken every day, it was about a month later before I learned that Ken was dating Barbie. The question he had raised with me that fateful morning was a precursor to him boasting that he and Barbie were dating. My crude and unwarranted response shocked him into remaining silent.

I still cringe at my stupidity, rudeness and unpardonable disrespect. It was a hard lesson learned because I can do almost anything, drive, watch telly, pick my nose and all of a sudden I'll cringe. The memory of my stupid comments flash into my head. I give out a thunderous groan; loud enough for people to consider calling an ambulance.

"Are your kidney stones back?" my wife asked me after one particular flinching loud groan.

"Just a twinge," I said to placate her, before going back to wincing at my gargantuan and gratuitous mouth - even although it happened years ago.

Today, Ken and Barbie are still together. I hope he has forgotten that exchange but in case he has not I would like to apologise wholeheartedly and unreservedly for my inaccurate and bad-mannered comments. I would also like to confirm that Barbie is a wonderful person. Not only is she a lovely lass, but she has remained slim, elegant and gorgeous. A catch in any red-blooded male's eyes. A lovely girl who blossomed into a beautiful woman who is still particular about her appearance and has remained youthful and elegant.

It is a valuable lesson for anyone to watch what you say. Even if the other person can forgive or forget your indiscretion, it might not be as hard for you to put it out of your mind. Nowadays, I am much more careful; such a question would have me ask, "Why?" before I gave any opinion. In fact, I am more likely not to say anything if I can't think of a nice word to say about someone. I use a technique called W.A.I.T. - before I open my mouth I think W.A.I.T., which stands for Why Am I Talking. It has saved me from groaning like an injured elephant in the most unlikely of places.

My only question is - what is Barbie still doing with Ken? I mean, he is no oil painting!

Another lovely lady I should apologise to is Rosie.

Rosie was my secretary. Not my personal secretary, she was the office typist come office clerk at a small station I worked at in the twilight of my career. I liked that station, I was the senior officer and had a great bunch of community cops to work with. I once made a little mischief by putting a plastic spider in Rosie's desk drawer. Two of the community team, a pair of wags, picked up on the fact I liked to play the occasional prank on Rosie and they did their own. They stapled jackets to her ceiling, turned her desk drawers upside down so that when she opened them, everything fell out, or filled them with the contents of the shredder - things like that. Unfortunately, Rosie always gave me the blame. She didn't believe the two nice community cops would get up to such nonsense. Which made it all the funnier for them.

Rosie was such a pleasant and obliging lady. She always made sure everyone else was okay and was entirely unselfish in every way. One morning I arrived for work at a tardy ten minutes past nine and as usual stopped by her office to say good morning.

"Good morning Rosie."

"Good morning," she replied, "do you like a quiche?"

"I don't mind it," I replied, somewhat noncommittal. Quiche isn't my favourite, but I could guess what was coming. Rosie produced a large quiche from her bag; she had purchased it at the local supermarket that morning.

"That's our lunch sorted, "she said, "I won't be able to eat it all myself."

I thanked her for her kindness and toddled off to my office.

It was a busy day for me, and I had to go out to follow up on enquiries I had. By lunchtime, I was more than a little peckish. I stopped and ate a hamburger at a roadside snack van, attracted there, at first, by the picture of a generously sized burger laden with onions and sauce and then sold by the aroma. No sooner had I consumed the burger I received a call from Rosie.

"That's lunch ready," she informed me.

I told her I had one more person to call on and would be back in about half an hour.

My call took longer than expected and it was over an hour before I got back to the office. Rosie had finished her lunch and was back at her desk.

"Your dinner is in the dog," she joked.

In fact, it was still in the oven. Rosie had just switched it off, "but it should be still warm," she informed me. I thanked her again. I didn't let on that I had already eaten.

I made my way to the kitchen and took the leftover quiche out of the oven. The pastry sides had collapsed in on itself as the egg filling had shrivelled up. The cut edges had blackened and burned. The tiny spots of ham on the surface resembled little black bottomed capsized lifeboats bobbing in a yellow ocean. Even on an empty stomach I couldn't eat the dried up offering. I considered discarding it in the bucket, but Rosie might find it and feel offended. I pondered what to do.

At the back of the kitchen, we had a window that overlooks an expanse of overgrown ground. There was a gap of about ten feet to a high wall that borders the office grounds. All I had to do was lob this quiche over the wall, and the evidence would disappear. The mice could have it. I took the half quiche out of its silver foil, opened the window and threw it.

Unfortunately, the quiche broke up the moment it left my hand and only half of it cleared the wall. That left a quarter of the quiche splattered, but still recognisable, sitting right on the top of the wall.

I couldn't get it off as the wall was too high and I couldn't reach it from the window. The quarter of quiche lay on the wall staring back at me in an accusatory manner. The next time Rosie came through to the kitchen, she would see the lunch she had generously provided me sitting on top of the wall. She couldn't miss it. She would know I had betrayed her. Her thoughtful gesture to provide me with my lunch just thrown away. I hadn't even tasted it. I had just thrown it out of the window, and now it languished on top a wall for everyone in the office to gawp in speculation.

Busted.

Anyone entering the kitchen would see this quarter of quiche on the wall and questions would be asked.

'Who on earth threw that quiche onto the wall?'

It wouldn't take long to figure out. They'd tell Rosie and she would forever remind me of my callous treachery. Ostracised for chucking an egg based pie badly. I would become a persona non grata. My credibility in the office would be as far out the window as the quiche. I wouldn't be able to look anyone in the eye ever again. Everyone would know that I did it. Inspector McEwan, the cold hearted bastard who threw the warm quiche out the window.

There was only one thing to do. 'Honesty' and 'best policy' came to mind. The right and proper thing to do in these circumstances is always to come clean. At least that way you are being honest about your deviousness.

I made my way to the front office.

"How was your quiche?" Rosie asked with a big expectant smile on her face.

"Delicious!" I answered, then I took the afternoon off and went to the gym.

Sorry, Rosie!

Every year thousands of 'Orangemen' march through towns and cities of Scotland. Originating in Northern Ireland, 'Orange Walks' commemorate the *Battle of the Boyne* when William of Orange defeated the Catholic King James II. But for many Catholics, the marches are contentious and sectarian. The marches on 12 July sees the Orangemen dressed in bowler hats and orange sashes stride alongside orange bands dressed in colourful uniforms. They can be a recipe for trouble, and during any marches, the police had to be on their toes.

It is no surprise that these marches are controversial. What place is there in today's society for a commemoration of a battle that happened in 1690? Perhaps it would be fine if limited to a celebration but they don't. The marches sustain bigotry, intolerance and hatred. Thrown into the mix is alcohol. On any day of a big march, individuals dressed in their affiliated band colours crawl out of bed and gather at the side of the road awaiting the minibus to collect them. I have seen them standing there as early as 6 a.m. scratching their balls and downing cans of beer. Later, at the end of the day's festivities, they pour out onto the same pavement in a dishevelled heap. Jackets unbuttoned, white socks soaked with the rain and flies open as they piss out the gallons of beer onto some innocent old buddy's footpath.

The itinerary for an orange band is to march through their home town in the morning, clamber aboard a bus that takes them to the main orange walk - providing another opportunity to consume more beer on board. The main march will gather hundreds of bands from lodges across Scotland.

The organisers of these events have to lodge requests with the police to hold a parade. They have to provide details of numbers involved, what stewarding will be in place, route and timings. The police can make stipulations based on previous problems that have arisen. In the small town where I worked during my early service the organisers always insisted in taking their march past the local Catholic church. One stipulation placed on them was that they must cease playing their flutes and drums one hundred yards before reaching the Catholic church and not start up again until they were one hundred yards past it. Invariably they ignored this and continued to play as they marched right past the church. I might have taken a more stern approach with them if it wasn't for the fact that the local Roman Catholic Priest being a character. He would stand outside his church and stamp his feet and clap in time to the music. Unperturbed by the glowers he received from the Orangemen.

My last involvement in an Orange parade was as an inspector in charge of two serials (two minibuses staffed with six cops and a sergeant) tasked to attend trouble spots where they arose and act as a Fast Action Response Team. Although we were officially called the Support Team, the acronym from the Fast Action Response Team kinda stuck.

We managed the whole operation from the Command & Control Centrer under orders from a Chief Superintendent and various other ranks. We had a dedicated radio channel for all personnel involved in policing the event. It was a big occasion, the biggest orange parade our force had seen. A lot was happening.

In charge of communications was Sally McNally an experienced female inspector, she worked in the Control Room for many years. Unfortunately, her radio manner wasn't the best. Out of the office environment, a nicer girl you couldn't meet. Put her in charge of the radio in an event like that, and her gruff demands and unapologetic scolding turned her into a nippy sweetie. She was never off the radio, every second she barked out orders or looked for updates re positions or developing situations. Coupled with the fact they had a live CCTV feed into the Command and Control Centre her grumpy persona took a snipe at anyone not seen to be doing their job as she perceived it.

I had my serials patrolling the outskirts of the parade where buses dropped off and picked up the drunk and often belligerent Orangemen. At one point we came across a bus load of Orangemen squaring up to a group of locals. The Orangemen wore black tunics with large silver buttons, orange sash, black trousers that didn't quite reach down to their ankles, showing off their white *Sports Direct* socks and various foot apparel. The shoes were the only things that didn't match. They had on Puma training shoes, white plimsoles and one even a pair of brown cowboy boots.The locals were all wearing Celtic Football Club colours.

This was a situation that could get nasty. There were about twenty youths all in green and about thirty band members all well-oiled and energised by the day's events. They spread out into the middle of the street and were facing up to each other. I needed to alert the Command and Control Centre. Alas, I couldn't get on the radio. The constant stream of orders and sarcastic remarks streamed unremitting from Inspector Sally McNally. There was no break in transmission. Every time I pressed my button to speak my radio buzzed to inform me that someone else was talking. I had a choice. I could either press the emergency button thus clearing up the airwaves for my transmission or sort it out ourselves.

I instructed my officers to grab hold of the ringleaders on either side. The Orangemen had been heading for a bus parked fifty yards back up the road. I sent an officer to instruct the driver start it up and leave in exactly two minutes. I wanted every band members on board and out of there. Anyone not on board would likely be arrested.

The removal of the two ringleaders confused both groups. There were a lot of protests from those that remained, but it was enough to confuse them and leave them uncertain of what to do next. The rest of my officers intervened and ushered them either onto the bus or away from the location depending on what colours they wore. It worked.

The two ringleaders received my finger wagging best lecture before I let them go. The leader of the Orangemen had to run after his transport home and just made it on before the bus hit the main road.

There were other pockets of trouble we dealt with the same way. On each occasion, I was thwarted from making our Control aware of the situation by the constant stream of commands from Inspector Sally McNally. It was frustrating, but we made it to the end of the day with no police officer injuries - always a bonus.

Most major events involve a debrief at a later date. It is the professional thing to do to learn from any mistakes and improve the way we police future such events. I attended the Chief Constable's meeting room a week later. Around the table was the Chief Superintendent in charge of the operation, various senior officers, several inspectors and a wizened old sergeant from the training department who'd had point duty. Inspector Sally McNally didn't appear, thank goodness.

In due course, the wizened old sergeant was asked how he thought the operation had gone.

"Well it was okay apart from 'Old Vinegar Tits' always talking down to us on the radio, other than that it was fine," he replied.

His description may have been a succinct and apt portrayal of our ill-mannered female inspector. However, I was a little surprised that the senior officers around the table (a superintendent and three chief inspectors) said nothing. Nothing, either in the way of reprimand for the inappropriate comment or in concern why one of their staff should bear such a label.

Inspector Sally McNally retired soon after and all those who worked with her breathed a sigh of relief. However, the same nickname got used for another female, Detective Inspector Mary McHarkin. It was a shame. DI Mary McHarkin wasn't an 'Old Vinegar Tits'. On the contrary, she was sparkling company, also she was a bright and competent officer. She moved to the CID on merit and progressed through the ranks to detective inspector.

A detective inspector has a high-pressure job. It calls for a lot of responsibility. They have to take charge, not only of the most serious crimes but also have the daily responsibility for performance in all crimes, no matter how minor. It calls for a lot of long hours, and it is one of the most stressful of roles in the police. I don't know if it was her role that induced the change. Perhaps we all get grumpy as we get older. Perhaps it was the company she kept, certain people breed a culture where they malign, criticise and castigate everyone. That was the culture in some parts of the CID. The after work cocktail hour spent sipping drinks and nibbling away on other people's reputations. Scorn is a currency used by those who think by doing so they raise their own regard - the more derision and mockery they can pour on others the higher the respect they earn.

The opposite is true.

People become wary of contemptuous people, knowing they will talk about them in just as derogatory terms as soon as they walk out of the room. Such a culture breeds distrust.

Detective Inspector Mary McHarkin fell into the way of the CID. She worked hard, but that wasn't enough. The police have glass ceilings and those ceilings are all the thicker in the male dominated environment of the CID. Mary McHarkin had to work twice as hard to get her promotions, she also had to fit in, toe the line, and in doing so she got tarred and the feathers stuck. In time, Detective Inspector Mary McHarkin could make as cutting a remark about colleagues as anyone. She became indistinguishable from the pack.

After many years in the role, the glass ceiling frustrated her, and she realised, like her bosses, it had become too thick to break. After much anguish, she walked into her bosses office and handed him her transfer request. She moved back to uniform and, with the weight of the world's problems off her shoulders, overnight she returned to being pleasant and agreeable. Mary McHarkin took on the role of uniform inspector in my nearest big town.

Now you have the background I will get to the story.

One day I set about organising staffing for a large funeral. We were expecting up to two thousand people to attend. The family organised a pipe band to lead the funeral procession on foot from the church to the cemetery. A distance of a mile and a half. The route passed through the town centre which could be busy. At a planning meeting, I asked Sergeant Rupert Wentworth Hamilton to see if we could borrow a couple of Traffic Wardens from Mary McHarkin's staff to assist in traffic control. Sergeant Hamilton requested the extra Traffic Wardens by getting in touch with the Resource Management Unit.

A day later, a reply came back to Sergeant Hamilton from the Resource Management Unit stating that Inspector Mary McHarkin had questioned why we needed two of her Traffic Wardens for three and a half hours. Sergeant Hamilton came to see me with a worried look on his face,

"Em. Old Inspector Vinegar Tits is asking why we need two of her Traffic Wardens for three and a half hours."

"Leave it with me," I said shaking my head in wonder at why anyone could be bothered to question the need for two Traffic Wardens, "I'll sort it out... oh and by the way 'Inspector Mary McHarkin' is competent enough to be a senior officer within this force one day - so you better not let her hear you call her that."

I later phoned the Inspector Mary McHarkin and explained the issues with the size of the funeral, and she accepted this with no complaints. She wasn't in the least bit bothered about giving up two of her traffic wardens. We had a pleasant conversation about old times; then I had an idea for a prank.

"How about we wind up Sergeant Hamilton?"

"Old Rupert Wentworth, how?"

"Well if I draft a spoof email on the subject and address it to you but copy Sergeant Hamilton in, I could make it really funny."

Inspector Mary McHarkin, contrary to her vinegary reputation, was all for it.

"You should expressly ignore my comments, though."

"Don't worry, I won't take offence," she assured me.

The email I drafted up took less than five minutes:-

TO: Inspector Mary McHarkin
CC: Sergeant Hamilton.

Dear Inspector,

We need the two Traffic Wardens because this is a big funeral and it will take a long time. Surely it is more important to ensure the safety of two thousand mourners as opposed to you having an extra few parking tickets issued in your area.

Why on earth should you be bothered about giving up a couple of Traffic Wardens for a few hours when your detection rate is so low. Perhaps you should spend your time concentrating on more important matters. Maybe then your detection rate would be as good as ours.

It is just another example of your desire to poke a stick in everyone else's wheel rather than help out.

I therefore respectfully request that you wind your neck in and stop pestering the resource management unit with your idiotic postulations. It is exactly for these reasons they call you 'Vinegar Tits' behind your back.

Kindest regards.

Inspector McEwan.

Within thirty seconds of pressing the 'send' button, Sergeant Rupert Wentworth Hamilton received it, read it, and rushed back to my office to see me. He laughed so hard at my impertinence that there were several officers nearby popped their heads in to check if he was all right. He had to read it over several times to believe I had the nerve to write and send such an e-mail.

He had no idea that Inspector Mary McHarkin was in on the joke. I didn't enlighten him.

A few days later I was sitting in the Headquarters canteen when Inspector Mary McHarkin spotted me. She gave me a scathing look before berating me.

"Do you realise that because of you I now have the nickname 'Vinegar Tits'?"

"But, but, it was just between you, me and Sergeant Hamilton," was all I could muster.

"Yes. That was until Sergeant Rupert Wentworth bloody Hamilton forwarded your email to the Resource Management Unit. Now it is being passed all over Headquarters with no explanation it was a joke."

Oops!

I never liked falling out with anyone. Unfortunately, there were occasions when I did. I would like to apologise to Inspector Mary McHarkin - for any upset this may have caused her. Although, I take no responsibility for coming up with the nickname in the first place.

THE MICHAEL PARKINSON TELEVISION INTERVIEW

Parky: Oh dear. Rather unfortunate circumstances.

Malky: Just a tad, yes.

Parky: Is Inspector Mary McHarkin still upset with you?

Malky: Probably.

Parky: Do you not think she would see the funny side of it now?

Malky: I don't know, she hasn't spoken to me since.

Parky: It is a funny story, though.

Malky: Yes, it is quite amusing, in an embarrassing sort of way.

Parky: Moving on, you also did some research I believe?

Malky: On?

Parky: On what it takes to be an outstanding cop?

Malky: Yes, I did.

Parky: How did you go about it?

Malky: It wasn't scientific or anything if that's what you mean. All I did was ask people who the most outstanding cops were and why.

Parky: Police officers?

Malky: Serving police officers, retired officers and some civilian police staff.

Parky: How many did you ask?

Malky: I surveyed a total of two hundred and fifty-five people. Not a definitive amount but it was enough to gather some interesting data.

Parky: Two hundred and fifty-five people is not an insignificant amount.

Malky: It was quite an interesting exercise.

Parky: How did you go about finding the people to ask?

Malky: I just asked people when they were in my company.

Parky: Did they choose the same outstanding officers?

Malky: There were two or three officers who stood out. A lot of people mentioned them but there were officers chosen who I hadn't worked with, and as a result, I saw them in a different light.

Parky: Did you learn anything from the answers you were given as to why they were chosen?

Malky: Now this is where it got really interesting. Four traits came up time and time again. Pretty much if an officer had those four traits, they were considered to be outstanding. There was one trait that stood out as a prerequisite, everyone in my survey who was identified as outstanding had this trait. It was to do with good communication skills. To be outstanding, they had to have good communication skills. It wasn't just about being able to stand up and talk to people; it was simply listening. When I broke it down the officers identified as the most outstanding had the ability to listen.

Parky: Sorry, what was that you said?

Malky: Hah, funny!

Parky: So, what were the other three traits?

Chapter 19

HOW TO BE THE MOST OUTSTANDING COP IN THE WORLD

I always wanted to join a wine club. I pictured myself opening the door to the Parcel Force delivery driver, signing for my case of wine and carrying it through to the dining room table. A sharp knife allowing me access to the delights of Shiraz, Rioja and Sauvignon Blanc. Each bottle consigned to a position in my (free with the first order) antique wine rack and admired each time I passed. In anticipation, I would lick my lips as I considered which bottle would match with dinner on Friday night.

In reality, I retired and joined a wine club that met at 7.30 a.m. every morning in the park.

Well, not quite 7.30 a.m.

Occasionally I meet up with old colleagues on a Friday afternoon. We take our dogs a walk, chew the fat set our destination to a dog-friendly pub. Our walk ranges from two to five miles, depending on which pub we fancy that week.

Modern technology is great. Rather than phoning around each of the old timers we moved with the times, set up a *WhatsApp* group, and the *Old Grumps Wine Club* was born.

We are all ex-cops - I look at them arriving at our meeting point and think we are quite a strange collection of beasts. Maybe we did all look like cops when we were on the job - all but one of us does now. Only ex-PC Prim looks like a cop now. I know it is a sweeping statement. Especially nowadays when cops come wandering along the street, hats off, spidery tattoos crawling up either arm in some misplaced struggle to create their own identity. Not PC Prim, he is your old style police officer. Tall, straight backed, short hair (actually not much hair) and a bearing that exudes confidence. The unmistakable-ness of his police manliness running through his veins further evidenced when he speaks.

You don't so much have a conversation with him as an interrogation.

"What have you been up to today, Malky?"

"Nothing much."

"Nothing much?" Pause for effect, "I saw your car down at Tesco's this morning?"

The look he gave suggested that this was a question not a statement, and it wasn't rhetorical.

"Er, well, yes. I was shopping."

"What did you buy?"

"Just some groceries."

"Just groceries?"

"Groceries, yes… and some beer."

"Beer?"

"Yes, beer." I was getting tetchy with his line of questioning.

"I noticed you had plenty of beer in the other day when I popped into your house."

"I like being prepared."

"Oh! Are you having a party?"

"Well, not so much a party. Just having some of the family around on Saturday."

"Saturday?"

"Yes."

"What's the occasion?"

"Well number two son is back up from London, and we thought we would have his cousins come to the house for a drink."

"Cousins?"

"Just the twins."

"… and?"

"And their Mum and Dad."

"Your Mum and Dad too?"

"Yes, them too."

"Uncle Bo coming?"

"Yes, I think he can make it."

"All the family coming then."

"Well, if they can make it."

"Are you having a barbeque?"

"I thought I might - if the weather is nice."

Jeezy peeps! I'd been in his company for two minutes and went from nothing much happening to telling him all about our upcoming family barbeque. I had this feeling (as I think most criminals did with him) that he knew what I had planned all along. He just had to interrogate it out of me. Now I felt guilty for not inviting him and his family.

"Do you want to come?"

"Shall I bring the wife?"

"Yes, bring the wife and kids too."

Ex-Sgt Barbeque Bill (who was so named because he didn't have a Barbeque) chipped in, "Can I come too?

Ex-Sgt Hop-A-Long looked at me with big moon eyes.

"What about me as well?"

I looked at my ex-colleagues and made an executive decision.

"Yes, why not, just all of you come along to our family get-together? You are more than welcome. I'll buy more burgers tomorrow."

"Better get more beer too," ex-Sgt Barbeque Bill chipped in.

On these walks we talk about all sorts of things; the state of the world, how things aren't how they used to be, what stupid things cops got up to during our service and the big question - can monkeys eat chocolate?

When we exhausted these topics, I asked the question; Who was the most outstanding cop you worked with?

PC Prim was first to respond, "The officer that springs to mind is Detective Sergeant Bill Black."

"He would be my choice too, but why?"

"He was a good communicator, he was competent, he was tough, and I liked him."

"I'd agree with all of that. I learned an awful lot from him when I worked with him. He never told me to do anything, he always asked, and because it was him, you jumped to it."

"He had a way with him."

"What do you mean?"

"Like he had a sixth sense, he just knew what to do. He was good at cutting out any crap."

"Not with his diet, though!"

"Naw, he liked a beer and as much chicken pakora as he could stuff down his throat."

"What about with the criminals?"

"Yes, he didn't stand any nonsense with them, but mostly he didn't stand any nonsense with the bosses."

"He was honest too."

"Do you think that is important?"

"It is essential that police officers are ethical. That is a fundamental truth. Cops have to hold themselves to a higher standard," PC Prim asserted.

"Okay, here is an ethical question for you. You are in a pub and you hand over a £10 note for drinks but the server gives you change from a twenty. What do you do?"

"Hm, do you mean should I tell the wife or keep it to myself?"

"I meant that Bill Black was honest with people. He didn't sugar-coat things."

"I think I know what his secret was."

"What?"

"This is something you can all use. He had a thing he did that always made me feel like I belonged in his inner circle. He brought me into his confidence. Occasionally it was a whisper in the ear, sometimes he would beckon me to his office and close the door, on other occasions he'd put his arm around my shoulder and take me to the side to tell me something. What he told me wasn't always a big secret but the way he did it was conspiratorial. It made me feel good."

"I liked Perry Deckman," chipped in ex-Inspector McMilligan.

"What was it about him that made him the most outstanding cop you knew?"

"He was the most conscientious cop I ever came across."

CONSCIENTIOUSNESS

According to psychologists, conscientious people live longer, get better grades, earn more, have higher influence, are more likely to succeed in their careers and are happier at work.

"Highly conscientious employees do a series of things better than the rest of us," says Brent Roberts, Professor of Psychology. He states that they plan to achieve their goals better: setting them, working towards them, and persisting amid setbacks. If they realise that they cannot reach an over-ambitious goal instead of getting discouraged and losing hope, they switch to a goal that they can achieve. That is one strong reason why they reach goals consistent with the aspirations of the employer. He further states that such people carry grit and shall remain persistent in finding a solution to a problem after repeated failures and traverse that extra mile to ensure that they achieve their aspirations. Also, they plan, decide, draft on paper, and write down important dates. Highly successful people like Richard Branson, carry a notebook in their pockets all the time.

Near the beginning in my service, I worked at a small station. I was on early shift, and a road accident occurred during rush hour. There were three cars involved, there were no injuries, so the drivers exchanged names and addresses before I got there. One driver left stating that he needed to get to work. He worked in a town eight miles away, covered by a different station. It was a busy morning, and it was 11 a.m. before I got back to my office.

In those days our bosses didn't like us to stray too far off our beats in case we were required to attend calls. Very much different nowadays where cops can arrive at their station, get changed into their uniform and then spend an hour or two travelling to where they will work (not efficient). I telephoned the office that covered where the driver I was looking for worked and spoke to another young cop, PC Perry Deckman.

"Hi, I'm looking for a little enquiry."

"Certainly, what is it?"

"There was a road accident this morning, and one driver left the scene before I arrived…"

PC Deckman was quick to grasp what I needed and interrupted me before I could finish.

"You want me to interview him under caution, obtain his driving licence and insurance details, examine his car and note any damage?"

"Yes, please."

I put down the phone and, from previous experience, had low expectations of a quick resolution. No matter where you go, cops are busy and their priority is the work they have on their own plates. Non-urgent requests like mine get put on the back burner, and the likelihood is that after a week or two my sergeant would chase me up to get the enquiry completed and I would have to make the trip to visit the driver myself.

At 2 p.m., before I had even managed to leave the office there was a knock at the door and in walked a young cop.

"Hi, I'm Perry Deckman, here is your enquiry.

PC Deckman handed me a brand new buff folder. Inside was the full typed statements from him and his corroborating officer. Photocopies of the relevant driving licence and insurance document, both of which were attached to completed production documents. There was a detailed diagram of the damage to the driver's vehicle and a further labelled production of a paint sample he got from the bumper. It was the most comprehensive documentation in relation to any enquiry I had ever asked of anybody. Twenty-five years later, I retired, and in all that time I still hadn't got such a quick, detailed and professional result from an enquiry request.

PC Perry Deckman walked out the door and I thought to myself that he would go far in the job, there won't be any cops more conscientious than him. One day he might end up a Chief Constable, I thought.

I was wrong. PC Perry Deckman went one higher. He ended up HM Chief Inspector of Constabulary. Even the Chief Constables had to answer to him.

"Who else do you think made an outstanding cop?" I asked.

"I think Rob Appleson was outstanding," suggested Ex-Detective Sergeant Goodman.

There was a general nod of agreement between us all.

"What was it about him?"

"Well, he was very thorough, he followed the ABC of policing."

"Assume nothing, Believe no-one, Challenge everything?"

"Yes, that and I don't think he got embarrassed about anything."

"You think that is a good trait?"

"Well, yes. I sat in on an interview Rob did with a sex-offender, and he remained entirely unperturbed all the way through. He just listened and never judged. I think that was how he got them to admit to their crimes."

"Yup, I experienced that with him."

"You were interviewed by him for a sex offence?"

"NO! I was with him one night when he dealt with something and he was totally unembarrassable."

UNEMBARRASSABILITY

Where do you go if you want to smoke dope?

Your parents are home, so you can't do it there.

There will be a car park in every town that the police go to for their easy pickings. Every now and again, when things are quieter than normal, police drive up and check out who is there. Invariably, they find minor drugs possession cases.

Rob Appleson was a thief catcher who had a nose not only for sniffing out thieves, but he had a singular ability for knowing when something wasn't just right. One Saturday night Rob and I were on patrol driving our marked police car. Rob drove to the easy-pickings car park. This car park was a regular haunt for cannabis users who would drive up, smoke a joint and chat. They were never big players on the drug scene, but we often found that they would cough up a name or two of their suppliers in exchange for a warning.

The car park was empty, except for one car. Normally, anyone who sees a marked police car would dispose of what they were smoking out the window and drive off. Those were the ones worth stopping. This solitary car stayed where it was. We sat watching it for a minute or two, waiting for it to move off - but it stayed put. There was someone moving about in the front passenger seat but, from where we were at the entrance to the car park, we couldn't quite make out what was going on.

Rob's nose worked overtime and curiosity got the better of him. He drove right up to the car and parked next to the driver's window. It took a second or two to realise what was going on through the fug of the car's steamed up window. The driver was sitting in his seat, the seat back was fully reclined and bouncing up on down on top of him was a female in her early twenties. Rob rolled down his window and waited.

Rob had this impregnable façade that allowed him to prank people like me. A face that gave away nothing. I never knew if he was joking or serious. He also used that impregnable façade on those less virtuous members of the community. It always amazed me how he could be so immune from embarrassment.

The female looked at Rob through the window but continued to bounce up and down. Rob waited, watching - his face impenetrable. After a moment or two, the female rolled the driver's window open. She was naked from the waist up (I also presumed naked from the waist down and bouncing up and down on the now distraught looking driver underneath her). We recognised the female as a local worthy from a notorious family of thieves and vagabonds. Rob held her gaze and raised an eyebrow.

"You can't be doing that here Tracy," he reprimanded.

Without missing a beat, Tracy continued to bounce up and down at an even faster rate of knots.

"Aw fur fecks sake Rob," she implored, "I'm just about to come."

Classy!

"I have a theory about what makes anyone outstanding," Ex-Sergeant Barbeque Bill announced. He had been thinking about the question.

I'd better watch he doesn't do too much thinking - it can't be good for him at his age.

"What's your theory?" Ex-PC Prim asked.

"I was watching a programme on the telly the other night, and it was all about how the SAS survive the tests they have to do. Apparently, it is a mindset they have. They turn everything into a game. It helps keep their mind off the hell they have to go through."

"Yeah, I saw that. They were sitting in a freezing muddy hole for days and made up mind games and stuff.

"They bet on which bug could crawl up their face the fastest, things like that."

"Seemed like it worked because they had a laugh."

DON'T PANIC

How do you become a confident police officer?

If I could train Police officers in one skill more than any other it would be the art of not panicking. When people panic they make mistakes. They can't think straight. They forget their training, ignore rules and disregard procedures.

Preparation is the key way to feel in control. It helps you make better decisions. Astronauts, deep-sea divers, and bomb disposal experts all do it. They are repeatedly put through systematic training for all the scenarios they might come across and have to deal with. Familiarity breeds a powerful feeling of control.

Controlling the panic emotion involves thinking about the worst that can happen and with that knowledge working back to a better solution.

It starts with breathing. The SAS teach their recruits to breathe. They put them in situations that spell danger and the first thing they are taught to do is monitor their breathing. Taking slow deep breaths in through the nose, holding it and breathing out through the mouth is a great way to calm the mind and get your attention on solving the problem. It promotes rational thinking.

Making better decisions in panic situations is helped if the brain takes an outside perspective. Ask, 'What would Inspector Clouseau do?' For all that he was a comic character, Clouseau didn't panic, he reasoned his way through a situation - not always with good results but that is where you can improve.

How do you get police officers to run towards danger while others are running away? You train them to know what to do. You put them in those situations in the classroom and run the scenarios so they have it in their heads. We all have the same human instinct of fear but that can be put to the side if they have practiced the scenario and have a plan to follow. Confidence comes with knowledge and experience.

I used to use briefings to run mock scenarios with my cops. I'd think of a situation I'd been in and ask what they would do. The discussion often resulted in the cops coming up with better solutions than the way I'd dealt with it. We all learned from it. I treated it like a game. We played the game in our heads so we were prepared when it happened for real.

Sometimes I played the game just for fun though.

One wet and windy night my shift were all back at the canteen for a warming bowl of soup and a cup of tea. It was unusual for it to be quiet enough for the entire shift to have a break together. Make the most of them when it happens. It was rare for eight of us to sit together in the one place at the one time.

It might be different nowadays when the whole shift always sit down together (both of them).

Anyway, we sat in the canteen, and I announced that we would play a game.

"Let's have a game," I suggested.

The shift looked at me as if I was daft; the pool table had long ago been taken away, the table tennis table was now being used in the production store to keep boxes off the floor. There were no darts for the dartboard, broken and never replaced. Nobody complained. Cops were too busy to engage in these type of pursuits when they got a break all they wanted to do was sit and rest because they never knew when they would get time to sit and rest again.

"What kind of game, Inspector?" Asked the sergeant.

"Let's play a word game."

"A word game?"

"Yes, a word game."

"What kind of word game?"

"I'll explain. I will pick a topic, let's say 'Animals'. Going in a clockwise direction around the room the first person has to say an animal and the next person has to say another animal beginning with the last letter of the animal that the person said. So if I said rhinoceros, then the next person would have to say an animal beginning with the letter 'S' simple. If you can't think of an animal, then you're out. You have five seconds to answer. Understand?"

Everyone in the canteen nodded their heads in agreement.

"Okay, the first topic is 'months of the year', sergeant, you can start."

"Um, March."

"Good, okay, you're next Mike."

Mike looked at me confused; everyone looked confused for a second or two as they ran through the months of the year in their heads. Then there was a general muttering of disgruntlement from everyone as their brains figured out it was an impossible task.

"Five, four, three, two, one. You're out."

Mike almost spat out his tea in indignation.

"What do you mean I'm out? How can I be out? There isn't a…"

I interrupted him.

"Look, you're out. No point in moaning about it. If you can't think of an answer in the time given, then you're out. That's the rules."

"But…"

"No 'buts', you're out."

The rest of the shift looked at me as if I had a bogie on my forehead.

"Okay," said the sergeant, "I'll think of a topic, and you go next."

The sergeant had spotted my ruse and decided that one-upmanship was the way to go.

"Okay."

"Right then! The topic is 'days of the week', I'll kick off with Friday, your turn, Inspector."

My sergeant looked smug. He eyed his shift and then started his countdown.

"Five, four…"

I smiled.

"Three, two, one."

"That's too easy," I said, "Yesterday!"

The shift burst out laughing.

"Aye, you'll need to get up earlier in the morning sergeant."

THE MICHAEL PARKINSON TELEVISION INTERVIEW

Parky: So, that is the secret? To become the most outstanding cop in the world, you have to be conscientious, unembarrassable and treat it like a game?'

Malky: Don't forget you have to be a good listener.

Parky: That makes perfect sense. Do you think that having those four traits will transfer to any occupation?

Malky: There is a good chance that those four behaviours are transferable to most occupations. They might not make you the most outstanding plumber in the world or the most outstanding mortician, but I dare say they might help.

Parky: Are those traits something that anyone can learn, do you think?

Malky: There are personality types who have an advantage, it is in their DNA. Although, it is possible for anyone to learn to get better by putting it into practice. Good listening skills come with practice; conscientiousness comes with effort, and anyone can start playing life like it is a game.

Parky: What about unembarrassability?

Malky: That is a little harder. Sometimes that is just in your personality; introvert or extrovert. Professor Richard Wiseman suggests that if you act like a certain person, you become that person. He called it the 'As if' principle.

Parky: Dunkers don't get embarrassed.

Malky: True, maybe if you want to get on you should act like a Dunker.

Parky: Is that why Dunkers sometimes rise through the ranks?

Malky: You might be on to something there. They think they are good listeners; they believe they are conscientious, and they don't get embarrassed.

Parky: Not many treat it like a game, though, do they?

Malky: Exactly, maybe that is the key to identifying whether someone is a Dunker of not.

Parky: Okay, if you could sum up all the advice we have talked about, what would you say to someone who wanted to be outstanding in any occupation, not just the police?

Malky: Two things spring to mind; have a backup plan and don't give a fuck about it or have absolutely nothing to fall back on and truly care about what you do.

Parky: Which one of those two do you fall into?

Chapter 20

GRUMPY OLD MAN

I'm not sure at what point I turned into a grumpy old man. I could have said - I'm not sure at which point I turned into my Dad - but that wouldn't be fair to him. Yes, he can be tetchy at times, but he is an awfully nice man. He is always pleased to see his kids and delighted when his grandkids turn up at his house uninvited.

"Hello, come in, how's about a cup of tea and a biscuit," he'll say, "Put the kettle on Maw."

My Dad keeps an empty tube of *Smarties* for each of his grandkids in a drawer in his study and puts a £1 coin in each one every Friday. When Grandkids pay a visit, they can take what is in their particular *Smartie* tube or a £10 note. It is always amusing to note that every grandchild knows precisely how long it has been since they last saw their Grandad.

My Dad, like most dads, never phones. So when my phone rings and the caller display reads *'Maw & Paw'*, I always pick up the phone and answer with a cheery, "Hi Mum."

"It's me, your Dad," said the voice on the other end.

"Is Mum okay?" I asked, concerned that she'd had another heart attack, fallen down the stairs or crashed her car somewhere. That was always a worry, my Mum, even at eighty-two, drives everywhere like Lewis Hamilton on a mission, which is quite a skill considering she drives a one-litre Suzuki Alto.

"Ha- ha!" my Dad said in as sarcastic a manner as he could muster, "We're going to Blackpool, and we need a lift."

"No problem, Dad, when are you going?"

He didn't need a lift all the way to Blackpool. Once a year they would book a coach holiday and the bus would pick them up at the Town Hall. My job was to pick them up at their house and convey them to their pick up point.

Exactly one week later I received my second call of the year from my Dad, this time on his mobile phone. He had a cheap old clamshell mobile. He didn't need a smartphone because he only used it twice a year. Once in January to test it still worked and once in the summer to call me to tell me he needed picked up at the Town Hall.

"It's me, your Dad," he said.

"Is Mum okay?"

"Ha- ha! We are on our way back up from Blackpool. We will be at the Town Hall about five o'clock."

"Okay Dad, no problem."

And at that, he switched off his mobile phone to conserve the battery.

The bus was delayed. I phoned my Dad's mobile at least a dozen times, each time the call went to his answer phone. He hadn't set it up correct so it would ring nine times then click through to his message:-

"I CAN'T GET THIS BLOODY THING TO WORK."

Then I had to wait a full sixty seconds listening to him tut-tutting while he clunked the phone on the table and had a moan to my Mum about technology being a bigger pain in the backside than haemorrhoids. A further click indicated I could leave a message. I didn't bother. He wouldn't be able to work the thing anyway.

When they eventually arrived, I stuffed their cases in the boot of the car and asked about their holiday.

"It was fine," my Mum would say.

Then my Dad would retell some jokes the hotel compère told while they played bingo.

"Did you know it was eczema awareness day last week?"

"No."

"No, neither did I," he laughed, "so they tried to raise money by selling scratch cards."

That was it. No hour long saga about the hotel being a dump (although it was). No massive monologue about the crappy British weather -and it was that too. Even on the odd occasion when the hotel was good and the weather scorching hot, all I got was, "It was fine."

That is my family. They are not pre-disposed to bore the living daylights out of everyone they meet with the further chronicles of Blackpool. There are no post-holiday parties where friends and neighbours are invited round to view several thousand pictures of out-of-focus seagulls and a beach or out-of-focus beaches and a seagull. Unlike Kenneth.

You might know someone like Kenneth. Kenneth was the invisible cop. The cop who spent his entire service doing nothing. Not a jot! Kenneth joined the police used up the two years of his probation watching his tutors do the job, the next five years watching his probationers do the job and then for some unfathomable reason he went in the huff. Perhaps his sergeant asked him to get his notebook out and take a statement, or an Inspector commented to him, in the passing, that he should tidy himself up. It would be something equally innocuous. Kenneth's huffing and puffing about the perceived slight on his character resulted in a Chief Inspector deciding to get rid of him. Kenneth transferred to a department, a department where he could remain invisible and do nothing for the rest of his service. Never heard of again. A police officer for thirty years without ever showing the least sign of enthusiasm.

That was until Kenneth retired.

As soon as Kenneth retired, he became the jobbie that wouldn't flush. Kenneth was everywhere. Facebook (with his holiday snaps), Instagram (with yet more holiday snaps) and Snapchat (that's okay though, I'm too old to get Snapchat).

I bumped into Kenneth in Tesco, and for half an hour I had to listen to how good a cop he was and how 'they' shafted him - who the faceless 'they' were he never said. He moaned about the job not being the same, then moaned about various people in various ranks that had done him a disservice. All the time I wondered what he had to say about me behind my back.

Without asking, Kenneth pulled out his phone and showed me pictures of his holiday snaps. I didn't need a three-minute running commentary on each photo - but he gave me a three minute running commentary anyway. I can look at an entire album in that time. He zoomed in on each picture as he thrust it in my face. I'm just not used to that kind of holiday scrutiny. After twenty minutes I was losing the will to live and interrupted him as I looked at my watch.

"Listen Kenneth, I need to get going. I have an appointment I need to get to. I wasn't lying. I did have a dentist appointment - the next week.

"Wait," he said, "You won't believe what happened to us, have a look at the next photo..."

A week later I bumped into Kenneth when I was walking the dog, he was out for a cycle. He spent half an hour boring me about the same old moans and groans he spoke about the last time we met in Tesco. I changed the subject.

"How often are you out for a cycle?"

"Every week," he said and his eyes lit up, "Today I started off at the house and went up the by-pass, then up round the Cathedral, blah, blah, blah. Then I carried on out the cycle network, that took me up to the dam, blah, blah, blah. Then I took the path through the forest and on up to blah, blah, blah..."

A few days later I bumped into Kenneth in the pub. I was about to buy a drink and without thinking I asked what he wanted, I was just too polite not to offer to buy him one.

Now I am his best friend.

He spent half an hour boring me about the same old moans and groans he spoke about the last time we met. I changed the subject.

"Have you been out for a cycle again?"

"Yup, I was out this morning. I started off at the house and went up the by-pass, then up round the Cathedral, blah, blah, blah. Then I carried on out the cycle network, that took me up to the dam, blah, blah, blah. Then I took the path through the forest and on up to blah, blah, blah..."

Geez!

Now, every time I meet Kenneth, he moans and groans about the police and then tells me every tiny detail of his last cycle.

It is good he goes for a cycle every week, it is good for his health, I am pleased for him. I am happy that Kenneth is keeping himself fit and healthy. My only annoyance is I don't need to know every last minuscule detail. I'm sure you will agree that he should keep it to himself unless he had something exciting to tell me.

- I got chased by a swan on the canal path.
- I came across an accident and had to drag a woman from a burning car.
- Thirteen vestal virgins were skinny dipping in the river.

But no. Nothing exciting ever happened. Kenneth cycled around the same countryside he cycled around every week and told me about it for the umpteenth time.

The next day I was back in Tesco's to get a couple of bits, and I bumped into Kenneth again. The jobbie that won't flush. I had another forty-five minutes of dreary moans and groans.

Give me that toilet brush, please.

The day after that, I took my car in for an M.O.T. I'll just wait I said. I had my book with me; I could happily sit and read for an hour while they checked my car over. You won't believe this but guess who walked in. Yup, Kenneth.

Kenneth plonked himself down beside me; I tried to act all engrossed in my book, but that didn't work.

"I've just booked up my holiday," said Kenneth interrupting my reading.

"That's nice."

"You will never guess where I am going."

"Where are you going?" I said, closing up my book and pointedly laying it on the table in front of me.

"Go on, guess."

"You just said I would never guess."

"Go on, guess."

"Okay, you are flying to Amsterdam to get a long-haul flight to Singapore, where you will spend three days at the Marriott before getting a connecting flight to Bali where you will stay at a five-star hotel with your own private hot tub in your bedroom. Then you will have a jungle safari before flying to Dubai where you have booked a champagne reception for your wife's birthday in the Burj Khalifa. Then you jump on a cruise ship and take a slow boat to China for a week, see the great wall, fly to Australia… "

"Um, no. We are going to Portugal."

"That's nice."

You may already know the meaning of, 'schadenfreude'. Schadenfreude is German for taking pleasure in someone else's misfortune. What a great word. There is no direct English translation for the word. There is, however, a direct translation into a Scottish word. The Scottish word for schadenfreude is 'getitupye'. The Scots, in fact, have two words for schadenfreude - 'getitupye' is the mild form of schadenfreude. The general taking pleasure from someone else's misfortune. The second more distinct form is 'getitrightupye' which generates a greater emphasis on the pleasure taken from the misfortune of another person. Thus if I were to see Kenneth trip and fall, I would think to myself, 'getitupye'. However, if I were to see Kenneth trip and fall and his face landed in a cow pie I would think to myself 'getitrightupye'.

Kenneth is still a human being and, despite him being the jobbie that won't flush, that thought stopped me from being ill-mannered. I kept my 'getitrightupye' thoughts to myself.

Kenneth didn't trip up in front of me; there were no cow pies lying in wait for him at the M.O.T. centre. Kenneth, in his annoying little way, bored me with a description of the holiday resort he was going to in Portugal. Five-star reviews on *Trip Advisor,* seven swimming pools, nine restaurants, ten-star entertainment, blah, blah, blah. Kenneth was rubbing it in - and he hadn't even been there yet. He promised to keep me posted.

"I'll send you a message on Facebook when I post the pictures; I'll try to do some every day, okay."

Not okay!!!

It was time for some getitrightupye revenge. It was time to set Kenneth up.

"So what part of Portugal are you going to?"

"We are flying to Faro then staying at the Dom Perignon Hotel and Spa in Lagos, right next to the marina."

"That's nice. Who are you flying with?"

"Air Generic."

"Is it just you and the wife that is going?"

"Yes, just me and the wife."

"That's nice. You know how to get an upgrade from them, yes?"

"An upgrade? No, how?"

"Don't tell everyone but if there are only two of you flying, you can get an upgrade if you ask for the right seats."

"What do you mean?"

"Well, it's like a code. I use it all the time, and it's never failed yet. I once got moved up to first class for a trip to New York."

"How? What do you do?" Kenneth's face was a picture of interest.

"It's simple, ask for seats 14a and 14c."

"Why?"

"That's the code."

"How is that the code?"

"Well, I think it has something to do with the fact you split up. People like to sit next to their family when they travel, they try to book seats together but can't because you have booked a seat apart. So they automatically move you to upgraded seats. It's the only way they can put a family together. They have to upgrade you."

"That makes sense."

"Of course it does. It is automatic. The airline recognises the code, and you get the upgrade."

"But I have already booked."

"That's okay, as soon as you get home, go online and change the booking."

"Can I do that?"

"Yeah, you can reserve those seats, it's only another £20 or something like that."

"What happens then?"

"They move you up to the first class cabin. I've had free champagne, free gourmet food and all sorts. One time we got free bottles of perfume and aftershave. They had all sorts of gifts you can choose from."

"And all I need to do is book those seats?"

"Well, there is one other thing."

"What's that?"

"You have to pre-order your food."

"Pre-order our food?"

"Yes, it's the last bit of the code. Order the Halal meal for you and a Vegetarian Lacto-Ovo Meal for your wife."

"Really, why?"

"Because your orders are so specific, the airline doesn't want to get it wrong. So they move you up to seats beside the stewards, and you get the best of service."

"Oh, right! That makes sense."

"Yup, but please don't let everyone know."

"Great, thanks. I'll try it."

Kenneth left thinking I was the best thing since sliced Bagels and jam.

A few days later Kenneth and his wife were at Glasgow airport drinking beer and cider. I know this because he posted a picture of each glass. Then he posted a picture of his breakfast. Next, there was the obligatory map showing the route his Air Generic aeroplane would take on its journey to Portugal.

I put my phone down, rolled over in bed and smiled to myself. I imagined Kenneth's wife leaning forward in seat

14a and suspiciously eyeing Kenneth in seat 14c. I even pictured the fat hairy man sitting in 14b. Kenneth's wife sitting the whole journey wondering why her husband had booked 14c for himself, instead of the seat beside her. Then I pictured the steward asking them which one was Halal and which was the Vegetarian Lacto-Ovo Meal? That brought a smile to my face and a chuckle to my belly.

THE MICHAEL PARKINSON TELEVISION INTERVIEW

Parky: Ho ho ho, I can't stop laughing. I have to try that.

Malky: Don't you dare, that is my wind up, I need it to keep me sane.

Parky: Ha ha ha. Okay, okay, my sides are sore.

Malky: Take your time, compose yourself.

Parky: Okay, right. Now then. Has there been anyone else that has annoyed you as much as Kenneth?

Chapter 21

SERGEANT MCBULLYBOY

There is good and bad in all of us.

You find good and bad in all walks of life. As reflected in society, there are good police officers and there are bad police officers. Some are the most dedicated and hardworking people, but there is also those who are lazy. There are intelligent officers worthy of Mensa membership; some not so bright. Some are kind-hearted, and there were those who are heartless, bullying, paranoid, schizophrenic spunktrumpets.

We live and die by our reputation. It is unfortunate that few people get to know their reputation. People are reluctant to tell you if you are an arsehole, so they beat about the bush, and the arsehole never gets to know. Even those with a great reputation rarely get to know; we are a nation that doesn't go in for high praise or ostentatious pats on the back. So those with a good reputation don't get enough praise, and those with a bad reputation don't hear how bad they are thus remain unchanged.

Then there are those who don't care about their reputation. Even if they got to hear of it, they wouldn't bother changing. That is fine if you have a reputation like Big Bob, nobody - not even the neds - said a bad word about Big Bob. Nobody said a bad word about Gentleman George or Sam Gordonson or Barbecue Bill. However, if you had a bad reputation (if you were lazy or crazy), it was often easier to not care what other people thought of you, and carry on being lazy and crazy.

My Mum told me I shouldn't care about what other people say about me. That differs from not giving two hoots about what kind of reputation you have. Which is a shame because if you are a bullying, paranoid, schizophrenic spunktrumpet, then you go through your life never having a close enough association with people willing enough to tell you to your face you are a bullying, paranoid schizophrenic, spunktrumpet. Thus your bullying and paranoia and spunk trumpery never get addressed. At least not by the people that matter.

That is what I experienced with Sergeant McBullyboy. Sergeant McBullyboy's reputation preceded him. I worked on the other side of the force to Sergeant McBullyboy, yet I had heard he was a bully, that he was paranoid and that he was not the nicest person to work with. When I first heard about him, he was a detective sergeant in the CID. Several officers complained about him - pretty much everyone that worked with him complained about him. Unfortunately, not all of them complained about him to senior management, but the ones who did found themselves conveniently transferred to another shift or another station so they didn't have to work with him.

When I received my promotion to sergeant, I got transferred to F division where Detective Sergeant McBullyboy worked. I didn't think much about him. I wouldn't have all that much dealings with him, and I always tried to take people as I found them. I believe it is a good way to be. Make your own opinions, and people will surprise you. DS McBullyboy couldn't possibly be as bad as everyone made out - surely?

I worked in F division for a few months and got to know my shift. I liked working with them, and I was just getting to grips with the new area and what my new job entailed. Then one morning, the first day back from my annual leave, PC Moustaffa asked me a question.

"Sarge, you know how there is a new order out telling us to write all our reports and send them to the typists to put on the computer for us, what is your opinion on that?"

Because I had been on holiday, I wasn't aware that the Chief Constable had sent out those instructions. The chief probably heard typists were not getting enough work and were twiddling their thumbs for part of their day. Before the introductions of computers, all reports went to typists. Technology moved on, and not everyone was computer illiterate. Younger cops spent more of their lives typing things on to a computer than they did writing. It is just the way of the world. Give a teenager a phone, and they can rattle off more words per minute with their thumb than a professional typist could ever hope to achieve.

I liked to have a common sense approach to policing. I remember people telling me when I joined that policing is all about common sense. Police officers should have common sense in abundance. Having a rational, reasonable and logical approach to things worked for me. I didn't always come up with the best solutions, but if someone else did and it made sense, I was always happy to change my decision or take the appropriate action because that was the common sense thing to do. I'll give you an example.

If you have thirteen heavy boxes on the ground floor of a building and you have to get them up to the twentieth floor. Because the boxes are so heavy, you can only lift two at a time. You take twenty minutes to carry two boxes up twenty flights of stairs but only nine minutes to carry one box up twenty flights of stairs. What do you do? The common sense answer is: take the elevator.

So when PC Moustaffa asked me the typing question, I reasoned this.

"Well, I know that some of you can type quicker than you can write. I am a slow writer and find it much easier and quicker to type my reports. I'm not bright enough to write a perfect report on my first attempt, so I like being able to amend it as I go. I find it is still quicker for me to type my reports than to write them. Therefore, if you can write your reports faster than you can type them, then you should write them and send them to the typists. If you can type your reports quicker than you can write them, I have no objection to you typing them."

It was my common sense approach. I didn't see sense in officers wasting time writing out a report longhand and sending it to a typist to get it back two weeks later when they could type it themselves in half the time and get it sent away that day.

There was a general nod of agreement from my shift, and PC Moustaffa looked happy.

The next morning Sergeant McBullyboy joined my shift as a temporary inspector. He was covering for my normal inspector who was off on annual leave. As I said, I like to take people as I find them so when he walked into my briefing, I welcomed him to the shift, and he sat down. I finished my briefing and turned to Temporary Inspector McBullyboy and asked him if he had anything to add.

"Yes," he said, and stood up behind the desk to face the shift, "I want to talk to all of you about typing your reports."

McBullyboy was an imposing figure. He was average height, but he was larger than average wide. He had dark hair and although clean shaven black bristles gave his face a dirty look as if he had wiped coal stained hands downs both cheeks and across his chin. The most intimidating thing about him was his hands. His hands extended out of his arms like a hammerhead shark. Great big bulbous paws. McBullyboy clenched his paws into fists and rested them on top of the desk. His furrowed brow made him look angry; he reminded me of a silverback gorilla defending its realm. It turned out he was angry.

"I'm angry," he said, "I hear that officers are typing their own reports. That is not on. We don't pay typists to sit on their backsides to admire the view."

McBullyboy ranted about it. The shift, in their entirety, turned their heads to look at me. It was the topic we had discussed the previous day. I had been clear on my answer to PC Moustaffa - I had taken the common sense approach. I didn't think there was anything else I could do but interrupt McBullyboy and explain my thought processes.

"Excuse me, Inspector. The shift asked me about this yesterday, and I already discussed it with them."

I explained my common sense approach.

As soon as I talked, I realised something was wrong. McBullyboy didn't look at me. His head bent down, and he stared at his clenched fists on the desk. I could see his fists tighten as his knuckles whitened. If that wasn't scary enough, he took deep breaths in and exhaled like a steam engine. Was this technique to prevent him going into a tantrum? It didn't seem to calm him any. His neck muscles tightened, and the tendons became more pronounced. We looked at each other quizzical and worried. It was like waiting for a volcano to explode and we had nowhere to run.

After my explanation to McBullyboy, I waited for his response. There was none. He stood there glaring at his fists on the desk, not saying a word. I waited a minute or two, and when still nothing happened, I decided it best to get the shift out. I opened the briefing room door, and McBullyboy turned and walked out, not once did he look me in the eye.

Had I been out of order? Was my reasoned explanation disrespectful? I knew McBullyboy was with my group for two weeks while my inspector was on holiday and it would be a long two weeks if he was going to be like this. I waited half an hour, plucked up courage and went to see McBullyboy in his office.

With any normal person I would have expected to have had a quick chat, and he would have agreed with my common sense approach, and that would be that. I realised that I wasn't dealing with a normal person. McBullyboy was a dam turbine with a gasket glued shut. At some stage, the build up of pressure would burst through, and I didn't want to be in the immediate vicinity when it did. I expected the conversation to go like this:-

"Inspector, sorry to bother you. I thought I had better come and see you and have a chat because I got the distinct impression you weren't happy with me during the briefing."

"No, Malky I wasn't happy. I was trying to make the point that we aren't using our typists enough when you interrupted me."

"I'm sorry, Inspector. It was just that I had gone over it with the shift yesterday and my opinion, based on common sense, was that it was more important that they save time."

"The Chief Constable will not be happy with that, not when he is paying typists."

"Yes, I understand, but if half the shift is quicker at typing, I would rather they typed their reports. It means they will spend less time in the office and get more done."

"I get where you are coming from. I would rather we took a more efficient approach as well but we are a

disciplined organisation, and sometimes, even when things make little sense, we just have to follow orders."

"Yes, I appreciate that point of view. Are you instructing me to tell them all to write their reports from now on, even although it will take them longer?"

"You know what, Malky. Let's just leave it at that. We have passed on the instruction, but it is not the Chief Constable who has to go out and deal with all the calls, is it? If half of them take longer to write their reports, then we could end up paying overtime. I think I'd rather they spent their time out there catching the bad guys than wasting time in here doing paperwork in slow time."

"Yes, thank you, Inspector."

But that wasn't how the conversation went. This is how the conversation went:

"Inspector, sorry to bother you. I thought I had better come and see you and have a chat because I got the distinct impression you weren't happy with me during the briefing."

McBullyboy didn't look up from his desk. He did that silverback gorilla thing again. Standing up, clenching his fists and leaning on them as he placed them on his desk. Then came the breathing. Loud exhales in and out like a steam train. I could almost see the fire explode from his nostrils as they flared in and out. His brow had more furrows than a tattie field, and the veins in his neck stood out. I'll admit it; I was scared - scared that he would turn around and pummel me with his big meaty paws. I have no doubt that was what he was thinking. My fight-or-flight response kicked in, adrenalin pumped through me, and my pulse quickened.

McBullyboy just stood there, fists planted on the desk glaring at them. He didn't say a word. The only thing I heard was his loud inhalations and louder exhalations. Like a bull waiting to go into the ring. What the fuck was wrong with this man?

I turned and left.

Honestly, that incident prayed on my mind for the rest of the day. I couldn't sleep that night. I kept turning things over in my head. What could I have done differently? Was that anyway for an Inspector to behave? Was he like this with everyone? Was this how he would be the whole time I worked with him? What was wrong with him?

Even when I think about it now, I find it hard to comprehend what was going on in McBullyboy's mind. Anger management issues? An overreaction? Did I misinterpret the situation? I'm just not sure. I got the impression that McBullyboy would need to buy a new alarm clock every morning and I pictured him at sunrise standing at his window telling the birds to fuck off. He wasn't a doggy person; everybody loves dogs - he wanted them all dead. I think he was the type to keep a loaded gun handy in case he heard someone slurp their tea.

In the end, I needn't have worried. McBullyboy tripped over a toy in his garden and went off sick in the huff for two years. It was something like that, anyway. I don't know the full details.

Skip forward a few years, bird flu hit Scotland, Daniel Craig made his debut as James Bond, and Shakira's hips were telling the truth. The big news, though, I only went and got myself promoted - say hello to Inspector McEwan. I was back working at F Division. The station I had worked at when McBullyboy had been my temporary inspector. He wasn't there anymore. Finally he stopped sulking and returned to work as a sergeant. The bosses moved him from the CID and placed him at a smaller station in the division. That suited me just fine. I wouldn't have to work with him. I still felt sorry for those that did. Maybe that was harsh, perhaps he'd changed? After two years off in the huff, he might have mellowed. There was the distinct possibility that our Health and Wellbeing Department arranged treatment for him or even that he obtained counselling on his own. I don't know - but I'm forever the optimist. I put him to the back of my mind. I had a job to do.

I had to supervise the constables and sergeants on my group. I had to take charge of major incidents as they arose and I had to deal with complaints about the police.

Guess who the subject of my first complaint about the police was?

'Edgy' Eddie Eccles was a toerag. He had a criminal record that spanned many decades and rivalled War and Peace for its length. Raised on the south side of London, Eddie slipped into the family business with ease. The family business being all things criminal; especially falsehood, fraud and wilful imposition. Such was his offending that the law of averages meant he was sometimes in the wrong place at the wrong time. Occasionally he got caught. On average he spent half his life living it at Her Majesty's Pleasure. Eddie was a despicable scroat of the highest order, and as a result of him falling foul of the 'honour amongst thieves' code, he found himself banished from his birthplace. Even the despicable scroats of London couldn't be doing with him. Eddie moved to greener pastures and found himself a little council flat in a small town in F Division.

It wasn't long before Eddie came to our attention. He became the suspect of several thefts in the area that started up not long after he arrived. Local officers interviewed him at length but got nowhere. Eddie was as fly as they came.

"I'm here to keep my nose clean," he told them, "I got out of London to start a new life, I'm done with crime."

It was several months before two determined detectives managed to get enough evidence to pin a housebreaking (burglary) on him. As soon as they charged him, Eddie instructed his lawyer to send in a complaint to the police. Eddie ignited his smoke screen. His complaint passed down the line and, as the new inspector, I got the dubious privilege of investigating his complaint. It wasn't just one complaint; there were twenty different complaints about police officers. Twenty separate incidents. Eddie complained about every single time he had come into contact with the police in our area.

To speed along my investigation, I emailed each of the officers concerned, told them what Eddie alleged and asked for their response in the form of an operational statement. In the meantime I checked things like CCTV. The first complaint I could dismiss as complete bunkum. Eddie alleged officers had assaulted him in the High Street. CCTV showed two officers assisting a drunk Eddie to his feet after he had fallen. They had then waited with him until an ambulance arrived and they helped him on board. In fact, all his complaints were easy to dispute. Some independent witnesses rubbished Eddie's allegations. There were inaccuracies in Eddie's statement; Eddie said an officer swore at him and called him a 'Cockney' something or other, a picture of the officer being kissed by Minnie Mouse in Florida at the time proved otherwise.

There was only one police statement I had to chase up - that of Sergeant McBullyboy. Eddie alleged that Sergeant McBullyboy swore at him, grabbed him by the scruff of the neck and threw him out his office. I tried not to make any snap judgements. Sergeant McBullyboy ignored my request to provide his statement, I emailed him three times, but it wasn't until I phoned him and threatened to speak to the superintendent about him that he submitted it. When it arrived, it was in the form of a memo, not the proper statement format; that seemed odd. It was also full of spelling mistakes and grammatical errors, which doesn't necessarily make you a bad person (I'm no Charles Dickens). Sergeant Bullyboy's closing paragraph stated that if had he known 'Edgy' Eddie Eccles was going to complain about him he would have locked him up. The tone of it was somewhat threatening. I gave McBullyboy a call. I informed him he might like to put his statement in the proper format and asked if he was sure about the tone (hint, hint).

Some people just can't take a hint, can they?

> *"What's your email address?"*
> *"www.goawayandneverspeaktomeagain.com"*
> *"w w w dot gee oh ay… what was the next bit?"*

Sad to say Sgt McBullyboy decided that his memo was in the appropriate format, refused to provide a proper statement and was adamant if he ever saw 'Edgy' Eddie again, he would lock him up. I submitted my report. I could prove nineteen of the complaints were complete nonsense, a smoke screen. Only the complaint Eddy made about Sgt McBullyboy smacked of being true. In due course, the Professional Standards Department sent a letter to 'Edgy' Eddie. It listed twenty separate complaints from him and detailed why each was unfounded. They dismissed the complaint against McBullyboy on the basis that as the other nineteen were disproved the likelihood was this was nonsense too.

A police force is forever evolving. People retire, people get promoted, and people transfer to different jobs. Personnel shuffle around to fill the gaps. I had been at F Division for nearly two years and felt settled. I was enjoying coming across things I had already dealt with and knowing what to do made me feel competent. I'd been there long enough to feel ownership of the problems. Not there long enough yet to feel bored or disillusioned with the place. I got the phone call at home.

"Malky, Chief Superintendent Gordonson here."

"Hello, sir." My brain was whirring away. Chief Superintendents do not routinely phone inspectors at home. What had I done wrong? Was something happening, and they needed me? Had one of my shift got into trouble? Do monkeys eat chocolate?

"Malky, I am looking to sound you out to see if you would be willing to transfer to S Division."

Ah, transfer news just in!. Good in the respect I had done nothing wrong, something wasn't happening. they didn't need me to come in and one of my shift hadn't got into trouble. I still didn't know if monkeys ate chocolate but all things considered I was better informed.

"We are a disciplined organisation, sir. I will go where I am told to go." I was happy in F division, enjoying my role - but I don't like to say 'no'.

Off I went to S Division. I had worked there before as a sergeant, and it was closer to home, so I didn't mind, not really. It was a bigger area, and occasionally I had to attend calls that required a two-hour drive. In those situations, I relied on what sergeants and cops told me. On one occasion a call came in from a holidaymaker who had seen what appeared to be an unexploded shell lying in two feet of water at the side of a loch. The only road into and out of the area ran next to the side of the loch some twenty yards away from where the shell bobbed in the water. A cop described the shell over the radio.

"What do you want done, inspector?"

I had to go on the information they told me. The closest he could get to the device, without getting wet, was about ten feet. The young cop confirmed that the device he saw looked like the tip of an explosive shell. It was cylindrical with a pointy end. It was about three inches wide, and about half of it was poking out of the water. He estimated it to be about twelve to eighteen inches. What to do?

Here is more information for you:-

It was evening and would be dark in about two hours.
The road served three towns and some small villages.
About two hundred cars, vans and lorries would pass by the side of the loch every hour. It might be quieter during the night, but it would get busy again by first light.
The EOD (Bomb Disposal Unit) would not arrive until the next day.
The shortest detour for cars unable to use the road was a distance of one hundred and forty miles.

So you see the problem.

The sergeant in charge of the area was only about half an hour away when the call came in, so he arrived just as I heard about it. They had already decided on an exclusion zone and instructed that no-one was to approach the device, cops were to stay off the shore and remain on the roadway at least twenty yards away and ensure that cars could pass.

Here is a tip for all supervisors in these situations. Cops need to do something even if it is nothing.

"Just stand there and make sure nobody gets closer than twenty yards."

Now they are doing something. Still standing around doing nothing much - but standing around with a purpose.

The second tip in these situations is - extend the cordon or exclusion zone.

Let's face it; I don't know if twenty yards is a safe enough distance for cops to stand or for cars to pass. I wasn't about to find out. I radioed in my instructions.

"I want an exclusion zone of one hundred yards either side of the device."

"Inspector, that means we will have to block the road and turn traffic back."

"That's correct. Do it and do it now. Nobody is to go anywhere near that device, and I mean nobody. Nobody is to drive past that road, not without my express permission."

Now they really had something to do. They had to figure out how to go about it, and that would keep them busy. Be clear about what they have to do.

Before I left the office, the sergeant sent me a picture of the device in the water. It did look like an unexploded shell. I was right to have believed the description given by the cop and my decision to extend the exclusion zone was spot on. No-one would die on my watch.

Two minutes later the sergeant called me on my radio.

"It's okay Inspector; it's just a toy."

"A what?"

"It is the head of a plastic toy. It just looked like a shell when it was sitting in the water."

The sergeant had put on a pair of wellies and waded out to see what it was. He used a pencil to tip it up and only then did he realise it was just a toy. On the one hand, I was glad he had resolved the situation on the other...

"Bring it down and let me see it, please."

I didn't need to see it, but I decided that would be his punishment for ignoring my instructions not to go anywhere near the device. I didn't need to give him a telling off after that, his two-hour round trip to show me what it was would be enough.

These things happen from time to time. Situations arise that create problems which can escalate into major incidents. Along comes a practical sergeant and solves it before it takes up a lot of time and effort. They might go against orders or procedures, but they have the best interests of the job at heart. On those occasions, it is often best not to make a fuss.

Things were ticking along nicely. I settled into S Division, and I got a new sergeant. A good guy. I knew he was a good guy because I worked with him before. Sergeant McNevis had just completed his sixth-month stint as Temporary Inspector working in the same office as me. I took over the helm from him. I got my handover from him. Thus I knew he was thorough and dedicated. I couldn't ask for a better sergeant although I knew it would just be a matter of time before he would be promoted and move on. Then I discovered who his replacement would be. Yup, Sgt McBullyboy was being made up to Temporary Inspector - again! He would work from my office as the spare Inspector. I would have to sit next to him most of the day when day shift and half the day when back shift unless he was covering for another inspector.

His first week as Temporary Inspector went fine. No issues. We politely sat getting on with our work. The problems didn't start until he was into his second week.

Sgt McNevis came into my office and shut the door. Never a good sign. His face said it all; he was flushed and angry.

"If that bastard ever speaks to me like that again, I'm going to put him on paper."

"Who? What happened?" I could guess, but it was a good ploy to let Sgt McNevis get it off his chest.

"McBullyboy. I was sitting getting on with my work in the sergeant's office when he came in and started his nonsense."

"What did he say?"

"He accused me of not getting the information he requested. For a start, he should do that himself. I mean I have just vacated his seat, and I did all that stuff myself."

I wondered if McBullyboy had asked him because Sergeant McNevis would know what he was doing.

"What did he ask you to do?"

It turned out to be research he really should have done himself. The thing was Sergeant McNevis was a good guy and obliging. He agreed to do it but had some urgent work to complete before he got started on it. The job McBullyboy had asked him to do wasn't required for a fortnight, so there was no hurry. I wondered why he was putting pressure on my sergeant. The work wasn't the real issue for Sergeant McNevis, though, it was the way McBullyboy had spoken to him. McBullyboy's attitude and manner left a lot to be desired. He might get away with that with young cops, but he shouldn't be speaking to a sergeant in that manner. Frankly, he was ignorant and unprofessional. Harrying people is not a good management style.

"Would you like me to take this further?" I asked Sergeant McNevis.

"No."

"I feel I should do something about it, now you have made me aware."

"No. I don't want you to do anything. I will just bear it in mind."

"If you don't want me to take it further, then the least I will do is speak to him about it."

"No. Don't get involved. Leave it. I don't want anything done."

"I don't know if I can. You are a valuable member of our team, and I don't want anyone speaking to you like that."

"No. It's okay. Just leave it."

"Are you sure?"

"I'm sure. But I can tell you this, if that bastard speaks to me like that again, I am going to put him on paper."

I considered the position. McBullyboy was out of order, and I should do something about it. Sergeant McNevis was adamant he didn't want me to do anything about it. Torn between doing my duty and my loyalty to Sergeant McNevis, who saw it as something he should deal with himself.

A day later, I sat in my office with McBullyboy in the chair opposite. We were on our respective computers doing what inspectors do. (We had to; they had taken solitaire off all computers throughout the force).

A cop wandered in and asked me a question. On his way out he shut the office door. McBullyboy and I were now behind closed doors. I decided now was the time to talk to him regarding the manner in which he had spoken to Sergeant McNevis. I did this for three reasons. First, I should do something about the fact he had been discourteous to a fellow officer. Sergeant McNevis had made me aware, and I had a responsibility to do something. Despite Sergeant McNevis being adamant he didn't want me to do anything, I felt it was still my place to do something. Second, I felt that McBullyboy was the way he was because no-one stood up to him. He got away with it, so he kept doing it. Last, I was going on holiday in two weeks, and McBullyboy was covering for me. I didn't want there to be any friction on the shift.

I didn't know McBullyboy all that well. What I knew was that he had been a sergeant, and he was now in his second stint as a temporary inspector. He must be highly thought of by someone. He must have a professionalism and leadership ability to have achieved that. I expected the conversation I was about to have with him to be short and reasonable. I expected him to see my point of view, to see why I had to raise it with him and that he would understand that I was keen to ensure that there would be no issues when he covered my shift.

"Can I have a word?" I asked him.

"What is it?"

"I thought I would take the opportunity because you are taking over my shift when I go on holiday in two weeks, and I don't want there to be any friction between you and Sergeant McNevis."

"What do you mean?"

"Sergeant McNevis told me, in confidence, you had an altercation with him yesterday."

"What the fuck has he said, like?"

"He wasn't happy with the way you spoke to him."

"I'll speak to him how I like."

"That's not very professional is it? Don't forget he just finished in the role you are doing now, and he is a good sergeant. He didn't have to agree to do what you asked him to do, but he was still going to do it. The only reason I thought I would mention it is to ensure that there are no problems when you cover my group."

"I'll speak to him how I like."

"Well, if you do, you will end up being put on paper."

"What do you mean?"

"If you speak to Sergeant McNevis in the same manner you spoke to him yesterday he will put a complaint in about you."

McBullyboy rose from his chair, his brow furrowed, his fists clenched and he planted them on the desk in front of him. The silverback gorilla was back. An intimidating pose, angry and menacing.

"He'll put me on paper? I'll put him on paper!"

"Look, just calm down. All I am trying to do here is prevent any friction between the two of you. If I had known you would be like this, I would never have mentioned it."

"Are you finished? Are you finished?"

"Listen, this is just a quiet word in your ear. Nothing more."

"Are you finished? Cos I'm going to put him on paper"

"What are you going to put him on paper for?"

"Are you finished? Are you finished?"

"How do you think it will look when you put him on paper just because he is going to put you on paper for your behaviour? You are just going to draw attention to yourself and your poor management skills."

"Are you finished? Are you finished?"

Now I was getting a little tetchy. As threatening as McBullyboy appeared, I wasn't going to put up with his antics anymore. I'd have a more reasonable conversation with a hungry crocodile. I'd had enough. I stood up too, and I planted my fists on the desk in front of me.

"It is exactly this bullying attitude of yours that people object to. That is no way to speak to anyone, especially those who work for you. I sat down to have a quiet word, inspector to inspector, to save any hassle when I am away on holiday, simple as that. You have completely taken it out of proportion, you are the one who has lost the plot, and you want to put him on paper?"

"As an inspector to an inspector, you should be telling me this."

"I can tell you, that I will not be telling you anything like this ever again."

"I am going to speak to the Chief Inspector about him."

"Really? You will run away to the Chief Inspector to tell him that someone is going to put you on paper if you speak to them in a rude and impolite manner again? You are just going to confirm to the Chief Inspector what we all know"

"Are you finished? Are you finished?"

"No, I'm not. You have just blown it with me. I will never let you into my confidence again because you are a totally irrational…"

I stopped myself before I called him a 'bullying, paranoid schizophrenic, spunktrumpet'.

"Are you finished? Are you finished?"

"No. Sergeant McNevis didn't want to put you on paper, but if I hear you speak to him or any other member of staff like that again, it will be me who puts you on paper. This job doesn't need…"

"What, c'mon what?" he stretched his head forward, straining the veins in his neck. A threatening move, a precursor to letting loose with his fists. A move designed to frighten me and make me back off.

"… this job doesn't need bullying, paranoid, schizophrenic, spumktrumpets like you!" I didn't care. It needed said. If it tipped him over the edge then he better be good - because I was ready for a fight.

"Are you finished? Are you finished?"

"No, I'm still not finished. Sergeant McNevis is my sergeant, if you want him or any of my staff to do anything for you, then you will have to come through me. I'm not having you speaking to any of my staff like that again."

"I'm going to speak to the Chief Inspector, and we'll see what he says."

"Good, because the Chief Inspector deserves to see what you are like."

"Are you finished? Are you finished?"

"Yes. Now I'm finished."

McBullyboy stormed out the door, straight through to the sergeant's office and grabbed one of the other sergeants that had been present when he had spoken to Sergeant McNevis. He bullied him a little and then went to the chief inspector. There was a furore of gossip that didn't quite evolve into a scandal. The Chief Inspector spoke to everyone involved. I felt bad. Sergeant McNevis asked me not to do anything, and I did, and it had failed spectacularly. The only good thing about it was the incident identified to the bosses that McBullyboy was a bullying, paranoid schizophrenic, spunktrumpet. I didn't doubt that now, through his own doing, he would finish his temporary inspector stint, transfer back to his old station and live out the rest of his police career as a sergeant.

How wrong was I?

They promoted McBullyboy a few months later. They transferred him to a department, and ten months later they promoted him again to chief inspector. How could that be? I understood that our force policy was we had to be in a rank for at least one full year before they could promote you again. It turned out that that policy changed. Who changed it? Well, guess what? The department McBullyboy transferred to as inspector was the department in charge of that change to the policy!

Maybe the problem was that bully boys found their way to the top - the very top. All eight Scottish forces were due to merge in April 2013. The Scottish Government announced as early as September 2012 that the new Chief Constable of Scotland would be Stephen House, the then Chief Constable of Strathclyde. House had a somewhat fearsome reputation. Wikipedia cites he has few interests outside his job and family, other than hill walking and reading science fiction. He is a keen motorcyclist and turned up unannounced at police stations on a motorcycle when he was Chief Constable of Strathclyde Police.

Rarely did the troops get any warning of his visit. If they got notification he was coming he would be nowhere near on time or not turn up at all (I had personal experience of that - on the second occasion I didn't bother waiting in for him).

One day in January 2013 the new Chief Constable for Scotland rode in on his motorbike to a small police office in Fife. He dismounted entered the office, removed his helmet and jacket. He only had his black wicking T-shirt on underneath. It displayed his shoulder crowns, but those were the only real sign of his exalted status.

The office clerk met the Chief Constable. She did not recognise him as he hadn't worked in her area before but she noticed the crowns on his shoulder. Guessing he was someone of much importance she ushered him through to the highest ranking officer in the station, Sergeant Smart.

The future Chief Constable of Police Scotland entered Sergeant Smart's office to find him with his feet up on his desk, leaning back in his chair and conversing on his mobile phone. The Chief Constable was put out and reddened about the neck as Sergeant Smart nonchalantly stuck two fingers up at the new Chief Constable of Scotland to indicate that he would be a couple of minutes.

Sergeant Smart continued his conversation on the phone - he was booking his car into the local garage for a service. The Chief Constable's neck reddened even more. Sergeant Smart remained in his relaxed position with his feet on his desk and pointed the Chief Constable to the vacant chair in front of him.

The Chief Constable screwed up his face, his anger spreading in flared veins across his brow. He moved to the front of the sergeant's desk and stood there glowering down at him, muscles tensed, veins in his neck bulging. Sergeant Smart. Sergeant Smart wasn't intimidated, he didn't put his phone down. His feet remained firmly planted on the desk. He simply turned his head away and looked out the window as he continued his phone call.

By the time the Sergeant Smart finished his call the new Chief Constable for Scotland was livid. Enraged, incensed and showing it.

"DO YOU NOT KNOW WHO I AM?" the new Chief Constable demanded of Sergeant Smart.

Sergeant Smart remained nonplussed. His feet still on the desk, he calmly stated that he did not know who was standing before him and that it would be nice if he introduced himself.

"I AM YOUR CHIEF CONSTABLE, AND I EXPECT MY SERGEANTS TO SHOW MORE RESPECT THAN THIS" his raised voice full of anger.

"You are not my Chief Constable, I think I'd recognise my Chief Constable.You must be the new Chief Constable of Scotland," Sergeant Smart surmised, still calm. "But we don't amalgamate until April, and since this is only January, you are not my Chief Constable yet."

Stephen House was even more infuriated that he had not got the desired reaction.

"MY GOD." He yelled. "I HAVE NEVER MET SUCH AN INSOLENT OFFICER IN ALL MY YEARS. ARE ALL THE SERGEANTS IN FIFE AS DOWNRIGHT IMPERTINENT AS YOU?"

"I don't know," Sergeant Smart smiled, "are all the Sergeants in Fife retiring next Friday as well?"

THE MICHAEL PARKINSON TELEVISION INTERVIEW

Parky: Do you feel better getting that off your chest?

Malky: I'm not sure. I worry that someone will tell Sergeant McBullyboy or the ex-Chief Constable about it and their blood pressure will go through the roof. I could be responsible for giving them a heart attack.

Parky: You wouldn't say that it is their fault for doing it in the first place?

Malky: It's not that, I worry that it might not even be what people want to read.

Parky: I think it is. I think people will find it silly and learn from it, don't you?

Malky: Yes, but my next chapter is so much funnier.

Parky: Do you think you worry too much?

Malky: Probably.

Parky: You promised to enlighten us as to why we should never keep a kiwi under the bed.

Malky: Yes, I did mention it.

Parky: I am intrigued.

Chapter 22

NEVER KEEP A KIWI UNDER THE BED

The Police Treatment Centres is a charitable organisation supported by voluntary donations from serving and retired officers. The charity provides two treatment centres where serving and retired police officers can receive recuperation and treatment following an illness or injury. I'm not sure why but some officers don't contribute to this worthwhile cause. When I joined the police, the recruiting sergeant laid a bunch of forms in front of me and asked me to sign each one on the bottom line. He then shuffled them back up, and ten years later I received a cheque from the Police Mutual Assurance Society (PMAS) when a 'ten-year money-spinner' investment matured. Just one of the monthly payments he had elicited from me.

Amongst the other monthly outgoings I'd signed up for was £2 for the Benevolent Fund, 75p for the Police Retirement Fund, £4 for the Police Club and £9.20 for the Police Federation. There was £1 for the Prize Draw (although I think I might have been duped into that later in my service), 87p for the St Georges Fund and £4 for the Convalescent Homes.

These payments came straight out of my wages at the source, so I didn't notice them. Probably recruiting sergeants are much less inclined to hoodwink new starts into signing up for these things nowadays, which might explain why some officers aren't contributors. However, it is not until you go to the Police Treatment Centres that you appreciate just how important it is to donate.

The Police Treatment Centre in Scotland sits in a quietish town in the rolling green countryside near Gleneagles Hotel, Spa and Golf Resort. The centre itself sits in idyllic well-kept grounds and provides officers with a place to go when they are recovering from injuries, operations and the like.

Age doesn't come itself. Towards the end of my service I hurt my back   - bending down to tie my shoelaces. My doctor decided that I required physiotherapy and instead of putting me on an NHS list and waiting for the world to end he suggested I go to the Police Treatment Centre. He signed a letter which stated that an intensive course of physiotherapy would benefit me.

It was the year when Colin Firth stuttered his way through *The King's Speech,* and Tony Blair looked decidedly dodgy in his interview during the Chilcot enquiry into the Iraq war. I drove to the Police Treatment Centre listening to the popular beat combos of Calvin Harris and Ed Sheeran. Adele also spun her magic by setting fire to the rain. I wasn't sure what the Police Treatment Centre would be like, but colleagues, who had been there, assured me it was, 'fecking brilliant!'

As a new admission, they showed me to my room, I unpacked and headed back to the TV lounge for induction. I didn't know a soul in the place. I take a little time to get to know people before I come out of my shell. Thus I sat on a chair at the back of the room, like a wallflower, and eyed my fellow patients, looking for a likely candidate that might have the same interests as me. Someone who could play snooker, have a laugh and perhaps enjoy an occasional pint in the pub.

A member of staff entered and began our introduction to the Treatment Centre. It was all very pleasant until he laid down the rules: No alcohol - a gasp went up from the gathering. There is a strict no-alcohol policy at the Police Treatment Centres, which makes sense. People are there to recuperate and recover. There may well be patients there because of alcohol dependency, so it wasn't just discouraged it was expressly forbidden. Anyone caught possessing alcohol would be grabbed by the scruff of their neck and marched off the premises. There were other rules too: No running in the corridor, no petting in the pool, no walking in the library and silence on the grass. I think they said; no talking with your mouth full, no elbows on the table and no batteries in the remote control - things like that, but after the first announcement I wasn't sure if I got the rest correct.

To encourage everyone to make new friends, the Police Treatment Centres operate a table plan for dinner. I imagine they choose our names at random, but we sat at a table with the same people all week.

I was second to arrive for lunch; Harry was already there taking up one and a half spaces at the table. Sergeant Harry O'Hare was a big strapping lad with a bald head and *Frank Zappa* (horseshoe) moustache. His general countenance best described as 'hangdog'. His moustache gave him an upside down smile that conveyed a mixture of misery and self-pity. His stony facial expression was of a dreary melancholy that never wavered. He looked like a cross between a depressed bulldog and a suicidal rugby player. My first impression was that it would be best to avoid him. I was there to recuperate and hopefully enjoy a week of rehabilitation. I didn't want saddled with the company of a dour and depressing misery guts. But there I was, sitting directly opposite Deputy Dawg. I had to sit there for the rest of the week, breakfast, lunch and dinner. How on earth was I going to survive?

The table sat four people and in due course Helen, a retired detective inspector and Wendy, a rather large serving officer in the Highlands sat down beside us, guided by the seating table at the entrance to the restaurant.

I initiated some polite conversation, and we exchanged names, years' service, places worked and injuries.

Helen had had a fascinating and exciting career in Special Branch, so fascinating and exciting that she wasn't allowed to talk about it - even although she retired three years previous. Still, I was impressed with her tales of the afterlife - life after the Polis. When she retired, Helen had taken time out to travel the world. She had decided that beach holidays and normal tourist destinations were not for her. So Helen stuck a pin on a map and went there. It turns out it takes about thirty pins to find a place you can actually go to (the earth is seventy percent ocean, thirty percent desert, ten percent ice, and five percent charity shops - so by my calculations that leaves a nice little place in the

Cotswolds). Helen regaled us with stories of the weird and wonderful places she had been, and it made me want to get up and see for myself - except maybe the place she went in Belarus - her diarrhoea story was perhaps inappropriate lunch conversation.

Wendy was quite a big girl. If she went to the pub, I'd be right behind her, which would be a good hiding place. She was gay in all senses of the word. Bouncy, bubbly, joyful, exuberant and animated. She enthused about everything, the Police Treatment Centre, the food, the weather, the nice cutlery and even the job. I wondered if she was bi-polar.

Harry was rather monotone, and it wasn't until Helen asked him, "What's the matter Harry?" that he opened up.

Helen assumed, from Harry's normal hangdog expression, that there was something wrong. It wasn't until he started talking that I realised he had a mischievousness sparkle in his eyes. With a poker-faced delivery, Harry told us what the matter was.

"Well it all started two years ago," he said, "I was involved in a road accident and broke my arm."

Harry demonstrated how he couldn't raise his arm any higher than to put the cup he was drinking his tea from up to his mouth.

"I was on night shift, and I got patched up at the hospital and taken home. When I arrived home, I saw a strange car in my driveway, and it was only then I realised my wife had been having an affair."

Helen sympathised, "Oh Harry, that's awful!"

Wendy joined in, "How dreadful - what did you do?"

I wouldn't like to have been the guy that came face to face with Harry after being caught in bed with his wife - broken arm or not.

Harry continued, "Well we tried to patch things up, but it was no use. After about another year we got ourselves a divorce. I had to move out the family house. I gave up half my future pension and had to pay her half my wages. I couldn't afford to buy another house, so I had to move back in with my parents for a little while. They had moved to a smaller house, so I ended up sleeping on the couch."

Wendy nodded with compassion.

"Then about nine months ago I got myself a small flat. My wife still wouldn't let me have access to the kids, but she let me have my dog. I loved my dog, but it still didn't make up for not seeing my two daughters."

Now Harry was pulling on the heart strings, and Helen and Wendy's gazes never left his face as his story unfolded.

"Then my Dad had a heart attack and died. He was the main carer for my Mum who suffers dementia, and I had to put her into a home. Every penny they had has gone to pay for her care."

Helen looked angry, "Damn the government, they'd steal your last meal."

"Then I had a fire in my flat, and it destroyed all the pictures I had of my kids."

Harry was laying it on now. Wendy and Helen remained engrossed in his story.

"Then my car got stolen."

Geez, you're an unlucky bastard

"Then my wife emigrated to Australia with the kids, and I don't think I will ever see them again."

The concern shown by Helen and Wendy was touching (yes they touched him to comfort the poor soul).

"Then to cap it all my dog died."

Wendy and Helen groaned in unison as if they had just slipped a disc.

With the most hangdog expression of all, Mike then told them, "I had no choice. Even although it was my wife who had the affair I got taken to the cleaners. I'd slept on a couch, didn't have access to my kids, my Dad died, and my Mum was in a home. I had a fire in my flat and to top it all my dog died. There was only one thing left for me to do."

"OH MY GOD!" Wendy said as her jaw dropped.

"What did you do? Asked Helen, with nothing but concern in her voice.

"I took twenty Paracetamol."

"THEN what happened?" Helen asked as she grabbed Harry's arm with both hands.

Harry stood up from his chair, spread his arms wide and smiled for the first time.

"OH, I FELT A LOT BETTER!" he declared.

I burst out laughing so hard I regurgitated my rhubarb tart and custard. There was a little confusion from Helen and Wendy, for a second or two, before they too joined in the merriment.

I had an enjoyable stay at the Police Treatment Centre. Sergeant Harry O'Hare was delightfully hangdog in his expression all week but full of mischief and fun. One evening, during a quieter moment, we sat chatting in the library. I asked Harry why he was at the Police Treatment Centre. I assumed it was something to do with his broken arm, but I never saw him get any physiotherapy.

"In our Force, we get a yearly check-up, everything seemed fine until the Force Medical Officer asked me if I was depressed."

An easy assumption to make, given his wretched and miserable look that DNA had given him. Harry, as usual, full of mischief, had replied, "I sometimes feel a bit like I'm on my own in the cosmos. Like a tiny fragment of nothing, in a deep-sea of meaninglessness."

His Force Medical Officer referred him to the Police Treatment Centre for respite with the intention of giving him some breathing space. Harry gave me a conspiratorial look suggesting that he had engineered his fortnight of recuperation through devious means.

I pondered his situation. I mean, he still looked morose but maybe glum wasn't his natural expression. What if there was more to it than he was letting on? Perhaps his Force Medical Officer was truly concerned about him. Perhaps there were other things he wasn't telling me. I considered it my duty to probe a little further and offer some empathy.

"..and were you depressed Harry?"

"Oh I occasionally have such thoughts, but then I have a cup of tea and a biscuit, and I feel much better. Just low blood sugar, I think. It crossed my mind I was down in the dumps, but it turned out I was just a little peckish."

I was at the Police Treatment Centre to sort out a back problem and had daily treatment from an excellent physiotherapist along with various exercise classes, including Pilates. If you haven't tried Pilates, then I recommend you do. It was a revelation for me. But be warned. The pain scale, from one to ten, starts at a dull ache - that's one. Then you go to eight (giving birth). Second highest, at nine, is standing barefoot on Lego or an upturned plug. The highest pain on the scale, however, (even higher than stubbing your toe) is Pilates. It might be the right exercise for a flexible six-year-old girl, but I was a stecky old man.

I much preferred the exercises that involved less bending. They had a small pool they used for light aerobic workouts, so I signed up for the afternoon sessions. Sergeant Harry O'Hare also signed up for the same sessions and together we took part in, what amounted to, splashing with style. Also in the pool with us was Tommy Gunn and all round good guy Gentleman George, who was recovering from an operation on his shoulder. After the Tuesday session, our instructor informed us that the Treatment Centre was to get a VIP visitor the next day, none other than Prince Charles. We were warned to be on our best behaviour. Harry O'Hare had other ideas.

Wednesday afternoon came, and the four of us were lined up by the edge of the small swimming pool while Prince Charlie was ushered through the building and shown through to the poolside., Harry suggested that the first person to laugh when our royal visitor came by had to take us to the pub and buy a round of drinks that night.

All four of us stood in the pool, elbows on the edge so as Prince Charles walked by he could bend down and have a chat with us. His entourage guided him over to where we were perched. He stopped and asked Harry his name and why he was there.

"Hello sir," Harry replied, "I'm Sergeant Harry O'Hare, and I lost my hearing in a shooting accident."

"Will you eventually get your hearing back?" Prince Charles politely asked him.

"Pardon!"

Without so much as a blink, Prince Charles nodded and moved on. I had to stifle a laugh.

"How about you?" Charlie asked Tommy.

"Hello Sir, I am officer Gunn, Tommy to my friends. I broke my foot in a chasing incident."

"Oh, who were you chasing?" inquired the Prince.

"Johnny Walker and Jack Daniels!"

I had to clasp my hands over my mouth.

Again this reply was resolutely ignored, and Prince Charlie moved on to Gentleman George who's position meant that his frequently operated on and battle-scarred shoulder was prominently displayed for our visitor to see.

"I take it you have injured your shoulder?" he stated, looking pleased with his deductive powers.

"Yes, sir. That's correct," Gentleman George replied.

"How did that happen?"

"It's a golfing problem," George explained.

"You injured your shoulder playing golf?"

"Well, not exactly, I had an awful slice when using my driver, and an operation was the only way I could cure it."

Prince Charles nodded and moved on none the wiser that any of the three pool pigeons had been winding him up. He walked off without even speaking to me as Harry, Tommy and myself were giggling like schoolgirls. Gentleman George was supplied with free drink all night for coming away with the best line.

The Police Treatment Centres, as I already mentioned, is a charitable organisation. It is therefore reliant on the donations it receives - mainly from that £4 that officers pay into it from their wages. It is not like we miss £4 a month. The patients themselves also do fundraising amongst themselves. Each week the patients pick a committee whose job it is to organise tournaments (snooker, darts, table tennis), quizzes, bingo and other entertainment. These evening get-togethers are good fun. The committee charge a small fee to enter which raises money for the charity. We donate prizes, and I suspect that several of these prizes were donated straight back to the prize fund for the following week's raffle. The dusty old bottle of *Warninks Advocaat* I received for winning the snooker tournament went straight back into the prize fund - I expect it will still do the rounds decades from now. *Advocaat!* I hadn't seen anyone drink that stuff since I was five years old when My Uncle Bobby arrived at our Hogmanay party with a bottle - wearing his tartan blazer, his Casio calculator watch and Brylcreem hair. Uncle Bobby was such a flash bastard.

On the night before we were due to go home, the consensus was we should celebrate our new found friendships with a mass exodus to the pub. I say pub (singular) because we had been warned that the village contained one police friendly pub and two not so police friendly pubs. Two no-go areas. Enter at your peril. Off limits.

So about thirty of us descended on the police friendly pub. It wasn't my first visit to the pub and to be honest it was not an appealing place. The atmosphere was cold and the beer warm. The pub had built an extension which served as a dining room - the owner's trying to modernise the place. Unfortunately, they purchased their furniture from a garage sale and the décor from 1974.

We were there to enjoy ourselves, so it didn't matter all that much. The committee that week composed of three good guys. Oliver originated from New Zealand and was now working as a detective in Scotland. He had a great accent and looked like he had just landed on the beach, all that was missing was his surfboard. Gordon was a firearms sergeant; he spent a lot of time in the gym but even more time in front of the mirror. Omid Djalili was the third member of the committee, that wasn't his real name, but I called him that because he was the doppelgänger of the comedian

Omid Djalili, the only difference - he was funnier than the real one.

Halfway through the night, the music turned off, and Oliver stood in the middle of the floor gaining our attention.

"Ladies and gentlemen," he boomed, "your committee would like to thank you for your generosity. It has been amazing. Together we have raised more money this week than any other time."

There was a loud cheer and a prolonged round of applause as we congratulated ourselves on the news.

"As a special thank you, all of us on the committee would like to regale you with a traditional dance from my home country. We would like to perform, for your pleasure, the Maori ceremonial dance called the 'Haka'. Originally a war dance to proclaim our strength and prowess you will recognise it as the dance performed by the New Zealand rugby team.

Oliver whipped off his shirt and planted both feet on the floor, slightly apart, knees bent. A cheer went up from the girls. Oliver waited until silence descended across the pub. Then he began chanting. Slowly, almost under his breath. Then louder, suddenly he stamped his right foot hard on the ground. It was the signal for Gordon. Gordon joined Oliver in the middle of the floor, stood to his left and a little behind. Gordon planted both his feet on the ground, mirroring Oliver's pose, feet apart and knees bent. He too whipped off his shirt to reveal a ripped and hairless body - another loud cheer went up from the girls and an even bigger cheer from a guy at the back who sold waxing products.

Oliver and Gordon hummed, and together they began a coordinated stamping of their feet. Then they crossed their arms in front of their chests right arm above the left. It was the signal for Omid to join in. Omid took up his position to the right of Oliver, slightly behind. Now they formed a V formation. The biggest cheer went up from everyone when Omid whipped off his shirt to reveal all his blubbery goodness, a body shaped from eating a curry five nights a week.

The three of them regaled us with their version of the Haka. They had obviously practised it. Oliver was grunt and chant perfect but with the limited time available Gordon and Omid had to follow Oliver's lead. The result was the funniest thing I had seen all week. The entire clientele of the pub mesmerised by the display. Hilarious!

It is times like that I just love life. Everyone in that pub was having a good time - our aches and pains forgotten. Surrounded by new-found friends, laughter and fun. Why didn't I stay where I was?

I'll tell you why. Wendy asked me if I wanted another drink - it was her round. I had just gotten a taste for it and nodded, but the bar was mobbed. The committee's rendition of the Haka meant everyone stood watching while they drank their drinks. Now everyone crowded up to the bar to get a refill.

"Why don't we try one of the other pubs?" she said.

"Yes, why not," I agreed.

We toddled out of the police-friendly pub and wandered down the street to the first place that had a large red 'T' above the door.

This pub had frosted windows so we couldn't see in, even if they weren't frosted we wouldn't have been able to see in for the dirt. The narrow entrance led to a wooden door with a porthole window; this too was frosted, so there was no sign of what it was like inside. A deliberate ploy of the pub owners to ensure that no-one about turned before they entered. Had I seen what I was walking into I would have been inclined not to have bothered. Wendy plunged right in, and I had no option but to follow.

You know the feeling you get when you think someone is looking at you and you turn around, and sure enough, someone is looking at you? They get embarrassed, and they look away. That happened when we walked in - except they didn't look away. There was no embarrassment, just sheer unadulterated hostility. We weren't locals, so they assumed we were from the Police Treatment Centre and therefore off-duty police officers - great powers of deduction. As I peeked at the clientele from behind Wendy, I saw a motley crew of ne'er-do-wells. If there had been a piano player in the corner, he would have stopped playing to look at us. All that was missing was a Wookie.

I was about to tap Wendy on the shoulder and suggest we leave, but before I could say a word, she stepped forward to the bar and ordered a pint of Guinness. The barman nodded in approval and poured her a pint.

"What do you want?" He asked me, begrudging.

I paused a moment to look at the selection of beers on tap. There were none that appealed. There were a small selection of whiskies and other spirits on the gantry but, again, none that took my fancy. The pub was still silent, and all eyes were on me as they waited to hear my order.

"Do you have a wine list?" I asked.

The clientele burst out laughing, and there were further guffaws when the barman bent down under the counter and produced two miniature bottles of cheap wine, holding one in each hand he asked, "Red or white?"

We found a dart board and two darts that still had their flights on them. Before long we were in a knockout darts match with half the pub involved. We had a great night.

My only reservation for anyone else who goes to the non-police friendly pub is to make sure that you have a Wendy with you. I felt safe with Wendy, but I'd have needed a riot squad team for me to go in there any other time.

As it neared closing time Wendy and I left. We headed back to the Police Treatment Centre, mindful that there was a curfew in place. They made it clear to us at our induction it was a capital offence to disturb any of the other patients. We bumped into the rest of colleagues leaving the police friendly pub and made our way back up the street, we were too noisy. The loudest coming from the ones trying to keep the rest of us quiet.

"SSSHHH! SHUSH! SSSHHHUUUUUSSSHHH!

"What?"

"Ssshhh!"

"Why?"

"Cos."

"Cos what?"

"Just SHUSH OKAY!"

Wendy and I bumped into Oliver and Omid Djalili, who were holding on to each other as they zigzagged their way back. They were closely followed by Raquel, a young cop from Fife with a generous personality and equally generous bosom. Raquel had taken a shine to Oliver, and her ample bosom thrust in his direction at every opportunity.

I smiled to myself. The police are supposed to be upstanding members of society, peacekeepers and upholders of the law. Looking at the drunken state of the party in front reminded me we were just like normal people. Police officers reflect society, there are good and bad, and there are those that like to have a good time too.

Then Wendy stopped.

"Guys, guys, guys - listen."

We stopped and listened.

"I have an idea," she said.

We nodded in approval; it is always good to have an idea. We like nothing better than an idea when we are drunk and in need of a good night's sleep. Ideas make us human. Acting on those ideas, however, can sometimes turn us into goats.

"I have a bottle of wine in my room," Wendy continued, "why don't you all come back and have a nightcap," she suggested.

We gasped in horror at her blatant disrespect and abuse of the no alcohol policy enforced at the Police Treatment Centre. However, it seemed like a good idea to Oliver, Omid and Raquel. I put on my sensible hat, and on our return, I made my excuses and headed off to bed.

In the middle of brushing my teeth I heard a quiet knock at my door. I hadn't yet got into my pyjamas (I don't actually have pyjamas, so you get the idea). I put down my toothbrush, wrapped a towel around myself and went to see who it was but, whoever it was had little patience and knocked again - rather too loudly. I threw the door open to prevent them waking any other patients. It was Wendy, Omid and Oliver. They pushed their way in and shut the door behind them.

"What's going on?" I asked.

Wendy, who had a bottle of red wine and a corkscrew in her hands (even although the bottle of wine was a screw cap), explained, "Raquel is after Oliver and went back to her room to spruce herself up. Oliver doesn't think it is a good idea."

"Why not, Oliver?"

"Because I'm married. I'm not into complications. Raquel is a nice girl, but there is no way I'm getting involved with her."

"Yeah, she told me to disappear by the time she came back. She wanted Oliver all to herself. Can we sit here and have a nightcap?" Wendy pleaded.

"Sure, why not?" I said - which would have gone against my better judgement had I been sober.

The four of us sat on the bed. Wendy dispensed the wine into a white coffee cup, a toothbrush glass and a plastic cup - all found within my room. She drank from the bottle. About five minutes later I heard another quiet knock at my door. We froze. Then I realised it was my room, and I should do something.

"Who is it?"

"It's me, Raquel. Can I come in?"

Oliver ditched his glass on the bedside table and scrambled under my bed.

"What do you want?" I asked Raquel, by this time I had made my way towards the door so I could keep the noise down.

Omid opened my walk-in cupboard and pushed all my clothes to the side to ensconce himself at the back. Wendy followed him in, and I wondered what kind of state my clothes would be in when they left because there wasn't a lot of room for anything other than those two.

"I'm looking for Oliver," said Raquel.

"He's not here."

"What about Wendy and Omid?"

"They aren't here either."

"Are you sure."

"Yes, I'm sure."

"What?"

"Ssshhh."

"Let me in."

"No, go away, I'm going to bed."

"LET ME IN!" Raquel shouted.

I checked that Oliver was well hidden beneath the bed and that the cupboard doors were closed over. They were all quiet and out of sight. Rather than have Raquel wake everyone up, I opened the door to her and prove that I was alone.

"Come in and keep quiet," I said, "look there is no-one here, and I am just about to go to bed. I think it probably best if you go to your bed too."

Raquel scanned the room with her glazed eyes and then, without warning burst into tears. She sat on my bed, and chest heaving up and down as she took in great big gulps of air in between her sobbing. For the next ten minutes, I tried to comfort her and persuade her to go back to her room. Raquel continued to bawl and blubber.

How did I end up in this situation? How could I have avoided it? I'm a responsible member of the police service in a position of rank. What if someone came into my room now and found me with a towel wrapped around myself sitting on the bed with a randy young female police officer crying her eyes out because she couldn't get a surfboarding Kiwi into bed. And little did she know all I could think about was getting her out of my room so I could get him out from under my bed.

Sometimes life gives you lemons. In those situations, I always try to make the best of it. If life gives me lemons, I put a little salt on my wrist and pour myself a Tequila. Glass half full kind of guy. Always look on the bright side. To be honest, though, at that precise moment the particular lemon life had given me wouldn't resolve itself with salt and Tequila. Wine might do the trick though.

"Would you like a glass of wine, Raquel?"

I handed her the glass that Oliver had left on my bedside table. I picked up my cup and took a sip. Raquel took a few deep breaths and then a gulp of wine. It did the trick. She stopped crying and calmed down. I put on a sympathetic voice as Raquel recounted the misery she had undergone to that point in her life. I was getting somewhere; my sensitive side came to the fore. The concern and understanding I showed Raquel made her realise that life wasn't all that bad and the best thing for her to do was to go back to her room and get a good night's sleep. A couple more minutes and I would have Raquel out of my room. I poured her the last of the bottle of wine, hoping she would swallow it down and bugger off. Then suddenly my cupboard door flew open and Wendy bounded out.

"What the feck, Omid!" she screamed.

In the process of opening the cupboard door, Wendy knocked the glass of wine Raquel was holding, and it splattered all over me. There were red stains everywhere. Omid emerged from the cupboard put his hands up in an effort to placate Wendy.

"I couldn't help it," he said.

"You do know I'm gay, don't you Omid?"

"I didn't mean anything. It was just that your bum was pressed right up against me. I couldn't help it."

The realisation of what had happened in the confines of my cupboard was confirmed by a quick glance down at Omid's crotch. My look was enough for Omid to put his hands back down and cover his enthusiasm. The absurdity of the situation overcame Wendy, and she burst out laughing. I couldn't help myself, and I joined in. Raquel started crying again.

It was time to get them out of my room. I stood up, held onto my towel with one hand - I didn't want any further mishaps. I threw my door wide and ushered them out.

"Time to go," I said.

Omid sidled past me, followed by Wendy who was still laughing and then Raquel who's chest was still heaving as she tried to keep in her sobs. It was only then, as I went to close the door, I saw the night watchman standing outside in the corridor, arms folded and a raised eyebrow. Goodness knows what he thought had been going on. I did the only thing I could think of and put my finger up to my mouth and said, "Ssshhh." At which point my wine-stained towel dropped to the floor.

I ducked back into my room and closed the door. I clambered onto my bed and turned out the light. What a night! I wondered what the night watchman would report back. I fancied that it would be my last ever visit to the Police Treatment Centre - thirty years of donations or not. Even if they didn't allow me back, I might be too embarrassed to revisit. I hope my sore back gets none the worse. All these thoughts were going through my head when I heard a loud snore reverberate around my room, reminding me that Oliver (the Kiwi) was still under my bed.

THE MICHAEL PARKINSON TELEVISION INTERVIEW

Parky: So that's why you shouldn't keep a Kiwi under the bed, ha ha.

Malky: Good advice for anyone.

Parky: So you have come to the end of your trilogy of reflections are there going to be any more silly police books from you?

Malky: I don't think so, time to move on.

Parky: What are you going to do with yourself?

Malky: I'm going to explore Scotland.

Parky: Is that something you are going to write about?

Malky: Perhaps, I have already found myself in some side-splitting situations.

Parky: Have you exhausted all your police stories?

Malky: I did keep some stories back that I didn't think appropriate.

Parky: What kind of stories?

Malky: Well, there was this one female police officer who was worried she might grow a willie because she was taking steroids.

Parky: Anabolic?

Malky: No, just a willie.

AUDIENCE LAUGHS

Parky: Last question, do you miss the police?

Chapter 23

After thirty years and two months in the police, I went from being a nineteen-year-old immature, naïve *'cocky little upstart'* to an immature and naïve fifty-year-old. I like to think I'm less of a *'cocky little upstart'*. The police gave me life experience, a reasonable income and some silly stories to tell.

It is a busy occupation being a police officer. We always had places to go and people to charge. Keeping the peace is not a peaceful pastime. Even more so nowadays, have you ever tried to juggle balls? That is what it is like being a police officer - police officers are master jugglers. Juggling six or seven balls at a time, sometimes bouncing them off the ground all the time watching them fly through the air. The secret is getting a rhythm.

Policing is the same. You juggle enquiries. Just when you think you are getting good, your sergeant chucks another two balls at you. You toss these in the air with the others. All balls requiring more height so they stay up a bit longer, giving you time to settle back into a rhythm again. You have to work harder; your muscles feel the burn and your concentration levels are the same as an astronaut on takeoff. It's all about keeping control. Then your radio crackles into life and the dispatcher tells you to drop everything. There is an emergency somewhere - and you are it. You have to go. It's your job.

Policing is a vocation that attracts amazing people who do extraordinary things. People who drop all the balls they are juggling to save the lives of others put themselves in danger and deal with the things from which most people would run away.

Just as soon as the emergency is over, the cops head back to where they dropped their balls, pick them up and start juggling again.

The Scottish Police College is still there in the heart of Scotland churning out new recruits. Despite the relatively stagnant wages for the past ten years and the extra ten years service required to earn a lesser pension, there are still remarkable people signing up to serve the public. People who work all hours of the day and night to protect life and property, detect offenders and put themselves in danger. People who juggle enquiries and workloads but drop everything to attend an emergency call. They will speed towards things that others shy away from. It is amazing what they do in the name of keeping the peace. We should all be thankful for their dedication to duty and be less critical when they get the occasional things wrong.

The number of police officers in Scotland has fallen to its lowest level since 2010. Scotland, however, has not seen the drastic number cuts endured by England and Wales. There are still over thirty percent more police officers in Scotland now than when I joined in 1983. The difference is that there are significantly less of them used on the front-line. The changing nature of policing points towards new forms of criminality such as cyber and economic crimes. The likelihood is that we have seen the best of political support for the police - at least for the foreseeable future.

I was lucky to have been a part of it during the best of times, although, sometimes it didn't feel much like it. What it felt like was to be in the biggest bestest gang. We supported each other, made each other laugh and had the occasional bit of nonsense. That all helped us deal with the adversity we faced. There were hard times, dangerous situations and sobering life experiences. When serious things happened, we became serious and professional. To remain sane afterwards, we let off steam.

I joined the police at the same time as Hoddit, Doddit and Bruce. Hoddit left to become a lawyer, Doddit left to avoid being arrested, and Bruce left to try out new careers all over the world. He settled in Liverpool, which he says is the best place to be.

As for the others who passed through my life and into the pages of my books I have tried to maintain their anonymity. There are some, who I am sad to say, are no longer here. Big Bob died of cancer, a gem of a man, helpful to a fault and a supremely nice human being. Big Bob was a father figure to many a probationer like myself and each of us grew to love him for his kindness, his larger than life personality and his mischievousness. Big Bob died at 12.34 and 56 seconds on the 7th of the 8th of the 9th. A remarkable man and fitting that his unusual time of death will not be repeated in a hundred years.

PC Penfold continues to amuse me whenever I am in his company - which is never often enough. His self-deprecating humour and mishaps give me much fodder. In a startling turn of events, PC Penfold became poacher turned gamekeeper when he took on a part-time job serving pints at his local pub. It suited him to the ground. He was in the company of his friends, continued to revel in the banter, and it prevented him from ruining his liver four nights a week. On the other three nights, he returned to the pub and spent all the money he earned whilst working behind the bar.

"They would be as well to pay me in beer tokens," he observed.

One evening, while sitting drinking with an old friend, PC Penfold ordered a pint and was served his frothy beverage without a penny changing hands. His old friend raised an eyebrow.

"What's going on? How come you didn't pay for that?"

"Oh, that was left in the tap for me by some of the other locals while I was working."

"What do you mean?"

"Well, some guys want to buy me a pint when I'm serving, but as I am not allowed to drink when I am working I save them up to drink them on my days off."

"How many pints do you have in the tap?"

"Normally about a dozen or so."

"What? Well, why don't you buy me a pint from those?"

"Oh, I can't do that. That wouldn't be fair. The guys have bought them for me, so I have to drink them."

Through the *Old Grumps Wine Club* (a *WhatsApp* group), I keep in touch with many retired officers I count as friends. PC Prim keeps me grounded and goes out of his way to include my family and me as an extension of his family. I can rely on him for everything. He is the epitome of a retired police officer. He organises ceilidhs, devotes time and effort to his favourite charity and there isn't a day goes by he doesn't go roaming the streets with his dog looking for someone to interrogate. We both wonder, sometimes, how we found the time to work.

Sometimes, out of the blue, PC Barbecue Bill sends me a text, a *WhatsApp* message or a *Facebook* message to remind me he is still alive. The messages are always derogatory, and utterly offensive - which is strange because I never take offence, it is hard to take offence when you are laughing. He is one of the funniest guys I ever came across. I have him to thank for proofreading my books and his encouraging comment, "Aye, quite entertaining!"

Gentleman George is another retired colleague who I wish I could spend more time in his company. He has the greatest wealth of stories and anecdotes. Also, he is one of the most generous of people. He is first to put his hand in his pocket and also the last. If it is at all possible for Gentleman George to attend an event, he will be there, no matter what. He is having a deserved and enviable retirement. He goes to as many golf outings as he can, he partakes in retired indoor sports events, he has as many fishing trips as he can fit in and with the rest of his time, he and his wife take their caravan all over the country.

I worked with many outstanding cops. I haven't mentioned them all because it would take too long. The silliness played a small part of our day - some cops weren't even silly at all. There were many characters I came across and I hope my books go some way to remembering them.

It is nice to catch up with all my retired colleagues and always a pleasure to speak to those who are still beavering away on the job.

Policing is a wonderful career, a life full of experiences and a fantastic way to earn a living. I am confident that the police will continue to produce extraordinary people and I wish them as much mischievousness, nonsense and shenanigans as they can get away with.

THE MICHAEL PARKINSON TELEVISION INTERVIEW

Parky: Thank you for your time, Malky.

Malky: No problem. It has been a pleasure.

Parky: All the best in your retirement and I look forward to reading more of your work.

CREDITS ROLL

MALKY LEANS ACROSS TOWARDS PARKINSON AND WHISPERS

Malky: So, who was the second most extraordinary person you ever interviewed?

Parky: That's easy - Billy Connolly.

According to Section 23 of The Scottish Further Powers Act 1974
If you smiled at any of these stories, then you are Legally obliged to spend two seconds giving it a five-star rave review
(Not really but it would be nice if you did).

Go to Malky McEwan on Amazon
Then scroll down to 'customer review'.

GLOSSARY OF SCOTTISH TERMS

- Ah - I
- Aw - All
- Awfy - Awful
- Aye - Yes
- Bairn - Child
- Bogie - A green snotter picked from one's nose
- Braw - Beautiful
- Bricht - Bright
- Couldnae - Couldn't
- Cos - Because
- Crabbit - Being a nippy sweetie
- Dae - Do
- Disnae - Does not
- Drooch - Thirst
- Druggie - A person who takes (drugs other than those prescribed by a doctor).
- Fae - From
- Fannybaws - a term of ridicule, in some cases of endearment (oi, fannybaws, gies a drink of yer scoosh).
- Fur - For
- Gie - Give
- Glaiket - Glaikit
- Glaikit - Stupid (As in: ya glaikit bastard!)
- Gob - Mouth
- Gonnae - Going to
- Haud yer wheesht - Stop talking
- Heid - Head
- Heids - Heads
- Hudnae - Haven't
- Huv - Have
- Irn Bru - Fizzy Scottish drink made from girders and commonly used as a hangover cure when accompanied by a roll with square sausage and brown sauce.

- Jist - Just
- Jobbie - A perfectly shaped torpedo of excrement
- Ken - Know
- Moonlicht - Moonlight
- Naw - No
- Nicht - Night
- Nippy sweetie - Crabbit person
- Och - Oh!
- On the piss - Partaking of a small libation (when used in this phrase piss means drink)
- Piss - Pee
- Polis - Police
- Sclaff - To scrape the ground rather than hit a clean golf-stroke
- Scoosh - Fizzy drink (eg Irn Bru)
- Scooshed - Squirted
- Scroat - Despicable person
- Spunktrumpet - A fannybaws (without the term of endearment)
- Stecky - Stiff and sore
- Tae - To
- Tattie - Potato
- Wee - Small
- Willie - Penis
- Wis - Was
- Wisnae - Wasn't
- Wouldnae - Wouldn't
- Ya -You (Normally used in the phrase 'Ya wee wank' - instead of ye)
- Ye - You
- Yer -Your

Malky McEwan writes to tickle, inspire, and make you think.

For police humour to tickle and delight:

'The really FUNNY thing about being a COP'
The exciting things, the funny incidents, the strange goings on, and the comic situations are what remains of a thirty year and two-month career in the police. So here they are, guaranteed to make you laugh out loud.

The really STUPID thing about being a SERGEANT
Read about PC Penfold (if there is a jobbie on the pavement, he will stand on it). The hilarious antics of Inspector Deadpan Dick and Superintendent Amnesiac will make you laugh out loud, and the hokey cokey in the pokey is not to be missed.

Keep your colleagues amused and never be bored at work again with the *Lateral Thinking Puzzle* books:

'Outstanding' Fiendish & Fun Lateral Thinking Puzzles
My favourite puzzle here is 'The milk container' which always gets the biggest 'AHA' moment.

'Even Better' Fiendish & Fun Lateral Thinking Puzzles
'My favourite puzzle here is 'Skiving' which was an absolutely, fit to burst, hilarious scenario that really did happen. It still makes me smile to this day.'

'The Ultimate' Fiendish & Fun Lateral Thinking Puzzles
My favourite puzzle here is 'How to deal with time wasters' which has such an elegant solution. I genuinely used at work

to stop time wasters in their tracks. It never offended anyone and worked every time. There is a slight twist if you want to get to the right answer.

14769803R00176

Printed in Great Britain
by Amazon